HOW TO BUY
AN OFFICE COMPUTER
OR WORD PROCESSOR

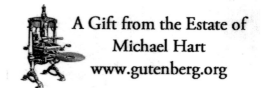

Brian C. Donohue is a practicing attorney in Manhattan Beach, California, and a member of the California State Bar. Formerly a systems analyst for Sperry Univac and chief of Data Processing Contracts for one of the largest users of data processing equipment in the U.S., Mr. Donohue has managed on a yearly basis more than $30 million worth of expenditures for computer and word processing equipment. He has negotiated with such major computer manufacturers as IBM, Univac, Digital, Honeywell, and Burroughs, and with such mini-computer/word processing suppliers as Hewlett-Packard, Prime, Data General, and Wang. He is a member of the American Bar Association, the Los Angeles County Bar Association, and the Computer Law Association, and is a United States Army Reserve Contracting Officer with the Defense Logistics Agency. In addition, he is an active member of the business community and a member of Rotary International. He teaches part-time at El Camino College in California and conducts seminars in computer and word processing selection, negotiation, and contracting at the University of Southern California. He holds an M.B.A. in Data Processing from George Washington University, Washington, D.C.

Brian C. Donohue

HOW TO BUY AN OFFICE COMPUTER OR WORD PROCESSOR

A SPECTRUM BOOK

PRENTICE-HALL, Inc., Englewood Cliffs, New Jersey 07632

Library of Congress Cataloging in Publication Data

Donohue, Brian C.
    How to buy an office computer or word processor.

    "A Spectrum Book."
    Includes index.
        1. Word processing equipment—Purchasing.
    2. Electronic digital computers—Purchasing.
    3. Small business—Data processing.   I. Title.
    HF5548.2.D589   1983   001.64'068'7   82-21526
    ISBN 0-13-403113-X
    ISBN 0-13-403105-9 (pbk.)

10   9   8   7   6   5   4   3   2   1

ISBN 0-13-403113-X

ISBN 0-13-403105-9 (PBK.)

Editorial/production supervision by Norma G. Ledbetter
Cover design by Hal Siegel
Manufacturing buyer: Pat Mahoney

Prentice-Hall International, Inc., *London*
Prentice-Hall of Australia Pty. Limited, *Sydney*
Prentice-Hall Canada Inc., *Toronto*
Prentice-Hall of India Private Limited, *New Delhi*
Prentice-Hall of Japan, Inc., *Tokyo*
Prentice-Hall of Southeast Asia Pte. Ltd., *Singapore*
Whitehall Books Limited, *Wellington, New Zealand*
Editora Prentice-Hall do Brasil Ltda., *Rio de Janeiro*

*to Ed, Mary, Linda,
Molly, Sean, and Megan*

CONTENTS

Foreword xiii

Preface xv

1
STEPS TO BUYING
OR LEASING 1

2
THE ENVIRONMENT 6

3
MEASURING THE JOB 27

4

PREPARING
REQUIREMENTS 46

5

SERVICES: JOYS
AND TRIBULATIONS 79

6

EVALUATION
AND SELECTION 98

7

NEGOTIATIONS 118

8

THE CONTRACT AND
OBTAINING COMPLIANCE 129

9

LEGAL ISSUES 146

APPENDIX A:
QUESTIONNAIRES
AND FORMS 161

APPENDIX B:
REQUEST FOR PROPOSAL
AND VENDOR RESPONSE 182

APPENDIX C:
EVALUATION FORM 200

APPENDIX D:
NEGOTIATING
MEMORANDUM 202

APPENDIX E:
SAMPLE RENTAL
AGREEMENT 205

APPENDIX F:
STATUS REPORT 209

APPENDIX G:
COURSE OUTLINE
FOR INSTRUCTORS 211

Glossary 216

Index 229

FOREWORD

With the recent upswing in interest in the small business computer and inexpensive word processor, it is no wonder that so many traditional computer suppliers, and even more upstarts, are producing these machines at ever-increasing rates. With all these computers and options to choose from, it is difficult for the uninitiated businessperson to make a comprehensive study of, much less a valid decision on, the best computer equipment for his or her application. For anyone who is interested in a small business computer but is unfamiliar with computer terms or has trouble asking the right questions, this book will definitely help to clarify many points.

The presentation of the material makes it easy to learn what questions to ask, how to ask them, and how to guarantee that they are answered correctly. Negotiating for any item, particularly a computer, can always enhance the buyer's position . . . if done properly. This book takes the reader on a step-by-step approach to specifying the requirements of a small buiness computer and following through with various vendors in obtaining the required hardware at the best possible cost.

Even those people familiar with computer terminology but not necessarily familiar with the purchasing aspects of computers will benefit from this book when it comes to contracting for computer equipment. Although the book is designed to assist the first-time computer user or potential user, it also brings out many points that even those of us with years of experience might otherwise overlook.

Chapters 1 and 2 provide an overview of the required steps in buying or leasing a computer, why office automation equipment is necessary, and what steps have been taken to improve its usefulness. In Chapter 3, you will find guidelines on evaluating the requirements for your particular application. After the individual requirements have been defined, Chapter 4 helps you compile them into a suitable request for proposal (RFP) to present to various vendors. In fact, the major emphasis of the steps in this book revolves around the effective use of an RFP.

Chapter 5 cautions about nontechnical problems that frequently disrupt a computer's purchase and subsequent operation. Chapter 6 gives guidance on the comparison and evaluation of vendors' responses to a typical overall evaluation of various systems.

After you make some decisions on the basis of the proposals, you then learn how to negotiate (Chapter 7) with various vendors on the different aspects of purchasing a computer. Chapter 8 cautions about contracts and tells how the contract can work in your favor rather than just in the supplier's favor, as is usually the case. Proper negotiations prior to purchase can guarantee much longer satisfactory performance. Chapter 9 presents the legal issues regarding the computer purchase and operation for those persons unfamiliar with specific restrictions, procedures, and possible pitfalls.

The appendixes contain numerous sample questionnaires and evaluation forms that will be useful in assisting you in purchasing all types of computer equipment—from personal computers to the small office business computer and even to large mainframe computers. A model RFP is in Appendix B, along with an example of vendor answers and a discussion on the rating of these answers.

In summary,the information presented here will undoubtedly prove financially rewarding to any individual or company following the principles and procedures outlined in this comprehensive book. In particular, the concepts can be used, as a minimum, to evaluate your requirements to guarantee that you do not end up with a computer having fewer capabilities than you need or with a computer that costs more than is necessary.

TERRY BENSON
Technical Editor
Interface Age magazine

PREFACE

The story of great successes of the computer age is not without its dark side. A friend approached me some time ago with a tale of gloom: his stomach had been bothering him, he had been drinking more scotch than he could handle, and he felt that his overall well-being was seriously declining.

The cause of my friend's maladies was his computer system. Customers were threatening to terminate long-standing business relationships that he had worked for so many years to develop. Computer reports were not reaching his customers on time, and the much sought-after computer guru who was responsible for the maintenance of the system was, more frequently than not, "out to lunch." My friend and his business were helpless and nearing the end of their rope.

What had gone wrong? Not the computer, which was the model of advanced technology. The computer was more than capable of handling the requirements of the small business. At the root of my friend's problem was his own failure to do the necessary homework before selecting the computer and signing the contract.

Buying a computer is not like buying a typewriter or a copy machine. A computer is at the heart of many contemporary businesses, pumping data back and forth through the essential arteries of the operating appendages. If the heart fails, so will the entire organization.

A business professional cannot simply say "I'll take this one." It is imperative that he or she understand the computer and word processing functions in relationship to *his* or *her* particular business. In order to do this, the purchaser *must*:

- Analyze the current business work load.
- Anticipate future business needs.
- Understand the basic principles about hardware and software.
- Learn whether his or her business can use a ready-made program or will require custom programming.
- Develop a plan for the installation of the system.
- Prepare employees to adjust their work patterns in a way that will complement the new systems.
- Consider provisions for adequate postinstallation maintenance and prompt repair of the system.
- Develop a healthy respect for computer contracting practices and the applicable laws.

The business professional must accept that a business or office will come to depend on its machines. This makes imperative a well-planned selection method, effective negotiations, and a complete and fair contract. If any link in the chain is broken, it can mean disaster for the office or business. If the computer system fails, the damage to the business may be permanent and irreversible. The risks of financial liability associated with a computerized office or business can be catastrophic. Choice of a computer system is serious business and should not be taken lightly.

I have written this text keeping the customer's point of view in mind. Having been a computer vendor for a number of years, I can also understand the vendor's side of the business, including problems of attempting to accommodate neophyte customers who have wishy-washy lists of specifications and simply do not understand what they need or want.

Computer experience among students in my classes and seminars has been varied, a mixture ranging from college freshmen, just beginning in computer science, to data processing professionals. Included have been business professionals, office managers, and many others who are interested in what the new office technology may have to offer. My experience with these students has convinced me of their displeasure with existing textbooks and other reference works—books that are too heavily slanted toward technical language, either of the computer trade or the law. The jargon of "computerese"—with its references to bytes, bits, RAM, ROM, modems, and microseconds, or the "legalese," laced with "caveat emptor" and "force majeure," UCC, TRO, and implied warranties—has no place in this book.

This book presents a step-by-step, easy-to-follow procedure that a person of average intelligence and common sense can follow with ease when tackling the complexities of computer selection. It is designed for the average business professional, whether shopkeeper, doctor, lawyer, executive or manager of a corporate group, educator, supervisor, and anyone interested in learning what steps must be taken to ensure getting the best system at the best price.

My experiences have indicated to me the type of knowledge these people need and want, how much theory is needed, and how much practicality is required. The organization of this book follows the normal and logical procedures necessary to a satisfactory agreement for purchase or lease of a computer or word processor. Each step is important and is discussed thoroughly, from the analysis of computer requirements for a business and the evaluation of the various systems available in the marketplace, to the fine points of negotiating and drafting of the contract.

In addition to giving a general overview of practices within the computer marketplace, this book focuses on several computer acquisition problems that recur most frequently, offering specific suggestions for ways by which the purchaser can avoid them. Also noted are steps by which business professionals can better ensure that computer vendors perform as agreed. Attention is also focused on certain clauses frequently used by vendors to gain a favorable position over their customers. Understanding of these clauses should be a particularly valuable asset to the layperson when negotiating a vendor's preprinted agreement form.

The law is changing rapidly in attempting to keep abreast of computer technology and the inevitable repercussions. This book describes legal issues currently being debated regarding computer technology: questions of patents, copyrights, trade secrets, crime, security, and privacy. Dramatic recent changes in these areas of the law underscore the need for even users of small computers to become familiar with a few simple and helpful legal principles.

The appendixes in this book provide model documents and agreements that are excellent practical guides. Appendix G is an outline for computer instructors whereby this text may be used in a semester course, which should become a prerequisite for all data processing degree programs. Even if you do not plan to buy a computer or word processor in the immediate future, I hope that you will enjoy and learn a great deal from this book. It should be fun. Let's begin!

ACKNOWLEDGMENTS

As with any endeavor, there are many people behind the scenes who truly cause the production to take place. This book is no exception. My father, E. A. Donohue, a practicing attorney for more than 40 years, was at first skeptical about computers and word processors being brought into the office. But he is a man with an open mind, enormous personal resources, and a firm commitment to his family. With his support and encouragement, this project got started and was brought to a successful conclusion.

Terry Benson of Redondo Beach, California, Technical Editor of *Interface Age* magazine, private consultant, and authority of business computers, provided the expert analysis of all technical areas of the text to ensure accuracy. Genuine professionals such as he are hard to find in this subject area, but this book has had the touch of one such individual and the end product reflects it.

Richard J. Stover provided valuable and timely input to a most difficult subject discussed in the text—namely, measuring workloads to size computer requirements.

I also extend my appreciation to California Law Office Automation of Manhattan Beach, California, and to Jeffrey E. Allen, Inc., Studio City, California, for providing the excellent sample reports in Appendix A; Chronometrics, Inc., Garden Grove, California, for the excellent input sample forms in Appendix A; Datapoint Corporation for selected definitions in the Glossary; Jeanne M. Perkins, winner of *The Office* magazine's Word Processing Award for the Questionnaires and Charts in Appendix A, and Michael Scott, Esq., publisher of *The Scott Report*, for his review of Chapter 9 on legal issues.

The last acknowledgment is for Linda, supportive and loving wife, mother, and friend.

1

STEPS
TO BUYING
OR LEASING

The procedure to be followed in buying or leasing a computer or word processing system is quite simple. In fact, it is not substantially different from what we all generally follow when shopping for a new refrigerator, car, or house. There are, of course, more variables to handle with the computer. The technology is one of the most difficult because it is constantly changing, and the rate of change is rapidly increasing. Most experts advise computer users that in terms of technology, everything one knows today will basically be obsolete in three to five years—a somber thought.

To illustrate the growth of computer technology, one industry expert analogizes that if the much-heralded technology of our air and space industries had progressed as rapidly as our computer technology, we would now be able to fly from New York to San Francisco in two seconds!

Along with the growth of computer technology, there has been an associated drive in the business world to maximize the profits in this new frontier of information technology. New creative financing arrangements and new and sometimes irresponsible marketing practices have all become a part of this new frontier. These forces are the catalyst for dramatic change in the business world. Some corporations constantly restructure their marketing and financing plans, while corporate giants such as RCA, Xerox, and Itel often cannot overcome their structural inertia, and they collapse in the cutthroat computer marketplace.

Another major change in the current environment is the new and very significant legal forces such as new statutes, multimillion dollar law suits, and recent Supreme Court rulings. These powerful legal forces, along with financial pressures and market economics, have created a tug-of-war in the computer marketplace.

Only by being aware of all these conflicting pressures can the buyer have an even chance in this environment. The following steps have been found to be the most effective ways to ensure that the buyer ends up a winner. These procedures do not guarantee choosing the perfect computer system. But they are the best way to protect against failure. With all the forces pulling and tugging on the buyer, the possibility of failure is greater than the possibility of success. This will be discussed in detail later; however, Murphy's Law reigns supreme in the computer industry too—whatever can go wrong, will go wrong.

This procedure has contingencies built in so that even if vendors fail in a portion of their commitments, buyers will have a readily available fallback position. With this procedure, the buyer will learn how and when to cut losses before being stuck in a no-win position where there is no retreat.

REQUIREMENTS STUDY

The first specific task is for the potential computer buyer to measure and define his or her requirements and the job to be done. Just as the correct size must be known before selecting the proper pair of shoes, the user must know how much data he or she intends to process. The measurement of data can be as relatively objective as measuring for shoes; however, the items measured are much more complicated. Yet the task is necessary. Use of a data processing consultant may be required in this task. For example, general examples of areas that must be measured are:

- How much data must be stored?
- How frequently will the data need to be retrieved?
- How many letters are produced per week?
- How many bills go out?
- How much time is spent typing and filing?
- How large is the inventory?

These questions might initially seem impossible to answer, even with the aid of an expert. But, in fact, there are many techniques for measuring data, several of which are discussed in a later chapter.

REQUEST FOR PROPOSAL

The information gathered during the requirements study is incorporated into a document referred to as a Request for Proposal (RFP). The RFP is sent out to a reasonable number of prospective vendors who may be able to satisfy the requirements.

It may seem that the RFP is too much work and not worth the investment in time. Nothing could be further from the truth. The RFP is the vehicle for creating the most favorable environment for selecting a computer system. This is where more than one qualified vendor is competing for the buyer's business. In this situation, the buyer will have the ability to extract concessions from a vendor because the buyer will have the ability to take his or her business to a competing vendor. Only by using the RFP will the buyer be able to have a backup vendor, which will give the buyer the upper hand in negotiating. It is essential for the buyer to understand that using the RFP will provide the flexibility in negotiating that is so frequently lacking.

The RFP sets forth to the vendor the requirements to be met. The vendor will then attempt to match product and price to meet the requirements stated in the RFP. One significant advantage to the buyer at this point is that the proposals made by the vendors may provide the buyer with more knowledge about the buyer's *operation* than ever learned during the requirements study.

Computer vendors are extremely knowledgeable about their products and about many different types of computer technology. The information that they provide in their proposals may educate the buyer about some dimensions of the operations that were never known before. The buyer would receive all this valuable information from the vendors at no more cost than the time and expense spent in preparing an RFP.

EVALUATION OF PROPOSALS

Probably the most difficult area in which to give concrete advice is how to evaluate proposals. There are certain basic criteria that will aid the buyer in approaching this problem.

How long has the vendor's company been in business?

> How many full-time employees?
> What do references say about the product? The company?
> How many local vendors' personnel will support the user?
> What does this vendor have that the others do not?

Attempting to keep track of all these variables is difficult. The time spent on quantifying the factors that are important to selecting a vendor and the relative weighing of those factors is well worth the effort.

Again, doing the vendor evaluation process will provide new options that may have never been considered, such as:

> If Vendor A has a certain feature that is missing in Vendor B, how should this affect your decision?
> How should you react to a new concept that you never expected?

The key advantage of this step is that Vendor A's product is competing against Vendor B's product. The buyer is essentially out of the firing line. The buyer is the judge, the passive third party being "impressed" by competing vendors. It is a nice position to have in this world of computers.

If the buyer fails to follow these procedures and begins dealing with only one vendor, with no backup, then every hour thus spent figuratively drives a nail into the buyer's coffin. Should anything go wrong, the buyer has no fallback position or competing vendor to use as leverage to obtain what is needed from the first vendor. The buyer has no backup, no aloofness, and little negotiating position. The buyer must take what he or she can get because so much committment to one vendor means that it would be too expensive and time-consuming to start all over with a new vendor—a bad position to be in.

NEGOTIATIONS

The next step is negotiations, and if done correctly, it may be hard work but very profitable and effective. The effectiveness does not come from cleverness at the negotiating table, or from a cagey body language, not even from studying all the new books on the "art of negotiating," but rather from the preparation of specific points that require a specific response from the vendor. If Vendor A does not deal in good faith and in a reasonable manner, then he or she can be thrown out and the next vendor brought in for negotiations.

Most computer dealers and salespeople are ready, willing, and able to deal on certain areas such as training, documentation, and modifying computer programs to reflect a customer's unique requirements.

Certain areas, however, are not easily negotiable (for example, certain liability clauses or damages clauses). In later chapters we will discuss which clauses should be negotiated and how they may be modified.

CONTRACTING

The last phase is the contracting process and ensuring compliance from the vendor. Boiler plate vendor clauses are written to benefit the vendor. It is up to the customer to understand some of the basic rights and obligations contained in the contract and to ensure that the contract is fair and equitable. The text analyzes a typical vendor's contract in a layperson's terms. Ensuring vendor compliance with the terms of the agreement is frequently a very difficult task. However, use of scheduled status meetings and written reports help to ensure control.

Let us take an overview of the computer marketplace and see what the future holds.

2

THE
ENVIRONMENT

THE COMPUTER AGE UPON US

Technology is defined in Webster's as the science or study of the practical or industrial arts; an applied science. Technology in the context of the computer industry means greater productivity at lower cost. These criteria—productivity and cost—are the driving forces behind the increasing use of automation in the broad spectrum of business and manufacturing fields in the United States, West Germany, Japan, and other developed nations.

At the root of this explosive demand is the capability of affordable electronically powered machinery to compute and transmit information, at the speed of light over any distance within human reach. This high-speed communication can improve customer services, raise the efficiency and volume of business, reduce expenses, and increase cash flow. Dr. Carl Sagan of the television program *Cosmos* says: "Computers rival the invention of writing as one of the most profound innovations in human history and are remaking the world at a phenomenal rate."

Although information processing machinery has been in use for several decades, its cost kept computers beyond the reach of all but larger organizations. However, sharp price reductions brought about by microminiaturization, combined with inflation in labor costs, have resulted in increasing growth in a labor-saving computerized society. The National Science Foundation reports that "information activities (both direct and indirect) account for more than 46 percent of the nation's gross national product." This information-oriented environment has created a climate in which those businesses that fail to automate will lose out to their competitors who have jumped on the computer bandwagon.

The United States has become the international leader in the research, development, and export of computer technology, yet business and industry, particularly the traditional office, have been slow to make effective use of automation. In contrast, West Germany and Japan, having rebuilt their destroyed economies from scratch after World War II, prudently equipped their offices and factories with the most up-to-date technology available. Resulting lower costs have given these countries a distinct competitive edge over the United States in overall productivity. Americans are beginning to realize that, in order to survive in the competitive world market, increasing use of computer technology in the economy is absolutely necessary to regain the productivity and profitability that have been lagging over the past years.

Productivity in the United States has been particularly inhibited in the typical office. General industry estimates show that during the 1970s the average blue collar worker's productivity increased by 80 percent, owing chiefly to automated factory equipment. Over the same period, the average office worker's productivity rose only 4 percent. This alarmingly poor percentage rate has focused attention on the office or small business as new arenas for vast improvement in productivity.

Some experts pin the blame for poor office productivity on inefficient allocations of resources. During the 1970s, says one researcher, 90 percent of office expenses went for salaries and wages in the typical office, 8 percent for space, and 2 percent for equipment. With a meager investment of 2 percent in the tools for the office worker, poor productivity rates are fairly easy to understand. By comparison, tools for the office worker equalled only 10 percent of the investment in tools for the factory worker. This trend must change if American businessmen are going to beat their foreign competitors. But we may ask "why automate now?"

Simple; machines reduce costs. With presently available automation, experts estimate that the business sector could cut operating costs 15 percent or more simply by improving the flow of information. Cutting costs is essential because modern business produces an avalanche of data. One report indicates that businesses make more than one billion telephone calls a year. They produce 75 billion documents and maintain another 300 billion. The annual growth rate exceeds 20 percent. This level of work load has extensive associated cost that must be reduced for businesses to remain competitive. It is this avalanche of data and information that paints such a bright picture for the immediate future of automation. Currently one in approximately 50 American workers uses a computer terminal. By the mid-1980s, according to projections, computer terminals will be the tool used by one in 10 of all American employees.

One industry authority cites that the cost of information processing is dropping dramatically and is driving up the demand for computerization. The cost of communications is dropping 11 percent a year; the cost of software is dropping at 25 percent a year; and computer memory is falling at a remarkable 40 percent a year. As one expert describes the phenomenon, computer-equipped businesses, in updating their automation since the early 1960s, have paid out no more for the replacement of the hardware and software, but have doubled the power, capabilities, and capacities of their systems every five years.

New pressures are suddenly being felt as microprocessor technology introduced in the mid-1970s has brought the cost benefits of computer systems into the range of small and medium-size businesses, even to the corner drugstore, small manufacturer, and professional office. Moreover, the microcomputers available now are capable of being programmed to meet future business needs. Says another authority, "By 1985 there will be an additional 10 million white collar workers using four times as many computers as now exist in the U.S. work force."

To that end, from the standpoint of physical compatibility between machines and people, emphasis has turned to designing computers and programs with as much convenience as possible for the users. "User friendly" is the term heard as engineers build more internal controls directly into computers, making the machines more responsive and less complicated for users. This means that persons untrained as computer users or programmers will be able to take advantage of many of the new data and word processing capabilities. These computers will be designed so that the neophyte can use them. Speed plus convenience will be measured when evaluating computers. In the final analysis, however, productivity cannot be measured merely by the speed of the equipment; it is the productivity of people that is the critical measure of success in any business. Without employee cooperation, a business can find itself in trouble very quickly. As the small computer finds growing favor in all levels of business, the primary challenge to the computer industry will be to recognize the computer's great limitations and to soothe employee resistance throughout the entire work force by finding a balance between the computer and the human being.

PEOPLE AND MACHINES
AND FUTURE SHOCK

Every revolution has its share of dislocations, and the computer revolution is no exception. For example, recent reports describe a company that laid off 550 of its 700 employees as a result of its new computer-directed automation. Workers fear for their jobs, and labor unions often resist automation in an attempt to save those jobs.

But the computer age is not the first technological revolution to be perceived as a threat to established values. The arrival of the automobile, for example, destroyed centuries-old professions and trades—horse dealers, blacksmiths, saddlemakers, and stablers. Yet, for every job ended by the automobile, a dozen others were created in manufacturing, sales, service, and repair, to say nothing of related industries such as highway construction, petroleum, steel, and rubber.

Indeed, all changes have rippling effects, for better or worse. Every level of society has benefited, in the long run, from that earlier revolution. If it were possible now to choose between living in conditions of the present or of the good old days, few would truly wish to return to the "good old days."

Like the automobile revolution, the benefits of the computer revolution are beyond calculation. Although computer capabilities have for some time held the attention of larger businesses, the American public in general is only beginning to comprehend the continuing trend toward computerization. Aside from financial advantages that computers can bestow on business and industry, these machines can provide invaluable information for the betterment of people's lives. Computers locate earth's natural resources and provide guidelines for world farming of land and sea. Computers can predict disasters and give warnings that can lessen the damage. Computers are frequently involved in rescue operations. Within computers are growing pools of knowledge about many vital fields, such as medicine, pharmacology, and law, forming libraries that are accessible through ordinary terminals. The impact of the computer industry on humanity defies analogy.

Nevertheless, it is only natural at this stage that computer capabilities described by some in terms of superlatives are frightening to others. Computer scientists herald the coming information age as that which "frees us from the weighty effects of ignorance." Yet the question to many is whether such control by the computer may be more of a burden than a blessing, whether it will rob our lives of other valuable qualities.

It is the viewpoint of Lawrence Heilprin of the University of Maryland that "increased interaction with computers diminishes the time spent in individual personal contact and tends to displace traditional cultural knowledge in art, history, and classic fields."

To the extent that individuals allow automation to take the physical burdens out of labor or recreation, their health may weaken. Much touted "shorter work weeks" may touch off feelings of boredom and, worse, uselessness. Terminal operators may be bothered by a lack of stimulating mental activity in their work. S. Zuboff of M.I.T. found that "when skills are no longer needed, especially in situations where the computer system is experienced as vast and incomprehensible, people begin to feel insignificant and overwhelmed."

Although people cannot help but marvel about machine intelligence, they grumble about machine invasiveness and errors. At present medical and financial histories and vital statistics of many households can be laid bare by the mere pressing of a few buttons. The potential for abuse is obvious.

Just as with the automobile revolution, this new revolution will introduce problems that the world did not have to face a century ago. Some of them will be very difficult, but deal with them we must. To begin with, men and women must understand just what technology systems are meant to do for them; they must understand the systems' strengths and particularly the weaknesses. Ultimately, people must run the machine and not the other way around. The computer is a mere tool, however stunning in its versatility.

As computers display their impressive abilities, it is easy to see how more power and influence may be imputed to computers than they actually possess. However, as more people become educated about the limitations of computers, most of the awe will be stripped away. Today's youngsters who are enjoying lessons in computer programming at their schools and even at summer camps should have few delusions about the capabilities and limitations of computers by the time they enter the job market. Undoubtedly, as a new generation grows up using computers, resistance to the concept of living in a computerized society, and its related problems, should noticeably lessen.

Thus, responding to the human factor is a very important element in all of computer science. Life is more than a series of computations that can be programmed into a computer. No mere machine can be the end-all to human problems. As H.L. Mencken put it, "There is always an easy solution to every human problem; neat, plausible and wrong!"

Many of the psychological effects that data and word processing systems may have on people, individually or in groups, will have to be studied by the successful manager. Especially on the job transitions from manual to automated systems, to be successful, will have to be balanced with care for human feelings.

Like it or not, the computer revolution is in motion, and there is no way to stop it. Automated systems are a fact of life; society must learn to adjust to the change. The course of technology may be set, but by understanding the forces that are driving the change, you will be better able to use the technology to your advantage. By being aware of some typical buyer mistakes, you can sensitize yourself to the technology and its associated problems.

TYPICAL BUYER MISTAKES

If you can identify some typical buyer mistakes that are particularly prevalent in the computer and word processing industry, you will be able to recognize them early and avoid them. More detailed discussion of these mistakes follows later, but for now an introduction to the most prominent ones may be most useful.

Minimizing the Risks

The impact of a computer on a business is always unique and the risks must be analyzed with respect to the particular circumstances. You must place your first priority on the capability and suitability of the system to your particular business or office.

Assume you feel that you can afford the new system, particularly due to the reduced prices. However, in six months the system turns out to lack the computing power needed for your work. The risks associated with an incorrect selection may be much greater than the loss of the relatively minor investment in the equipment and software. The downside risks of a wrong decision can be pretty grim, but they should be described and understood completely before proceeding. For example, the poor customer service that can be associated with a faulty computer system can result in lost customers, lost inventory, late reports, incorrect billing and a host of other devastating effects. Even when vendors fail to perform, monthly payments to them will be expected. Failure to make payments on the system can result in even poorer service from the vendor, not to mention the threat of a lawsuit by the vendor for past bills. A lawsuit can mean years of trial preparation, attorney fees, and exorbitant amounts of time. One expert reports 500 computer lawsuits in progress in the early 1980s; and predicts by 1985 there will be 5,000!

All of these risks are present with the implementation of any computer system. The mere cost of the equipment and software is really just the tip of the iceberg. All too often the initial investment is mistakenly considered the total risk involved. This is simply not the case.

It is important to understand what options are open and to decide just how your dollars can best be spent. Having vendors propose their solutions to your list of specifications allows you to maintain decision-making flexibility. You can select the solution that best fulfills your organization's needs.

Let us suppose, however, that several computer vendors, after studying your specific business needs, all propose systems significantly more expensive than you had budgeted. This would clearly indicate that you had better "rethink" your plans from the top. If the decision is made to go ahead, it may be wise to obtain the budget increase needed in order to buy an adequate system, rather than acquire a smaller, less powerful system just because it will cost less. The key is to recognize and understand the full array of risks associated with the selection of the wrong system.

Cost Only

Traditionally, uninformed buyers have operated on the theory that cost is the most important criterion in purchasing equipment. Within the computer market, this is a serious misconception because computer installations require extensive vendor support and service, lasting long past installation.

The contract will involve services such as software maintenance and documentation, equipment maintenance, training programs, vendor responses to trouble calls, and various other service-oriented functions. All of these support and service functions are required for the computer system to operate successfully. It is a serious mistake to look to the cost of the machinery alone and lose sight of these required services.

Cost is always an important factor, however, and, of course, it does set the parameters for purchases. Most small businesses would not invest in the "Cadillac" of computer systems when a "Volkswagen" system would do. However, "you get what you pay for" as the old adage goes. Far too many computer system failures are attributable to the customer's decision to go with the lowest priced system without recognizing the need for performance and functionality. You must learn enough to differentiate between the Cadillacs and the VWs in the computer marketplace. If a computer on the VW level will do the job, fine! If the Cadillac level of system is needed, you should understand the necessity and make the financial commitment.

Overdelegation

Problems can begin when the prospective customer fails to become fully involved with the process of computer choice and procurement. All too frequently computer failures in a business have involved the misdirected efforts of consultants hired to take on the job of computer selection and programming for a client firm. Serious problems arise when the expert concentrates too exclusively on the computer side of the problem, while failing to learn about the client's operations.

The break in communication may occur at the outset as the expert begins designing a new system without working closely with the client and the client's first-line operators. The business professional who has totally delegated the project to the consultant without retaining any control may eventually find that he or she has wasted time, money, and effort in having developed a computer system that fails entirely to meet the requirements of the first-line functional personnel.

A number of companies have failed because of oversights by consultants who were unacquainted with the basics of the clients' business. Programs have lost payrolls and inventories, misplaced customer lists, missed shipment dates, skipped orders, delayed billings, and jumbled accounts irretrievably.

The point is that the shopkeeper, manager, doctor, lawyer, realtor, insurance agent, stockbroker, manufacturer, and any other business man or woman who turns to business automation is going to have to learn the basics about the computer. Such responsibility is not wisely delegated away. The mere act of delegating has been the root cause of many failures that could easily have been avoided. Without an excessive amount of effort, you can learn and understand the principles of purchasing an office computer or word processor in sufficient detail to make your own decisions in this important area. This book provides necessary tools to enable nontechnical persons to cope with the inevitable encounter with the computer or word processor.

Shopper's Syndrome

Shopping from store to store may be adequate for buying certain items, but in the computer marketplace it can result in a poor selection and later failure. The uninformed buyer who goes from one computer store to another, having no conception of his or her requirements, is asking for trouble. The buyer may be persuaded to buy based on the assertiveness of the sales representative or the buyer's own mood at a particular time. The shopper may rush to buy what he or she naively perceives as a "great bargain, this week only, while the stock lasts." Without realizing it, the buyer will probably end up with whatever model is overstocked in the salesperson's inventory, whether or not the system is correctly configured for his or her unique requirements.

The first step in effective computer acquisition is the requirements study discussed in Chapter 3, an examination of the operational functions within your business as it already exists. You also analyze prospective functions and plans for future expansion. You consider such factors as active accounts, number of bills sent monthly, type and size of inventory, letters and reports generated, and so forth. From this study you can comprehend the approximate amount of data that, currently and in the future, will need to be processed. This information is essential. From this step the entire process of selection will follow.

Rather than shop without definitive requirements, the informed computer purchaser uses the information gained from this analysis of his or her current business procedures as a basis for fashioning a list of requirements to present to vendors. The object is to select the computer system that can best meet those explicit requirements. The various vendors will base their proposed equipment, software, and services on this list.

Trust Me

Although it may seem unbelievable, the same old "hype" that sells used cars may successfully sell computers. The actual lines and delivery may not be quite as obvious, but the concept is the same. A computer salesperson endeavors to develop a personal relationship with the buyer. Phrases are used such as "We'll get this system in, don't you worry about it!" or "You just let me know what you need and you've got it!" or "We have all of our resources available to you; we'll make it work!"

Trust is not bad, of course. However, it is of utmost importance for the purchaser to keep in mind that most companies owe their existence to their ability to sell. The moment that the agreement is signed, the marketing people may move on and a new group of players, the technicians, enter the scene. Any sense of personal relationship that has developed with the sales representative, any "trust me" feeling can evaporate upon the mere mention that your sales rep has just been transferred to a new account.

The answer to the "trust me" pitfall is that all commitments, promises, and deliverables to be produced by the vendor must be clearly documented in the written agreement between the parties. This sounds very simple, and it *is* simple, provided the buyer can avoid misplacing his or her trust in a particular vendor's verbal representations.

Vendor Demonstrations

The customer's primary reason for having vendor demonstrations in his or her office or shop should not be to evaluate vendor products. Rather, the chief value of a vendor demonstration is that it offers a chance to learn about the technology and to see it in action.

A vendor demo is an excellent opportunity to discover what capabilities are being developed and becoming available in the industry, such as new types of printers, the latest in word processing systems, and other new communications technologies. Any information of special interest gained from these demonstrations can be added to the Request for Proposal (RFP), enabling a complete comparison of the latest capabilities.

Step-by-step timing is very important to the selection process. A mistake frequently occurs when the customer tries to reach a decision prior to collecting the facts needed for an objective evaluation. The buyer becomes genuinely enthusiastic about the product during the demonstration (of course, the vendor is trying cause that effect), and the decision begins to go in one direction too early.

Sometimes the enthusiastic purchaser becomes the salesperson's best advocate, encouraging other demos for fellow employees and explaining the superb capabilities of the vendor's product to all parties. But with every enthusiastic statement or recommendation, the buyer makes it more difficult to arrive at an objective decision.

Remember to look at a vendor's demonstration in the early stages of the procurement as an educational opportunity, not a decision-making forum.

We have discussed just a few of the most important and common mistakes that frequently occur: minimizing the risk, cost only, overdelegation, shopper's syndrome, "trust me," and vendor demonstrations. Others are discussed in later chapters; however, as in every endeavor, there are certain "tips" that, if followed, can make your experience much more comfortable.

TRICKS OF THE TRADE

A few years ago I attempted to install heavy duty shock absorbers on my car. The first shock took almost eight hours; the second took 20 minutes. The task became easy once I learned the trick. The same is true of selecting computers or word processors. Once you know a few important tricks, the entire job will go much easier.

This section describes the more important tips. Other good tips are discussed in later chapters, but this overview covers some of the key points.

Competitive Buying

One cornerstone of successful computer procurement is "competitive buying," that is, having vendors compete against each other for your business. All too often the purchaser attempts to deal with one single vendor, with no alternative or backup, and, therefore, is unable to negotiate successfully.

The way to successful competitive buying is to distribute a Request for Proposal to a reasonable number of qualified vendors. Responding vendors will attempt to propose a computer or word processing system that they believe will meet your requirements. You are then able to study and compare the various vendor proposals, using a variety of evaluation criteria. During this phase, you merely invest time, not money, but in return you receive a wealth of information that may become very important in your selection.

With additional knowledge obtained from other sources, including vendor demonstrations and visits to a number of vendor business sites, you are ready to begin negotiating with whichever vendor is determined to be the best qualified, based on your objective criteria. Before negotiations, you should identify specific areas that bear discussion between you and the highest ranked vendor.

Should it happen that during the negotiations the highest ranked vendor fails to negotiate in good faith, or fails to address your concerns, you can easily move to the next ranked bidder. If negotiations with that vendor are also unsatisfactory, you may opt to negotiate with the third ranked bidder or return to the highest ranked bidder. You retain the options as to whom you will deal with and when. It is by retaining the ability to negotiate one qualified bidder against the other that you keep the essential bargaining edge over the vendors.

Financial Leverage

The number one rule for ensuring vendor compliance with the terms of the agreement is through the use of financial leverage, which is to say withholding payment until after the work is done. It seems remarkable that so many people pay for a computer system prior to its being installed and made operational.

Vendors are entitled to reasonable payment terms. They may also be entitled to payments of a percentage of the full price when deliverables are accepted by the customer and the system is installed.

However, before signing a contract, the buyer should negotiate for the right to withhold payments for the hardware and software until all of the components are installed, tested completely, and working according to the specifications. Thus, according to their bargain, the vendor should receive payment when the computer system is operational. At this point there should be two satisfied parties, the buyer and the seller.

Contracts as Planning Documents

Many people see a contract as a collection of meaningless "legalese" that only lawyers can comprehend. Accordingly, they often seem to feel that the less involvement they have with the contract the better. Much of this negative feeling stems from lawyers' tendencies to use legalese that is at times difficult or impossible to understand. However, the plans to install a computer or word processor can be managed in such a way that planning sessions can double as negotiating sessions. As ideas are discussed between the purchaser and the vendor, and plans become firm, the paperwork involved can easily become the contract and, conversely, the contract becomes the essential planning document. Opportunities for planning and documenting the computer installation and operation will focus the attention of both the seller and the buyer on details of the contract provisions. You may be able to obtain additional commitments and promises from the vendor, and these also will be incorporated into the agreement/planning document.

The installation of a small business computer or word processor is a difficult challenge, but a detailed plan will help to ensure success.

By participating in the planning sessions, you can be involved with the important decisions that must be made. It is safe to say that every moment spent in the planning phase, before the agreement is signed, will reap its reward in efficiency during the implementation and operation of the computer or word processing system.

In its finished form, the contract should include, by incorporation, all of the working specifications, drawings, charts, and price lists, letters between the customer and the vendor, and any other material that may be of value as reference.

It is extremely important in contracting to require the seller to document details identifying who will be responsible for what. For example:

Who is to order the required cables?
When and where is the training to be conducted?
Who will ensure that proper electrical connections will be available?
When will acceptance testing begin?
Who is to obtain insurance?

Which individuals from the vendor staff will help to train employees at the customer's site and when will they begin?

Every pertinent detail that can be identified, if at all possible, should be incorporated into the final agreement.

The best time to formulate detailed computer installation and operation plans is during contract negotiations. In that way the planning document is incorporated into the agreement before the parties sign it. If the planning document is postponed until after the agreement is signed, the planning will probably never be done because by that time the vendor will have one main goal—to get paid. Normally the buyer will not be able to plan after the contract is signed because all of his or her available time will be involved in reacting to problems and vendor requests. The tip is to make the contract become the master planning document.

Control of the Vendor's Activity

One professor teaches that the rule of thumb for estimating the cost of a computer installation is to estimate the original cost, then multiply by two. His statement is intended to generate attention, but it contains a foreboding of a recurring problem. It warns of the difficulty in completing the installation of the system within the stated budget and time schedule. Computer installation problems that find their way into newspaper headlines almost always concern budget overruns. A few simple guidelines can help to mitigate the problem:

1. A high level representative of the buyer must be appointed as the project manager.
2. An equally high level representative of the seller must be designated as the vendor's project manager.
3. Regularly scheduled meetings should take place between the two project managers, every two weeks usually being sufficient, more often if necessary. This is the important communications link between the two organizations, which must be kept open and responsive.
4. Written reports should also be prepared by the vendor at two-week intervals. They specifically describe: progress toward milestones, progress toward budgeting dollars, and problems encountered.

These simple status reports and meetings allow the user to keep track of the vendor's performance. Even more important, close monitoring allows the project direction to be changed when the need arises.

Installing a computer for the small business would appear at first glance to be simple; "plug it in and away it goes!" is the sales pitch. However, installing operable and satisfactory software for that machine, that is, the programming that directs the machine to accomplish the required task, is not easy at all. Priorities may change, decisions will have to be made, and schedules adjusted as the installation effort progresses. The frequent, regularly scheduled status meetings and reports are the most effective method to allow flexibility in the installation process. The two project managers are high level problem-solvers, and they must be delegated the authority and be held responsible to facilitate changes as the need arises. Experience has shown that this method is the best way to supervise the vendor's activity on the project and to see that the job is completed within the budget.

Other tips are discussed later, but the most important to remember are those just detailed: competitive buying, financial leverage, contracts as planning documents, and control of vendor's activity.

At this point, a few examples of successes and failures may add some perspective to our discussion.

EXAMPLES OF FAILURES

Nobody likes to think about the prospect of failure, but before approaching the computer marketplace it is important to realize what a devastating effect a computer failure can deal a business.

Usually the computer or word processor becomes central to the operation. The organization can come to a screeching halt when the computer "goes down." Most people involved with computers have experienced the typical problems: "the computer is down," "sorry, computer error," "the computer goofed."

But before becoming bogged down in the term "computer failure," let us consider the nature of typical failure situations.

Rarely, if ever, is a "computer failure" thought of as a permanent catastrophic collapse of an entire computer network. This is because the more critical systems produce sufficient and quickly accessible duplicates of all important data and information. For example, certain vital agencies, such as medical, defense, and space systems, and some financial entities, ensure a consistently reliable service by having entire backup computers available for emergency use. The most frequent failures, however, are much more subtle.

Less Bang for the Buck

The most frequent cause of computer failure in the more typical business occurs when there is "less bang for the buck." The purchaser of the computer simply does not receive enough computing power. A failure of this sort is more accurately described as a "computer procurement failure." The computer or word processor does not have sufficient capabilities to meet the customer's requirements. The purchaser continues along in a dissatisfied and angry mood anyway. That is the failure.

Defective Software

Another typical customer purchasing failure occurs whenever the buyer is led to believe that the new computer's programs will handle more functions than they actually can. Once installed, with the purchaser contractually committed to payments, the software deficiencies become apparent. In these cases, the vendor usually promises to "fix the bugs," but the software expert's time is spread so thin, among so many other accounts, that corrections are not forthcoming in a timely fashion, if at all. Many computer purchasers suffer from this type of failure.

At this point the business professional often tries to improvise "around" the deficiencies. He or she gets entangled in a sort of fire-fighting mode of operation, constantly trying to stamp out little problems that flare up, using solutions that skirt around the software problem. This situation is also a failure.

Paying Too Much

Failure may be too strong a word to use when a buyer has simply paid too much for a computer system that satisfies his or her needs. Like success, failure is often difficult to measure. However, if a comparable system could have been purchased or leased at a cost far less than the final price, then indeed there has occurred a failure in the procurement of the computer system.

Federal Government

A classic example to teach businesspeople what *not* to do is taken from a 1979 *Report to the Congress,* entitled "Contracting for Computer Software Development" (FGMSD-80-4, November 9, 1979, p. 51), which describes a federal agency's commitment to pay $378,147 for a computer system over a projected nine-month period. Forty-four months later, after having spent $2,200,000, the government cancelled the project. It abandoned all attempts to use the system contracted for, turning instead to a relatively uncomplicated system developed by the federal agency itself, at a cost of $20,000.

Why do such catastrophic failures occur? Let us examine this particular example more closely in terms of previously stated mistakes and tips.

The federal governing agency in this case had envisioned contracting for only a small management information system, designed to allow one federal bureau to monitor its own activities. Later changing its plans, the government broadened its specifications to become capable of monitoring the agency's additional six bureaus. Because of the original contractor's "experience and knowledge" gained from previous dealings, the revised plans were "sole sourced" to the same vendor. The contract failed to define, satisfactorily, the performance and acceptance testing criteria. Although the plans did require monthly progress reports, no documentation standard had been established. As it turned out, the people who had worked on the initial agreement no longer worked for the vendor. Thus, the benefits of experience accumulated by vendor personnel in the earlier planning sessions had been lost.

Shortly after the contract was awarded, the vendor reported to the federal agency that the small system initially bargained for could not be adapted as planned.

The remaining problems reported to the Congress were typical in that the contractor continued to request additional funding to cover:

> Constantly changing requirements requested by the government agency.
> Lack of executive staff support for the new system.
> Software problems.
> Production problems.

Upon the government's audit of the project, it was discovered that:

> The agency had assigned six different project managers during the life of the contract.
> The contractor had assigned at least three different development teams.
> The contract was modified 16 times.
> Agreements were unofficially made between the contractor and agency officials, without the project managers' knowledge.

Fundamental rules of successful computer procurement had been ignored. In its preliminary negotiations, the government agency had failed to:

> Assign one person as project manager who would head the agency's negotiating team through completion of the project.
> Designate that only one project manager should represent the vendor.
> Bid competitively.
> Control changes or modifications during the project.

You can avoid computer failures—that is, computer procurement failures—providing that there is no failure in following the established rules of procurement, rules born of reason and good common sense, and based on experience with the customs within the computer industry.

Commercial

Among minicomputer procurement failures is the classic predicament mentioned earlier of the frustrated man who ended up trying to chase down the "computer guru" who had designed the software for his business. The machinery in this case was a small business system. The software had been "sole sourced" to a software vendor who simply failed to live up to the software contract specifications. It became evident that certain bargained-for and essential functions had not been programmed into the system at all. As each error was identified, a "patch" was installed by the vendor's maintenance person. A patch is a small programmed instruction entered into the computer and intended to correct a known software failure. However, each patch in this case caused other errors, which created new sets of problems, further complicating the situation. As each of these "bugs" appeared, the operational reliability of the entire system degenerated, and the businessman's irritated clients began to take their business elsewhere.

Most intolerable was the fear that if the buyer were to have sought legal redress, the vendor's support services—as sporadic, limited, and unsatisfactory as they were—would have terminated immediately, leaving him in a worse position.

Rain or shine, however, monthly payments for the system were due based on the computer contract.

With fears for his business survival uppermost in his mind, in this no-win situation, the only solution was to continue to seek whatever help he could get from his vendor, biding time so that a software replacement could be found.

In another typical example of computer procurement failure, a microcomputer rests idly on an office desk, shoved to the side, unused, because the office personnel lack training to operate it. The machine, in fact, operates reliably and its software does exactly what it was advertised to do. However, the business simply does not know how to utilize the computer for that particular business.

Conclusion

The rate of business disasters laid at the computer's doorstep is high, with related financial losses often overwhelming to the business. Yet the record shows that the machinery involved in business failures has seldom failed to function as designed. Almost without exception, the fault has rested with failure to follow the necessary steps for a trouble-free selection, installation, and operation.

A prudent businessperson may well conclude that unless responsible computer selection procedures are followed, some degree of "failure" should be anticipated. The procedures will require effort. However, they are the time-tested steps toward a successful computer choice.

EXAMPLES OF SUCCESS

Often success and failure are difficult to define. What criteria define a successful computer system? What gives a business the ability to increase its work load, to reduce its overhead, avoid mistakes, or improve efficiency? Criteria will depend on the circumstances.

It is important for each businessman or woman to analyze his or her own situation in order to determine what features are necessary and desirable in a computer system. A system that works successfully for an associate, a competitor, or a neighbor may be ineffective or may even bring disaster to another operation.

Certain categories of criteria call for particularly careful consideration in a successful computer procurement.

Customer Service

Businesses in which service to customers is paramount need computer systems that process information with such speed that no customer will be made to wait beyond the absolute minimum. Customers ready to engage in business have certain expectations in mind as to the reasonable amount of time required before attention is paid to them. Furthermore, customer expectations are keeping abreast of changing times and technology. Consider, as compared to years ago, the speed and ease with which one can do banking errands or make airline reservations.

One large bank recently invested several million dollars to upgrade its existing computer installation because it was slower than that of the bank's competitor down the street. An unusually large number of the bank's accounts had been withdrawn and transferred to the other bank. Why? It was determined that customers had become impatient with waiting. Customer service may be the key criteria for success.

Reducing Overhead

Studies conclude that overhead reductions made possible by information processing are already evident and will continue to benefit businesses at an advanced rate in the future. A machine that can outperform an employee can substantially reduce a company's overhead. This is true particularly in the office environment where at least half of the work force is involved in data handling.

Reducing overhead does not directly mean that current employees will be laid off. It can mean, in most cases, allowing greater increases in the work load without an associated increase in the work force.

It is clear that the labor element of overhead is significant, typically 90 percent of all office expenses. Overhead itself frequently accounts for 50 to 60 percent of revenues for the typical office, while most offices cannot keep up with the administrative and typing burdens. Profit is restricted, not because of the productivity of the principles but rather by the limited capability of the office staff.

By making administrative people more efficient, the principal can increase his or her productivity without an increase in overhead. This is what we define as success, when overhead is reduced as a percentage of revenue.

Ensuring Accuracy

Owing to the speed and accuracy of the machinery, automated systems have been replacing manual systems for information processing. Tasks that traditionally required hours of laborious effort and that were made even longer by frequent arithmetic errors can now be done on a computer 100 percent accurately and within seconds. As an example, consider the relative ease of filing personal and business income tax returns calculted with the help of computers!

Speed

Approximately every five years since the 1960s advances in technology have caused computer processing power and speed to double, while computer prices have remained fairly constant. The rate and increase of speed and power now possible among computer systems almost defy description. Tasks that 20 years ago required days of work can now be done in minutes or even seconds by automated machinery. Far from being behind in customer billing, in keeping inventories, in paying bills, or in making payrolls, many businesses find that they are having difficulty in fully utilizing their computing capacity.

Efficiency

Some businesses suffer from just plain inefficiency. Manual procedures or outdated machinery can restrict effective growth of a business. Antiquated methods may cause the same problems to recur routinely. In such an organization, improved efficiency is a realistic goal and a measure of success. Offices, particularly, are inefficient and are prime targets for the new automated systems. Let us review examples of success.

AIRLINES

Most people are familiar with airline use of computers for passenger flight reservations. Stored within the computer are facts that can be accessed in an instant in response to almost any pertinent question. For example:

What accommodations does the passenger want?
_____ Aisle window?
_____ Smoking or non?
_____ Special menus?
_____ Movie?

Connecting flights?
_____ On same airline?
_____ Transfer to another airline?
_____ Arrival time?
_____ Departure time?
_____ On schedule?
_____ Behind schedule?
_____ Ahead of schedule?

Prices?
_____ First class?
_____ Tourist class discount?
_____ Economy plan discount?
_____ Family plan discount?
_____ Super-dooper special?
_____ Excursion discount?

Passenger information?
_____ Names?
_____ Addresses?
_____ Phone number?

Special problems?
_____ Need pet carrier?
_____ Need wheelchair?

You want to change your mind? Okay, let's do it again! Consider also that business projections are made from the travelers' decisions, such as aircraft scheduled, crews assembled, air routes planned, food prepared, and a host of other decisions and actions. And customers are free to change their minds as many times as they choose. Airline computers offer the epitome of customer service in our times and make possible the volume of traffic that improves our lives and our work.

BANKING

Another example is the new automated tellers that banks are providing for convenience and services. Most of them are open around the clock. These machines take deposits, disburse cash, transfer funds between accounts, and provide instantaneous balances—usually with no waiting! Merely push a few buttons and most of these transactions can be completed in minutes. Why bother with banking hours, parking the car, and long lines inside of the bank?

However, many people do not use the automatic tellers. When asked why not, the main reason given has been "I don't trust the computer." However, the convenience for depositors and the accuracy and convenience of electronic data processing are overcoming customer hesitancy. Similar success with computers is possible in a multitude of fields, provided, however, that the proper methods are followed in selecting, contracting, and managing the computer resources.

SUMMARY

Indeed, the "computer age" is upon us; the smart businessman or woman has embraced the new technology and will continue to do so. The interface of people and machines is a relationship that takes attention and care to ensure a comfortable transition. There are typical mistakes to avoid and tips that will help in encountering this most complex decision. There have been great failures, yet there are important and significant successes attributable to this powerful technology.

Success takes work and effort, and it starts with conducting a requirement study of needs. Chapter 3 discusses how to accomplish this.

3

MEASURING
THE JOB

"A problem well stated is a problem half solved" said inventor and one-time employee of the National Cash Register Company, Charles Kettering. Those words were penned almost a half century ago, but they are still as valid today in relation to the computer business. One of Kettering's fellow employees, Thomas Watson, had similar ideas for solving problems. His famous slogan, "Think," became popular in offices throughout the country. "To start thinking," Watson said, "start with the goal and work back. Picture what you want, define the purpose, the need, the goal—the objective that is desired. Then try to devise ways to build that machine, to outline its method of measurement, to devise a process of operation—to reach the goal for which you start." This statement and many other maxims from Watson probably are partly responsible for the success of the multibillion-dollar company he founded—IBM.

In order to define your goal, you need to evaluate your present office work load and then, deciding what you want to do about it, look for ways to improve it.

MEASURING THE CURRENT WORKLOAD

The most difficult part of defining the problem is in finding or making the time to analyze the current work load. There are always the demands of the business to be taken care of, customers to be attended to . . . right now! But determining the current level of work is essential because it is from this information that all other steps follow. The types of information requirements differ greatly with each business, but the information *can be* quantified. It may be inventory part numbers and current stock reorder points, or a directory of customers and all the associated customer data. It may be sales figures, payroll data, or the number of letters produced each week. The key is that time must be made to measure this information load. Relying on what is done next door or by the competition will not be good enough. The effect must be particular to your individual need. You must think about your needs because from your figures vendors will propose products to you. If your initial information is incorrect, or based on competitors' requirements, or those of a friend or family member, the result may be that your vendors propose the wrong type of equipment, which would mean ultimate failure.

If you take the time to properly determine the amount of work presently done, you should be able to evaluate the impact of any additional work load during peak periods. You should also be able to estimate the savings in time, and consequently money, by improving the work flow. It is important that you include not only those activities presently performed, but also those procedures that, although they might be desirable, are often not done in order to expedite the current work flow.

To better determine what areas to evaluate, let us look at a hypothetical office that is presently converting to automation through a variety of equipment and procedures that will streamline production flow. In demonstrating the office automation capabilities, keep in mind that in addition to clerical and secretarial productivity, there can also be a greater increase in managerial and professional output.

OFFICE STATISTICS

Every typewriter in this country is a potential market for an office computer or word processor. The impact of the computer or word processor on the traditional office will be greatest on the principals.

It has been shown that less than 30 percent of a principal's time is spent on actual thought work, such as, reading, creating documents, or solving problems. Much of the time is consumed searching for information, arranging meetings or conferences, and waiting for the preparation and delivery of reports and studies. Many of these tasks can be improved through the use of an office computer, and there is even greater productivity possible with a computer that is connected through some network to subordinate computers.

Several studies have shown that 60 to 70 percent of all of the businesses in the United States with sales of $5 million or less are still using manual methods for their accounting procedures. Better than 80 percent of the 2.2 million small businesses still handle their basic administrative and information processing tasks manually. In fact, one study indicates that wasteful office activities cost American business as much as $300 billion a year. We need to understand that a large portion of these costs are associated with misuse of professional resources so that we do not dwell too heavily on merely the secretarial inefficiencies.

It is interesting to note that since the early 1970s, manufacturing productivity has increased almost 40 percent due, in no small part, to the use of industrialized robots and other computerized systems. It is unfortunate that the same technology has not been applied to the office environment where productivity during the same decade increased by only 4 percent.

Much of the focus on improving productivity in the past has centered around the secretary. Both vendors and users tried to increase the output of the average 50- to 60-word-per-minute secretary, but that is not enough to increase the overall office productivity. Managers and professionals were paid $500 billion dollars—more than double all the other office costs including salaries for clerical staff and office space. Yet while white collar workers enjoy high benefits, increasing 10 to 15 percent per year, productivity remains low. Office automation is not simply a matter of installing equipment. It involves careful planning, equipment selection, employee education, and office design. It requires products that will win over staff members by adding more functionality and ease of use.

Offices will be going through all of the traumatic changes that result in the transition to computer-based systems. Therefore, systems must be selected so that the users, and particularly the managers, are comfortable with and enthusiastic about the new machines. One source in the office automation field puts it quite simply: "The challenge of automation is to keep the goals of the office humanly oriented, while at the same time being concerned for the business enterprise."

To more easily identify the problems in your own situation, let us look at a typical office that represents a microcosm of most of the problems, challenges, and opportunities in the real world of computers and word processors. The case study in the next chapter relates to this office and can be considered typical for a small operation. It can even be extended to larger business environments using the same concepts. The requirements of your own office will be unique, but they can be compared to this typical office.

Most of us are familiar with the activities that occur in any office. The ones of particular note here in evaluating the work load pertain to generating letters and forms, making personal contacts, correspondence, accounting reports, invoicing customers, and managerial reports. Traditionally, accounting operations are the most common and usually the only use of computers. In many cases, the accounting automation is not even performed on-site. A bank will usually handle payroll, and some other computer service will handle other accounting tasks. It may be possible to consolidate these functions into an on-site computer which also provides word processing functions.

This typical office, the ABC Firm, is comprised of six principals and has a staff of four secretaries and two assistants. The associated problems are comparable to those in any office of like size, whether made up of lawyers, accountants, bankers, real estate agents, travel agents, or many others. The ideas also relate to those involved in manufacturing companies and service-related firms. The most important consideration, regardless of application, is to remember that *information processing techniques* remain constant although the actual data content varies greatly, depending on the type of business. As you work through the case study, attempt to make the transition to your particular business. If your business is smaller, adjust the figures downward, and if your business is larger, adjust accordingly.

The techniques and procedures followed here have worked in a variety of office applications and have been tested extensively in actual use. As you go through each of the steps and procedures, note the salient points and apply them to your business requirements. The appendixes contain forms that may be easily modified to accommodate an actual situation and can prove very helpful in evaluating your particular requirements.

WORD PROCESSING WORKLOAD AND QUESTIONNAIRE

Several areas should be evaluated when looking at the general word processing overview of any office application. One of the initial evaluations will probably be the *volume of work* produced in the office. Essentially, "how much paperwork is generated per day or per week." You want to get an accurate accounting of how much data, including correspondence, documentation, interoffice memos, and other similar items, are generated on a regular basis.

After you have identified the amount of paperwork output, you need to evaluate the amount of typical *revision cycles* that one of these documents goes through before it can be considered final. Some documents may be correct on the first try, others may be revised once, and in some cases a document or even a simple letter can be revised as many as 10 times. What is typical in your environment? The nature of the changes should also be considered. For instance, are just a few words changed here and there, or are entire thoughts changed?

You then need to consider the *repetitive type* of applications where similar output is repeated over and over. There may be common business letters that are sent to a variety of business clients where personalized letters are preferred. The only differences between letters are the person's name and, perhaps, a reference to an account balance. Generation of invoices is also typically repetitive where perhaps only the name or address of the client changes. Just how much repetitive work do you do in your office?

Let us get back to work flow and see how it is affected by *backlogs*. Are there frequent cases where backlogs occur with consequent delays in important documentation? Is it possible to get higher priority documents out quickly or do they have to be placed in the typing queue and thus delayed until other less important documents are completed?

And what about *quality* of the documentation that leaves the office? Is the goal to have absolutely perfect, no white-out, no erasure letters? Do you sign anything if it is placed in front of you, or do you proof it first, looking for typos and spelling errors? Most people regard a signature on a document as indicating that the signer agrees with the contents of the paper and its presentation. Therefore, you want to make sure that it is correct in every detail. In fact, you will probably find that the more meticulous you are, the more revision cycles will be encountered on a particular document.

Everyone is aware that the computer is very good at performing rapid, repetitive operations, and the application of computers to typing chores is no different, particularly in generating redundant documentation. How many paragraphs in your particular business are retyped over and over on different letters or documents just because they are always included? These *standard paragraphs* may be considered "boiler plates." How many times do you generate a standard paragraph describing your company or employees? How much boiler plate do you have in your business? In almost every business there is going to be some form of duplication of typed material.

"I need it yesterday!" How many times have you heard that assertion? It seems that everybody needs to respond quickly and everybody wants documents generated at the same time. Which documents need to be turned around quickly and which can be delayed? How easy is it to terminate one typing project, insert another, and then resume the original project? There are certainly going to be applications where *responsiveness* is an important parameter in the generation of a particular report, such as one that a doctor or nurse might generate in a hospital environment. And, finally, you need to evaluate the method for *transmitting reports* and documents to the typist. Is the information given to a secretary in person, with the data being copied in shorthand, possibly creating time-consuming interruptions with such things as a phone call? Or do you generate material using machine dictation, where there is a smaller impact on job throughput by minor interruptions in the secretary's schedule?

All of these parameters affect overall throughput and need to be evaluated individually. There may be some particular circumstances that apply to your particular business and, therefore, should be included in the evaluation list as well. To simplify the collection of this information, questionnaires will help spot the major problems from both the viewpoint of the originator or principal and the secretary or typist. The Originator's Questionnaire (A1) and the Typist's Questionnaire (A2) as well as other forms, are shown in Appendix A and can be considered a guide to evaluating your own requirements.

Originator's Questionnaire

General data. After the general information of name, title, and department, list the secretary/typist most often used by you. This information, when completed, can help balance staff workload.

Clerical support. Now you need to evaluate present clerical support. This question is extremely valuable because it identifies if there is a problem in the first place. It may also immediately indicate where the more serious problems exist. Conversely, if all the principals report that they are satisfied with the secretarial support, this information could also have a significant impact. This is the first step in defining your goal.

Employee reporting structure. In any medium-size or large office the reporting structure may not be as clear as originally thought. By identifying others in this structure who share your staff, you can pinpoint potential bottlenecks in work throughput. A person in one department may use someone from another area for clerical support. One of the purposes of this questionnaire is to identify who is reporting to whom for office procedures and office support.

Paperwork generation time. How much time out of each day is spent generating data?

Work generated. The originator indicates what percentages of his or her work is generated by longhand, shorthand, or machine dictation.

Work outside the office. You will need to know the frequency that your principals work outside the office because there are many different types of equipment that can be used to satisfy this requirement. The method of creation can be compared to the in-office generation. This will help in evaluating overall work load needs.

Rough drafts. Many people simply prefer using a rough draft in essentially every circumstance. Knowing what percentage and how often will help in planning such things as the quality of paper purchased for the drafts plus what standards of quality should be used on a draft document.

Revising correspondence. What is the frequency of revising correspondence sent from your support staff?

Repetitive correspondence. Do you create form letters that must be sent to a comprehensive mailing list?

Fill in. Do you create forms or letters that require completing a different combination of blanks for each different piece of correspondence?

Standard paragraphs. Do you use standard, nonchanging boiler plate clauses in your correspondence? Word processing machines can store these clauses and instantaneously retrieve the clause or paragraph on request.

Merge text with your work. Do you use previously prepared text and incorporate it into new correspondence?

Satisfied user. Are you always late in correspondence or invoicing due to the typing backlog? If you are satisfied, should you be?

Backlogs in typing. How frequently must you live with a backlog in getting typing done?

Do you send work out? How much do you spend for outside help with typing? Are you sending work out or hiring temporary help?

Are you satisfied with the quality? How frequently do you send a letter knowing full well that it could be improved but lacking the time to redo it? Does the typed document present you in a professional manner or is it frequently of inferior quality?

Do you do secretarial work? Recent studies show that many highly paid managers or principals spend an excessive amount of time doing secretarial jobs. Typical examples are photocopying, research, filing, sorting and posting, or bookkeeping. With many of the contemporary office tools, principals may find it faster to do things themselves than wait for secretarial help. The principal is frequently making four or five times the salary of the secretary, but the principal simply does what must be done, despite the unproductive, or at least inefficient, nature of the work.

Do you have work currently not being done? A principal may be rescheduling priorities so that the typing can be kept to a minimum.

Peak periods. One common problem is the "peaks and valleys" of many jobs and offices. The questionnaire attempts to identify these swings so that the work can be transferred to minimize the impact of a peak or valley. One principal's peak may be another's valley. This question-naire will help exchange this type of information.

Anticipated personnel changes. The frequency of personnel changes will directly affect the amount of training that must be planned.

Suggestions. The best ideas for improvements frequently come from the first-line worker. Suggestions are not often freely volunteered, so you must ask. This gives each person a chance to identify personal ideas for improving office situations.

This Originator's Questionnaire is the first source of input about the amount and quality of data that must be processed.

Typist's Questionnaire

Since the typist is the one most closely associated with the office work discussed here, the typist's point of view should be evaluated in de-termining possible improvements in the office automation area. The typist's views on the office work load will give a different picture of your office procedures and, in some areas, will help to identify goals that management may not normally consider.

General data. After name, title, and department, the supervisor and names of persons to whom the typist reports should be listed. This provides for cross-reference information and potential rescheduling of duties.

Equipment. The present typing equipment will give some indication of which equipment the typist is familiar with and whether such features as proportional spacing will be required on any replacement equipment.

Work presented. The different percentages of types of input will be important in analyzing typing work loads whether machine dictation, shorthand, long hand, or copytype.

Rough draft. This relates to output and can help to determine the amount and type of paper required. It may also be that rough draft material could be printed on a high-speed printer rather than on a letter-quality printer normally reserved for the final document. Understand-ing the amount of rough draft may help to increase work throughput considerably by using two different types of printers.

Revision cycles. How does the typist handle a large number of revision cycles?

Amount of revisions. The typist should also identify how the revisions are made and whether a page needs to be completely retyped. Specific change methods are discussed below.

Author changes. Does the author actually change the material or are the changes due to typographical errors?

Typographical errors. This primarily relates to the final, clean copy and should identify the percentage of pages that need to be completely retyped due to typographical errors.

Previously typed documents. This refers to the boiler plate type of information where many paragraphs are copied or used in multiple documents. The higher this percentage, the more emphasis should be placed on the ability to store previously typed documents that can be easily recalled with a few keystrokes.

Cut and paste. Can pages be cut apart and reassembled in proper order at least for rough draft review? A word processor provides this capability with just a few keystrokes.

Erasures. Are erasures, whiteouts, or self-correcting type permitted? Where are they allowed?

Types of documents. For each of the following types of documents, estimate the average length and average number of copies required of each. The major categories are: straight text; statistical information, particularly relating to charts; forms and envelopes; and standard or repetitive paragraphs. Answers to this question will help to identify the capacity and capabilities of some of the word processing features.

Photocopying machine. If it is near the typist's desk, less time is spent in each trip to the copy machine, but it is more likely that more frequent trips are made rather than consolidating all copying chores for one period or even having a subordinate perform the copying chores.

Time away from desk. This will help in identifying actual availability for typing tasks.

Paper width. This will help identify the type of printer required when specifying a system.

Special type styles. This will help define required printer capabilities. Styles relating to a particular industry, such as engineering symbols or Greek letters, should be included here. As we will see in the next chapter, there is a special section for specifying unique symbols required for your applications.

Average timeline. The typist should estimate the amount of hours per day or the number of days per week normally spent on general correspondence, statistical work, and miscellaneous forms and reports.

Peak periods. The typist should specify any major typing tasks that occur periodically, such as a month-end report.

Backlog. Does work pile up at regular intervals? Is it always piled up or is there an opportunity to catch up? Daily? Weekly?

Overloads. Is overtime used or is outside help obtained for handling overload situations?

Daily schedule. The typist should estimate the amount of time per day, over a weekly average, for the normal office functions. The two tasks related to the type of word processing activities we are discussing are typing tasks and proofreading tasks. There are other time-consuming functions in a secretary's day that may detract from the apparent output of an individual typist. Tasks grouped under major administrative functions include sorting and handling mail, answering telephone calls, photocopying, posting/bookkeeping, filing, research, assisting others, reception duties, taking dictation (shorthand), and any other special projects or duties not listed. If the typist indicates only a small amount of time in any one of these categories, it may indicate that the principal is doing some of the tasks that the typist or secretary could be performing more cost effectively. Two other areas that should be addressed in this daily schedule are personal time and the all-important waiting for work. Does the typist have extra time waiting for someone to assign a task or looking for other duties to perform?

Nonroutine work. This section addresses those special projects or assignments that may occur sporadically, such as generating a proposal every few months. The amount of time spent on this or other related projects should be estimated so that total secretarial capacity can be compared with total requirements over, let us say, a one-year period.

Suggestions. This category can help to identify major goals that the secretary/typist can define so that these goals can be incorporated into the overall goals of the office.

When the Originator's Questionnaire and the Typist's Questionnaire have been completed by each person in the office, the total picture of the office requirements can be developed. In evaluating the overall work load, remember to include all office personnel that will be using the equipment you anticipate obtaining. If you are looking for a simple word processing system, you may not need to check with the accounting department. If you are anticipating a computer system that will include the versatility of word processing in addition to accounting applications, you must broaden the scope of the activity evaluation.

Selling the Staff

When presenting this form to a typist, you may have to be somewhat diplomatic and not overdemanding in what is required on the questionnaire. How would you feel if your boss said to you, "I want a log of every single item that you do today." You would be suspicious, to say the least! There may be some resistance to doing the requirement study, but if you anticipate it and handle it properly, there should be no major problems. Before such a study is undertaken, be certain that full management approval has been received and make the individual employee aware of this fact.

You should be aware of the psychological implications of word processing and data processing functions and, therefore, should be sensitive to employee resistance. You should explain that the purpose of the study is to evaluate a need for a computer or word processing system that will, in the long run, make individual jobs easier. It will increase overall productivity and, in all likelihood, will not replace any one typist. You just want to assure employees that in order to decide on the proper equipment, you need to measure the overall work load and that there is no intention to try and eliminate anyone for poor performance. The questionnaires have been designed in such a way as to be as unthreatening as possible to the individual employee. It is an attempt at an objective measurement of work and will not directly address the individual employee or the employee's work output. Indicate that employees can help to contribute to a smoother running office.

Sample Summary Charts

Using the information collected from the questionnaires, you can put together comparison charts. These charts can present an easy-to-understand picture of the overall office workload. In the Typed Document Input Source (A3) you see that the majority of input is provided in longhand and, in particular, no machine dictation is used in this office. In the Typed Document Classification (A4) half of the typed material is straight text and 15 percent of the total is standard or repetitive. A full 30 percent of the typing chores is devoted to statistical generation, which is probably one of the most time-consuming activities.

The distribution of this pie chart will vary greatly depending on your type of business. An engineering office, for example, will have much more statistical output than, say, a lawyer's office. A lawyer's office will probably have a much larger amount of boiler plate than in this example.

Straight text could vary greatly depending on particular applications. All of this information will be very useful and even essential when defining the requirements for your new office automation system— especially when you need to describe your goals to the vendors who will be providing the equipment. In particular, you want to make sure that the right kind of software is available to support your major needs.

In the Secretary/Typist Time Distribution pie chart (A5) you see how the normal activities of your typists are used throughout the day. The chart is very helpful in evaluating the utilization of employees and perhaps in rescheduling work loads, particularly where waiting time for one typist may be applied to a potential overload situation for another typist. In evaluating the actual time, be careful not to overreact to the "away from desk" time. Most of this time is used for productive work, such as filing, taking dictation, or working on special projects away from the desk. It is difficult to determine from this chart whether all time periods spent on the individual tasks are productive and perhaps a separate study would be required to evaluate those particular cases.

Note that the administrative functions represent almost half of the secretary's time. If the same chart were made of the principal's time, how much of the corresponding administrative functions could be transferred to the secretary, thereby increasing the principal's effectiveness? The functions represented in this group include handling mail and phone calls, photocopying, bookkeeping, filing, and other similar activities.

The Length of Typed Documents chart (A6) shows the overall percentage based on the number of pages in each document. In many offices where proposals or technical manuals are generated, documents of 50 or 60 pages to hundreds of pages are more common and shorter documents would have a much smaller percentage. These numbers will help to define the system requirements when evaluating the word processing capabilities of your intended system. (More on this in the next chapter.)

COMPUTER WORKLOAD AND QUESTIONNAIRE

After measuring the word processing requirements, we turn to computer requirements, namely, billing, timekeeping, accounting, cash processing, payroll, and miscellaneous items. The same basic approach of providing a questionnaire to the principals and staff should be used. The work requires a small amount of analysis of current operations and a review of current forms and sample reports so that the amount of data can be measured. Based on these findings, the computer's size and operational requirements can be determined.

Let us briefly review forms A7–A21 in Appendix A, a sample questionnaire and associated forms. The Computer Questionnaire (A7) is divided into four major sections: billing and timekeeping, accounting, cash processing, and payroll. Following it are many sample forms and reports. The samples were provided by leading office automation companies and should give a good idea of the power, flexibility, and usefulness of office computers.

The normal procedure in the study is to ask the principals to provide samples of their current reports. You can use your time better, however, by reviewing some of the typical forms used and the reports produced by an actual office computer rather than reviewing the typical nonautomated forms and reports found in most offices. Thus, the sample forms and reports will provide two perspectives; they will:

1. Present an example of a form or report that would be produced by the principal or secretary for analysis during the requirements study.
2. Illustrate what new forms could be used and what reports could be generated by an office computer.

These forms and reports provide superlative models to compare to your unique circumstances. The model reports have been prepared for an office that bills customers or clients based on the time expended by a professional, such as a doctor, lawyer, accountant. Many of the forms come from a law office example and refer to clients. This is a good model to use because most business people can understand the normal operations of a law office. These same programs can be converted easily to fit almost any other office environment. As you review the materials, think about how the forms should be modified to meet your own particular situation.

BILLING AND TIMEKEEPING

What must the computer do to ensure that the principals get paid for services rendered? Let us review only the more important questions:

How many characters of data do you retain per customer for billing purposes? (Attach sample form.)

We need to determine how much storage must be reserved on the computer for customer data. New Business Memo (A11) is a form that could typically be prepared for each new customer or client. The form contains name, address, and phone number, and also includes customer number, billing preference, description of services requested, estimated fees, detailed information about costs, and so on. Your business may need all or only part of this type of information retained in the computer.

How many customers do you have at the current time? How many in the next three years? (Attach sample report.)

The Client Directory (A12) is a sample report that lists pertinent information about current customers. The number of customers and projected growth in data over the next three years are very important in planning your computer storage sizes. How much storage will be needed? You must make plans now to meet future needs. A computerized listing of customers can easily be produced in alphabetical sequence and updated in seconds. Once on the computer, the customer list can also be sorted based on any criteria you desire, for example, customers that use a particular product, customers that reside in a particular geographic area, and the like.

How many time entries are logged in each day? Week?

The time log in A13 is similar to most others. Date, customer, case number, time, and activity are usually required in most time logs. The sample time log shows that a computerized system allows for additional comments to be included in the customer's bill, for example:

10 02 81 Jones 15324 1.5 Research in State Library

Remember also that once data are stored within the computer, the information can be retrieved, processed, modified, and repeated over and over without additional typing. This particular question addresses how many input data are typically created so that storage space within the computer can be properly apportioned. Some principals may only have six or so entries per day; others, depending on work load, could have dozens of entries each day.

A major improvement in billing systems is now available which incorporates a billing device into the office telephone system. Upon the conclusion of a telephone call a red light or tone is engaged which reminds the principal to bill his or her time. The principal then merely suppresses a button on the phone which engages a microcassette tape recorder. The principal may then dictate the billing information using as much descriptive language as needed to summarize the phone conversation or meeting. Each day or week, the secretary collects the cassettes and keys the data directly into the office computer which produces a complete set of bills and accounting reports. Such a system obsoletes the traditional manual time log method.*

How many characters of data are recorded per time entry? (Attach sample form.)

In addition to data, customer name, and so on, there is space for 37 characters of comments for each entry.

How much time is spent each day recording or correcting time entries? Each week?

This question attempts to analyze how much wasted, nonproductive time (and expense) is used in the billing process. Most people would be surprised to learn how much time is lost in this clerical work, or how much money must be paid for bookkeepers to maintain a correct and timely billing system.

How many different types of bills do you use? (Attach sample form.)

This question relates to the storage requirements needed for the generation of bills and most importantly to the computer programming requirements to allow the principal to make a selection of different styles of bills. Form A14 illustrates a type of bill that can be generated by the computer.

Do you need fee structures stored in the computer and automatically generated on bills? Or will bills be prepared from manual input only?

*For more information on this system, contact California Law Office Automation, Manhattan Beach, CA 90266.

Some computer software is able to store many different fee structures or price lists and automatically have the computer do a "table look-up" to establish the correct price. The computer programs needed to perform this function may cost more, but they save a great deal of time because price checking and the like are done instantaneously. When a bill is prepared based on the rate in effect for that particular customer, the computer will do the automatic look-up and create a correct bill.

Do you want dunning notices?
The computer can automatically prepare dunning notices ("Why haven't you paid your bills?") based on failure to record a payment after a certain time period, which the computer can track.

ACCOUNTING REPORTS
Accounting reports are extremely varied and unique to each business. However, let us review different types to illustrate what a computer can do for you.

How much time do you spend on accounting reports each week? Each month?
This question is important because it once again focuses on how much time is spent on clerical tasks.

How many accounting reports are generated each month? (Attach sample reports.)
This question requires the principal to collect all of the current reports and analyze them, with the help of a consultant, in terms of the amount of data that must be stored and processed. Also, based on the types of reports that are analyzed, certain determinations can be made about the types of computer programs that will be required.

Do you need. . . ."
Forms A15–A19 contain examples of the types of reports that can be produced by an office computer. By analyzing each sample, you will better understand the capabilities and information handling powers available from these machines.

AGED ACCOUNTS RECEIVABLES REPORT (A15).   This report shows accounts receivables from 0–10, 11–30, 31–60, 61–90, and 91-above days owing. It can draw attention to customers who need extra attention in terms of collecting moneys.

PRINCIPAL'S EARNING REPORT (A16).   The computer can

automatically generate an earnings report for the current period and year-to-date. The percentage breakdown of earning among principals can easily be produced to provide valuable management information regarding the productivity of the members of the office. This in turn can lead to improvement in the productivity of poor performers or at least begin some discussion on problems that may exist.

STAFF SERVICE REPORT BY MATTER (A17).   This report allocates the effort and time spent on each individual customer or client. The report lists, by customer, exactly what is being accomplished for this customer. Remember, all of these reports are generated from the simple one-time input of a New Business Memo plus the time log entries. The information is never typed a second time. The computer stores the data and prints the report when needed.

ACTIVITY SUMMARY BY STAFF MEMBER (A18).   This report can give exact data about the productivity of each member of the office. It provides valuable management data, and its preparation requires essentially no additional work because the information is all stored in the computer.

STAFF PRODUCTIVITY REPORT (A19).   This is a consolidated listing by percentages of the comparable productivity of each staff member.

All of the accounting reports are valuable in identifying trends and problems in the office. The reports give the manager the tools and insights into what is going on so that the resources can be properly applied to increase productivity—which is, of course, your goal.

How many copies of accounting reports do you need?

This question helps in determining the required speed of the printer as well as whether multipart carbon paper or xerography will be used to produce the reports.

CASH PROCESSING

Cash processing, like other clerical functions, takes time and costs money.

How much time do you spend on cash disbursements each week? Each month?

Cash processing is particularly slow because it is usually a manual process and clerical errors can be very costly. However, to analyze lack of productivity, you should answer this question as accurately as possible.

How many characters comprise an entry in your disbursement log? (Attach sample form.)

Cash Flow Application Adjustments (A20) illustrates an automated method of recording cash transactions. The customer number is identified and the date, source, and amount of withdrawal are set forth. Receipts of cash are recorded by amount, source, and date. There is also available space for comments that can be stored in the computer. Note that only one entry on this form is required. The computer makes all the correct postings to the correct customer account and reflects the transaction automatically in the customer's bill.

How many cash transactions do you have each week? Each month?

Once again, questions that measure the volume of transactions relate to the need for additional storage space as well as whether special equipment (for example, a terminal) is needed by the office bookkeeper. All the information has use during the later stages in the procurement process.

PAYROLL

The type of information that can be stored on a computer for a payroll process can vary enormously. Office computers can store and access personnel data that can greatly reduce clerical time.

How many characters of payroll data are stored on each employee? (Attach sample form.)

The Staff Master File report (A21) illustrates a limited amount of data that can be stored and automatically used where needed. For example, a payroll program could access this type of information and automatically generate all needed payroll data.

How many employees do you have now? In next three years?

This question addresses the storage capacity of the equipment and future growth plans and requirements.

How frequently do errors occur in the current payroll system? Each week? Each month?

Do you currently have a problem with your payroll program? This answer should help to identify problems in this area.

CONCLUSION OF COMPUTER STUDY

The data collected from analysis of model requirements for an office computer will be analyzed, measured, and presented in the RFP document. A vendor will then be able to understand your requirements for word processing and data processing. With that understanding, the vendor will propose the best product at the lowest competitive price.

The programming functions and reports that you learn about in your requirements study will enable you to make a knowledgeable selection about the software capabilities you will require. Understanding what comes out of the computer and what must go into it is the best way to make a knowledgeable choice of software.

Here is a special note to the one- or two-person office: the smaller the office, the smaller the requirements study. A one-person office could accomplish a requirements study probably in one week with the aid of a data processing consultant. The key is to do a requirements study. Vendors need to know your work load before they can effectively help you.

In the typical office discussed in this chapter, we assume six principals, plus four secretaries and two assistants; with an office that size, the overall requirement study may take as long as three weeks. To do a thorough and meaningful job during this period, it will probably be effective to hire a consultant at least for a portion of the time to assist in using the forms and evaluating the data. In the following section we discuss the value of a consultant and how such experience can be used to accurately measure the work load.

USE AND SELECTION
OF CONSULTANTS

During the fact-finding and evaluation phase, a consultant or computer professional may be most helpful. The effort in measuring requirements is an objective exercise so the consultant does not need to be given much independent discretion during this phase. A consultant can be hired on an hourly basis and, with your cooperation, should be able to generate a report that summarizes your information work load without great expense.

Depending on the complexities of the operations, a study of this nature could range from eight hours for a small office to a month or more for a large organization. The report should describe how many people generate how much data in what amount of time. This information will help you define the number of terminals required in your system. The amount of data generated will dictate the capacity of storage devices—both on-line and off-line. You are interested in the elements and quantity of data, not the content of data.

Let us look at a simple case in determining total computer file size for one operation. As an example, the consultant, or anyone doing the investigation, will determine the size, in characters, of one customer record. Then the total number of customers, plus some expansion room, will be used in computing the required computer file capacity. There may also be a separate inactive customer list kept for archival purposes in a storage media. The advantage to using someone competent in this field should be obvious: from the consultant's experience, the right questions will be asked.

The best way to select a consultant, just as selecting a doctor, lawyer, or auto mechanic, is through references and interviewing. Education, an impressive résumé, or membership in a particular society do not necessarily make for cost-effective consultants. Consultants from blue chip, prestigious firms may sometimes do unsatisfactory work for their clients, while relatively inexperienced, sole practitioners, perhaps with little formal education, can be superlative.

You should look for a consultant with some or most of the following attributes:

Excellent references.

Experience in your particular field.

A knowledgeable person who can speak your language—the days of the "computerese wizard" are over.

An enthusiastic, customer-oriented individual who expresses a keen awareness of your needs.

The consultant should be involved from the beginning of your work load study. He or she may even have suggestions on how to improve the forms or may have a similar set of forms. Perhaps forms will be developed that are more suitable to your particular situation. In any case, the consultant will help to evaluate the particular needs of your office.

During the evaluation period, the consultant may only be involved a few hours a week to make sure the work load study is progressing well. At the end of the fact-finding period, he or she will compile all the information and perhaps even generate charts similar to those already described. This graphic approach may help to sell the idea to management and may also be helpful in defining your problems to the potential vendors.

Vendors bring us to the next step in the process of procuring a computer or word processing system. In Chapter 4, we compile the information collected here into the Request for Proposal.

4

PREPARING
REQUIREMENTS

Alice in Wonderland asked the Cheshire Cat to indicate the correct path to follow. The cat asked where Alice desired to go. Alice replied that she didn't care. The cat said in that case it didn't matter what path Alice took!

In selecting a computer system, you do not want to make the same mistake as Alice. Unlike Alice, you do care, but you also need to know which way you are going. Electronic technology is racing ahead with more and more companies entering the computer industry all the time. There are presently more than 140 companies in the office automation business. Yet it was only in the mid-1970s that the first stand-alone word processor became available!

How can you tackle and control such a profusion of competing companies and technologies? The answer is a Request for Proposal (RFP), causing vendors to compete against each other for your business.

USE OF AN RFP

The purpose of an RFP is to, as accurately as possible, set forth your:

- Current work load.

- Current problems.
- Current plans.
- Current technical requirements for a new system.
- "Blue sky" future plans that you may not be able to afford today.

The RFP opens the door so to speak on your organization and your plans for the future. Vendors are invited to take a look at the operation and its problems, then, using their resources and knowledge of computer technology, to determine which of their products and services can best fit your requirements and plans.

The objective of an RFP is to place the burden on the vendor to devise a solution in your particular circumstances. In an RFP, you do not want a preconceived solution to your problem. Do not fool yourself into thinking that you know enough about the computer industry to make a correct decision without thoroughly surveying the current marketplace. By placing the burden on the vendors through use of the RFP, you relieve yourself of many of the burdens of trying to keep up with the computer industry. The RFP will result in written binding proposals from the vendors, which will "freeze" the technology and prices for a period of time, usually 90 days, during which you can do an in-depth analysis of the best technology and prices the vendor can propose.

During the evaluation period, you can obtain additional clarification and demonstrations from the vendors to better understand their technology, service, and pricing. The important point is that these rapidly changing variables of technology, service, and price are "frozen" during this evaluation period to allow some thoughtful and detailed analysis.

A frequent mistake, as previously mentioned, is that people so often have preconceived products or selected companies in mind in preparing the RFP so that the exercise is really not worth it. In both large and small procurements, frequently a vendor who was not even considered presents a proposal that satisfies the needs better than all the competition. Maintain an open mind in preparing the RFP so that no one vendor is given preference over another. In particular, make sure that the features and specifications meet your needs and are not just copied out of one of the vendor's data sheets. The vendor community does not need help. They have enormous marketing resources that can be utilized to compete for your business. By allowing vendors to compete openly in a clear, understandable RFP, the consumer will come out the winner. First, the vendor will show how the equipment does or does not fulfill your requirements, and second, when the vendor knows there is competition, the prices will be more competitive.

WORTH THE EFFORT?

Is an RFP worth the effort? By all means. It is a mistake to attempt to select a computer or word processor without one. You would lose the advantage of being given the choice of the various systems at the varying prices. You would lose the negotiating leverage between competing vendors, which is so valuable in extracting additional concessions from the selected vendor.

The effort involved in preparing the document itself is straightforward and easy. By using the model RFP in Appendix B as a guide, you can prepare an RFP document for your organization without much difficulty, time, or expense.

The model RFP for the small firm is relatively simple, yet it contains specifications for a total office automation system. An RFP could be much smaller than this model and still have the significant benefits associated with this tool. The RFP should define the specifications for hardware, software, training, maintenance, programming support, documentation, and various business programs. Depending on the operation, sophistication, and money involved, your RFP could be abbreviated from that shown in Appendix B. The expense for its preparation can be returned a thousandfold in potential savings to the organization by making a wise selection of the right proposal—but it must begin with the RFP.

BUYING PERSONAL COMPUTERS

Much has been said and written about the "personal computer." Let us first try to define what that term means, then discuss the best method of buying one. "Personal computer" means different things to different people. Each of the more than 140 companies in the computer/word processing business has its own definition. Perhaps the most useful definition is a computer designed for personal use—not an office staff—that can be obtained for less than $10,000. Home computers certainly fall into this category and usually have a large number of entertainment programs and games that make these machines highly attractive. Mathematical capabilities are available, but they are less in demand because the home usually does not require a great deal of computational power. Home computers can be purchased with checkbook, mailing lists, home budget programs, recipe storage, and other homemaking routines, but clearly the entertainment value is an important characteristic. The definition of a personal computer is predominantly keyed to use and not necessarily its cost or its computing power.

Thus, if a personal computer were taken out of the home and put into an office or business, where it was required to perform the normal office and word processing functions, its proper name would then be a "small business computer." Such a machine would still cost below $10,000. However, it could perform word processing, accounts receivables, accounts payable, payroll, general ledger, and inventory. As you can see, the difference in home versus business computer is more a matter of what software is used than the makeup of the hardware.

The procedures described here may be too elaborate for purchasing a personal computer for home use. On the other hand, the procedures should apply equally well to a single user system, which might be used to do work at home, just as they apply to a small business computer for the office or shop. In fact, many offices, both large and small, are purchasing personal computers for the staff to reduce the work load on the larger computer systems. In some cases, these personal computers can communicate directly with the larger computer systems.

As for personal computers in the home, the best advice is simply to shop around for prices. There are many excellent machines and programs available, as well as clubs comprised of personal computer owners who trade programs and discuss common problems. The machines are generally reliable and usually work without much trouble. If a part fails, a replacement can be purchased without large expense at a local computer store.

The only word of caution is to recognize that many home computers are primarily designed for entertainment and limited homemaking functions, and they may not be as expandable as the more costly office machines. There is little business risk with a home computer because its uses are limited. It is when you begin to plan on automating a business that the business risks mount quickly, and you must have a more thorough analysis of options and pricing before making a selection.

Small Business Microcomputers

A small business microcomputer is priced usually at under $10,000, is small enough to sit on a desk top, and is designed for the small office or business. Such names as Apple II, TRS-80, Commodore, and Atari are familiar in this range of machines, but the list of companies now in the market includes many computer giants, energy companies, banks, and others. A primary supplier of microcomputers is the computer store, where many different brands and prices are displayed or available off the shelf. The growth of microcomputers has been about 24 percent each year and more companies are entering this marketplace all the time. Japanese firms (Sony, Sharp, NEC, Panasonic, and others) now market microcomputers for personal and small business applications.

Software for microcomputers is also an explosive marketplace, from the choices of programming languages such as BASIC, COBOL, FORTRAN, and PASCAL to application programs such as VisiCalc, a popular financial planning package. There are thousands of other "packaged programs" for accounting, inventory, word processing, cash register, and mailing list programs.

Although this book is about the procedure in selecting and purchasing an office computer or word processor, it will be helpful first to review some of the basics about computers.

HOW COMPUTERS WORK

A microcomputer operates on the same principles as a larger computer and even most multiuser word processors. The principles of data processing and word processing are essentially identical; only the functions are different.

A microcomputer's "brain" usually fits on a chip of silicon less than one centimeter square. It typically manipulates "words" that are eight *bits* long, a bit being a binary digit, 1 or 0. An eight-bit word (usually called a *byte*) can represent a character of text, two decimal digits, an instruction, or numerous other things that need not concern most users. The memory capacity of a microcomputer is specified in *kilobytes* or Ks (K = 1,024 bytes). Most machines have two kinds of internal memory. Read-Only Memory (ROM) contains instructions that allow the machine to communicate with users and input/output devices and to keep its internal operations in order. Random Access Memory (RAM) is used to store programs and data. A typical microcomputer in a business application might have 48K of RAM. That is enough memory to store about 8,000 words of English text.

A microcomputer system usually consists of the computer itself, a typewriterlike keyboard, a televisionlike CRT (cathode ray tube) screen, a printer, and some external memory or storage. The most popular form of external storage for small systems is the "floppy disk." A thin, circular piece of flexible plastic coated with metal oxides, a floppy disk works like magnetic recording tape, except that rather than reeling through hundreds of feet of tape to find the part it wants, the computer simply shifts its read/write head like the arm of a record player to the desired track.

Depending on size and sophistication, floppy disk capacities vary from about 70K to more than 500K bytes. Floppy disks are popular because they are easy to handle, simple to use, and convenient to store in an ordinary filing cabinet. Systems requiring quick access to larger amounts of data—a larger inventory of letters, documents, parts numbers, or customer numbers—need more expensive hard-disk systems with capacities in millions of bytes. A floppy disk is similar to a small 45 rpm record; a hard disk is more like a large 33⅓ rpm record. The hard disk holds more data and provides faster access to data.

It is difficult to compare microcomputer systems for many reasons. Some package the keyboard, CRT, computer, and disk drives in a single unit; others sell all parts separately, like components of a stereo system. Prices vary according to capability, sophistication, ruggedness, and market factors.

A typical small business microcomputer—with 48K of memory, a CRT, one or two floppy disk drives, and a printer—will generally retail for between $4,000 to $10,000. Adding a five-megabyte, hard-disk drive might cost another $5,000. For more information about computer workings and "buzzwords," refer to the Glossary.

As with everything else, there are disadvantages to the microcomputer, some of which are:

A microcomputer may be too small from a hardware side to meet the data processing and word processing requirements of a business.

It may not have sufficient software to meet growth needs.

The training provided to the novice is usually inadequate, so a tremendous amount of time can be wasted by trial and error.

Programs for a microcomputer may not be flexible enough to allow easy modification when there is need to make changes to reports.

Some smaller microcomputers are not supported by technicians that will come to your office. You must bring the machine in for repair and hope that the store owner can fix it.

When you need to move on to a more powerful and larger machine, the transition from the microcomputer may be expensive and difficult.

With the number of products available, it is difficult to select which micro will be best for you.

Care must be taken when selecting a lower cost system to make sure that it not only will meet present needs, but can be expanded in the future. Be sure to have software compatibility between the low cost version and the next larger system.

Many small business computers can mislead the prospective buyer with a low price—for just the computer. Do not neglect the cost of proper peripherals and software.

For many small businesses, however, the microcomputer is the very best way to go. Microcomputers provide the key attributes important to the small business: they are inexpensive, they are powerful, and they work!

How To Buy A Small Business
Microcomputer—RFQ

Once you have decided on a particular computer system for your small business (after doing a limited requirements study and surveying the marketplace), rather than prepare an RFP, you may prepare a Request for Quotation (RFQ). An RFQ is a document that asks for *price quotes only*. For example, you decide that an Apple II will be more than adequate to meet your current needs and those over the next few years. You have selected several packaged programs that you are convinced will meet your requirements. You prepare a letter (the RFQ), which identifies the product that you want, and you send the RFQ to a dozen or more local computer stores and suppliers. The letter basically says "I want an Apple II; please give me your price." You send the RFQ to stores usually within driving distance since you will have to go to the store to make the purchase and pick up the equipment.

The goal in sending the RFQ is much like the goal of the RFP—to create a competitive relationship between stores to lower your price for the equipment. By mailing the RFQs, you save time by avoiding the need to drive from store to store. Quotations received from the stores will remain firm for 30, 60, or 90 days so that you have time to analyze the price quote and attempt to negotiate any other terms you may need.

Hundreds of dollars can be saved by using an RFQ in procuring a microcomputer. Aside from price, it can set forth other important factors. Examples of negotiable items may be: hours of in-office training, an additional set of manuals, customizing the reports so that your company name will appear, additional discounts on supplies (paper, ribbons, diskettes), and many others.

Now let us analyze in more detail the use of an RFQ.

REQUEST FOR A QUOTATION

An RFQ is used when you have a specific product in mind and are predominantly concerned with obtaining that product at the lowest possible price. There is usually little negotiation in an RFQ method of procurement. You would draw up the specifications of the particular product you desire and solicit vendors to meet or to exceed the specifications at the lowest possible costs.

Once you determine that a vendor can meet the specifications, you should buy the system from the vendor with the lowest price or best service or a combination of many parameters that can be weighted as you desire.

The essential requirement in using the RFQ is that you know exactly what you are looking for. The RFQ requires that you come to a decision about what you need. It thus assumes that you really know what you want. In many cases, of course, you *will* know exactly what you want, and the RFQ is the appropriate method of procurement. However, in cases where you are uncertain about your needs, the RFQ is not an appropriate method. The RFP, allowing the vendors to propose their best product and services and then to negotiate, is a better method when dealing with unknowns and uncertainties.

ADVANTAGES/DISADVANTAGES OF THE RFP AND RFQ

Do the advantages of the RFP or RFQ outweigh the disadvantages? Let us look at some of the pros and cons in dealing with the RFP and RFQ in order to get a better perspective on their relative values. Some of the obvious advantages of the RFP are:

1. Causes vendors to formulate a solution.
2. Provides more flexibility.
3. Encourages negotiations.

Disadvantages of the RFP are:

1. More difficult to select a vendor.
2. More work in evaluating vendor proposals.
3. Takes time to prepare.
4. May prolong the procurement process if you specify something that does not exist.

The advantages of the RFQ are:

1. Easier to evaluate by merely determining the vendors who can satisfy the specifications and then choosing the lowest price.
2. More objective; you can determine if the vendor satisfies the specifications.

Disadvantages of the RFQ are:

1. Assumes the solution to the problem.
2. Less flexible in negotiating new points that are uncovered during the process.
3. May not allow you to obtain the newest or best product because you are unaware of those products.

BIDDER'S CONFERENCE

What is a bidder's conference? What can be gained? Is it worth the effort?

A bidder's conference is a meeting to which all vendors are invited to discuss your RFP and to ask questions to gain a fuller understanding of your operation, problems, plans, and especially requirements. The objective is to educate potential vendors with sufficient knowledge about your operation so that they will be able to propose their best product and services to fulfill your requirements.

Lack of communication and misunderstanding abound in most human relationships. The deeper an understanding of your operations and plans, the more responsive the vendors' proposals will be.

Usually a bidder's conference is held after the RFP has been sent to the vendors, giving them time to review it and to prepare a list of questions. The conference, therefore, is an opportunity for vendors to ask questions or to clarify points that may seem ambiguous or are unstated in the RFP. The opportunity for face-to-face conversation about the RFP is absolutely essential to ensure that you have clearly described your operation and that the vendors understand your requirements.

Another key point about the bidder's conference is that all the vendors should be given the same supplementary information and, therefore, will be bidding on the same statement of your needs.

The bidder's conference usually should take a couple of hours, depending on the number of bidders present and the adequacy of your RFP. It is a small price to pay to ensure a better understanding between consumer and vendor.

REVIEWING THE RFP

Let us look at an example of a comprehensive Request for Proposal. Appendix B contains a model RFP for the procurement of an Office Automation System, which we will use to illustrate particular points. The model RFP in Appendix B presents the system features desired by the buyer in the left-hand column, set in lightface type. (The right-hand column, set in boldface type, presents model vendor responses to each point.) In the following discussion we will review each of the sections to provide a better understanding of just what is required and why a particular point should be included.

Throughout the review, all aspects of the RFP along with distinct features are discussed. Using the ideas presented, you can decide which sections apply to your situation and which need not be included. In many cases, particularly for smaller companies, it may not be practical to generate such a comprehensive RFP as one that might be required by a larger company. The model RFP should help to define your specific requirements and to optimize an RFP for your needs.

As each section of the model RFP is discussed, you may refer to Appendix B to associate the specific point with its place in the complete document.

Introduction

The Introduction (Section 1) is intended to give vendors some idea as to the intention of the system and the major reasons for generating the RFP. It is important to include a discussion of the principal points considered in deciding to invest in the new system. If the reasons are well stated, vendors will have a better understanding of your goals for the system. Vendors will be aided in determining, first, if they can satisfy your major objectives and, second, in highlighting those major points in their proposals.

Background

The Background (Section 2) gives vendors an overview of your company. The ABC Firm example in this book is a partnership, but your company could be a sole owner, a corporation, a subsidiary, or any other form of a business arrangement. This information gives vendors an understanding of who will make the decision regarding the new system and, perhaps, how that decision will be made.

The Background should also provide the vendor with an understanding of the history of the operation and the objectives of the new system. ABC Firm desires word processing capability and an automated timekeeping and accounting system. Your objective could be to reduce overhead, improve inventory control, improve productivity, or reduce staff. The vendor will do better if the goals and objectives are understood. Vendors, like you, will be working backward from your objectives. They will try to answer all the salient points of your RFP and, at the same time, illustrate other important features of their system.

It is also desirable to identify any current problems the organization is experiencing. ABC Firm is having a problem with excessive overhead in terms of salaries and benefits. In addition, the work load has increased over the last five years and current staff levels are just barely able to keep up. The RFP indicates that the future is not bright for the firm unless a solution to its problems is found.

You want the vendors to be aware that you may need additional capacity in the near future. If you anticipate a significant expansion, the vendor that can provide additional work stations at a later date may be the optimum choice for you now. If the vendors do not know your future plans, they may try to sell you a system that will just meet current needs but have no expansion capability. This nonexpandable system may cost a little less now, but it may cost a lot more in the future if you have to order a complete new system. The results of the requirements study are summarized in Workload (section 2.3) which lists as much detailed information as possible about the quantity and type of work to be performed.

Requirements

The Requirements section (3) is the essence of the RFP. It contains a description of all your requirements, in detail. It explains to the vendor what they must tell you and how to respond to the RFP. You want to make sure that each vendor will be quoting on the same set of requirements and in the same way so that you can more easily compare all of the responses.

In the sections on equipment configuration and optional hardware (3.2 and 3.3), you want to show vendors what you think are the minimum requirements for your application. You also imply that there may be other features of a particular system that could be used in your application or that could be considered for expansion later.

REQUIRED VS OPTIONAL RATIONALE

This RFP shows required features preceding the optional sections. The required features are just that—required, sometimes considered *mandatory*. You must inform the vendors of your minimum requirements so that they can configure a computer system to satisfy your basic needs at the lowest possible price. The optional section provides vendors with an opportunity to present some of their "bells and whistles," which usually cost more. But it is important to take a look at these options because you may discover that for a relatively small increase in expenditure, you can obtain some new feature that can provide a significant improvement in your operation.

The required section has a definite purpose, which is to identify minimums to the vendor. For a car, we might tell the sales representative that you want a V6 engine, air conditioning, power brakes, AM radio only, and bucket seats. You intend to obtain a minimum price to meet your minimum demands, but you are interested in what the cost will be for the many optional features.

The other advantage in using the required/optional methodology is that comparison between vendors' products can be simplified when all vendors are bidding to your required minimums. The number of vendors and the myriad of services and features make comparisons almost impossible. But if you identify your minimums and ask all vendors to bid against them, you will be comparing "apples and apples."

The list of features in this model is rather comprehensive, but there may be some not addressed here that you should consider for your own application. On the other hand, there may be several features that you will not need. In any case, these examples give an idea of how to discuss certain features and how to determine whether they are really necessary for your application.

This section also helps to explain some of the more common word processing terms and jargon. It should not be considered all-inclusive; but it is rather a guide in preparing a list of our own requirements.

REQUIRED WORD PROCESSING FEATURES (3.4)

The many functions of word processing are divided into four categories for ease of understanding and evaluation:

1. Text input—the features required while entering the text or data into the system for the first time.
2. Text edit and merge—the manipulation, alteration, and movement of previously entered information.
3. Miscellaneous software features—the functions that pertain to the data once stored in the system, for example, security (restricting unauthorized access), operational characteristics, and how long a wait to access data.
4. Software printing features—printing data using the high-speed, typewriter-quality printer and many sophisticated features to optimize the printing process.

These categories pertain to the three essential functions of a computer—input, processing, and output.

TEXT INPUT FEATURES (3.4.1)

Communication seems to be the most intimidating aspect of operating a computer. If you do not enter the proper command at the appropriate time or if you misspell an instruction or if the punctuation is wrong, the computer will respond with something like "illegal command" or "unrecognized format." It is extremely frustrating to think you have done everything correctly and then to have the computer come back with "What?"

The goal is to make the communication with the system as easy as possible with the fewest number of keystrokes. You want to make sure that the system is going to be easy to use and that it will support those items you have found necessary in the past. You must specify, as a minimum, those text input operations and features that you require. Usually many others that simplify text entry will be provided, but you want to identify specific ones that cannot be eliminated.

Now let us see how each of the features in the model RFP will be used.

1. AUTO PAGE NUMBERING.   Upon completion of the entering of data, the system automatically numbers each page.

2. AUTO PAGINATION.   The ability to use different length documents by having the operator establish the page length in number of lines per page, then having the system end the text so it fits correctly on any sized document. For example, the operator can set the line number to be able to use half sheets of paper or special forms.

3. AUTO WORD WRAPAROUND.   The system automatically moves a word that will extend beyond the right-hand margin to the beginning of the next line. The operator can type continuously without being concerned with margins.

4. AUTO CENTERING.   After keying in data or text, the operator presses a control key that automatically centers data in the form. The operator no longer needs to be concerned with counting spaces to the center of page.

5. AUTO DECIMAL TAB.   The ability to enter various numerical data upon which the system will automatically align the data by the position of the decimal point. For example, the operator can key $1,550.06 and $3.50 and the system will create the numbers in a column as follows:

1,550.06
3.50

This allows the operator to type numbers without regard for alignment.

6. TABLE OF CONTENTS/MENU.   Similar to a restaurant, the operator is presented a "menu" of various procedures to choose from, also referred to as "prompting" because the system prompts the user by

presenting various options. The operator either positions the cursor by the selected option or types the selected number and the system takes it from there. This allows the operator to use the system without extensive amounts of training. For example, the terminal screen might look like this:

TO INITIATE WORK, SELECT ONE OF THE FOLLOWING
1) ENTER DATA
2) EDIT DOCUMENT
3) PRINT DOCUMENT
4) STORE DOCUMENT

7. AUTO FOOTNOTE.   The system automatically ties together a footnote to the designated text. Thus, if the paragraph is moved to a different part of the text, the associated footnote reference is automatically moved also. This feature may give the ability to automatically provide for the footnote to fit at the bottom of the page and the text to automatically fit in the available space at the top of the page.

TEXT EDIT AND MERGE (3.4.2)
As described above, these functions pertain to the movement, editing, and manipulation of the data after having been keyed into the system.

1. ABLE TO EDIT 400-PAGE DOCUMENT.   Many systems are limited to a certain number of pages that can be edited in one document. In this case, let us decide that since many of our documents are lengthy, 400 pages would be the minimum required. For example, this capability means that a paragraph from page 1 can be moved to page 400 in one simple operation.

2. PARAGRAPH AND PAGE BLOCK MOVE.   The ability to automatically move either one paragraph or a series of paragraphs that comprise an entire page to any new location within the entire document. For example, move page 53 to a new position on page 351; with one simple instruction it is done. Additionally this feature would allow page 53 to be moved to a totally new document. It permits the operator to move paragraphs or pages without having to retype the entire text for proper sequence.

3. GLOBAL SEARCH AND REPLACE.   The ability to search through the entire document to find a particular sequence of text; the system can then automatically (or manually by allowing the operator to enter data at that time) replace old data with new data. It allows the

operator to use boiler plate documents and letters and automatically generate completely new documents with new names, addresses, and such, all in a matter of seconds.

4. COLUMN MOVE/DELETE.   The ability to take columns of data and move them on the document as you desire. It allows the operator to move columns of data so that reports can be changed and new data added without the need to retype the entire report or to move the data in a series of awkward commands. It allows the operator alternatively to delete entire columns instantaneously and then print the new report in seconds.

5. DOCUMENT ASSEMBLY/MERGE.   One of the most powerful capabilities of word processors and typically thought of in the preparation of form letters; the ability to take a variable document of data, for example, names and addresses, and to merge the data with a form letter. This may be done automatically and instantaneously or the system may pause and allow the operator to "fill in the blanks" on the form letter.

REQUIRED MISCELLANEOUS SOFTWARE (3.4.3)
This section pertains to the operational characteristics of the system.

1. STORE MULTIPLE FORMATS AND SPACING.   This elementary function provides for the storage on the system of many different formats or documents to be retrieved by the operator as desired. Spacing is the typewriter function of tabbing from field to field by a single keystroke.

2. THREE-SECOND SEARCH.   This system must not make the operator wait more than three seconds from the menu display until the required document is found on the system and presented to the operator to be worked on. (Performance standards such as these are important to incorporate into the RFP so that vendors know your expectation of the speed required for your operation.)

3. REVISION, STATUS, AND REPORTING.   There needs to be a method to automatically create an index, listing the documents stored, and keeping a record of each revision. The index can be used as a status report indicating the present state of each document and the date(s) on which it has been revised. You should also be able to keep track of how many revisions and who has worked on each document. This information is helpful in analyzing the work flow and the peaks and valleys

of the typing load. The production data can be very helpful in determining what changes can be made to even off the peaks and valleys and other managerial decisions that could improve overall efficiency.

4. SAVE FILES FOR BACKUP PURPOSES.   The ability to rapidly make a duplicate copy of a work file so that you will be able to maintain a complete set of data as backup in the event of a total loss of data, often referred to as a "crash;" caused by machine or operator error. Files will need to be saved either once or twice a day, and you want the capability to save them quickly without major interruption to normal processing.

5. UPGRADED TO HIGHER CAPABILITY.   Technology, as we know, is growing at a tremendous pace and usually work load will also. Thus you must recognize in the beginning the likelihood that the new system will need to be replaced. This requirement provides for the vendor to explain how your system can be upgraded when the need arises. This is extremely important because the likelihood of upgrading is usually great and you must ensure that the systems, programs, and data you work on today will be compatible with systems of greater capability you may need tomorrow. Frequently, this need is addressed by choosing a system that is at the low end of a "family" of computers all upward compatible. In this way you can start with a system at the low end and grow into a larger system with ease.

Caution: The upward compatibility of systems is a criterion to be considered. A frequent mistake is to overlook this factor and to "outgrow" the current system without the ability to convert the current programs and data.

6. SYSTEM SECURITY THAT PREVENTS DOCUMENT ACCESS. Depending on your need for security, you may elect to require that certain documents be individually protected by a password. This would mean that even an authorized user of the system may not be able to access certain highly confidential documents, for example, payroll records, personnel files, and so on. A small office may not need this feature, but it is shown here to demonstrate additional capabilities that are available.

7. SYSTEM CAN RESTRICT UNAUTHORIZED USERS.   The larger the system, the more important it becomes to ensure against unauthorized access. A computer/word processor that you envision purchasing will have enormous storage capacity and will contain many documents of a confidential nature. Remember that each terminal is an

access point to most of this information. Thus, depending on your particular circumstances, you may require the use of a password before a user can access data. There are other techniques being investigated for more sophisticated computer systems, such as voice comparisons, fingerprints, and security guards, but in the typical office environment, the password will provide a reasonable amount of protection.

8. PASSWORDS ARE NOT DISPLAYED.   A password is easily lost if one needs only to look over the shoulder of an operator as the password is keyed in. To ensure against this, you require that the password is not displayed on the screen when it is keyed in.

9. DISK ERASE.   This feature provides for an instantaneous erasure of all data stored on the disk. Remember that when the computer is turned off, the data remains stored on the disk drive and is susceptible to be stolen. By erasing the data, you can provide greater security.

10. SOFTWARE UPDATES MUST BE AVAILABLE.   As explained, the software itself, as with the hardware, is under a constant state of change as new improvements and features are added and as new "bugs" are discovered. Therefore, you want to ensure that as new "releases" or revisions of software are available from the vendor, you receive the releases at no additional cost. For example, the sort routine may be rewritten so that the time it takes to sort a file is reduced to one-half the normal processing time.

Note that releases of improvements in the operational characteristics of a particular software program should be at no additional cost. However, if the vendor announces a new functional capability, such as a new office personnel system not previously announced, the customer would have to pay an additional charge to obtain that particular piece of software.

11. MACHINE DIALOG/MENU PROMPT.   As discussed earlier under text input features, the menu prompt is the capability to present to the operator the various optional procedures that may be used. Machine dialog refers to the capability to use a question-and-answer format, or "dialog," between the system and the operator. For example, in the event of an incorrect entry by the operator, the system will flash a message that the information keyed was incorrect and to rekey the correct information. The capability is also used to assist the operator through the various procedures available on the system. This can be especially helpful in training new operators.

12. SPECIAL KEY.   Depending on your business, you may have need for special characters or symbols. In the required features section, you list each special symbol. Word processors have the capability of creating many special characters and can also be made to operate in a foreign language.

SOFTWARE PRINTING FEATURES (3.4.4)

This section pertains to the required software features that control the printing of the text or data, not the equipment capabilities of the printer.

1. PRINTOUT QUEUING (EIGHT DOCUMENTS).   Typically, the number of printers will be less than the number of terminals because the high-speed printers are so much faster than the operator keying rate. However, depending on the work flow, documents may be ready for printing, but the printers are in use with a large print job. What happens? Is the job lost? No. You require that the system have the capability to "line up," or "queue," one behind the other to wait its turn at the printer. This requirement is for eight jobs to be lined up or queued. You may not need this capability, but the number of documents per day or week can be used to help define the requirement.

2. DIRECT OUTPUT TO SELECTED PRINTER.   You require that any document may be directed to any printer you desire. One printer may be involved in a lengthy report and the boss may want another report right away. The operator can merely redirect the document to another printer available at that time. If one printer has a malfunction, you will want to be able to redirect the document to an operational printer.

3. PRIORITY PRINT ASSIGNMENTS.   The print queue may have as many as eight documents waiting to be printed. You want to allow the operator to select which priority the documents will be printed so that the highest priority documents are printed first. This requirement allows the operator to establish the priority for each document in the queue.

4. PRINT BEGINNING AT DESIRED PAGE.   If you desire to re-work a document beginning at page 105, for example, you will require that your system permits the operator to do just that. It is a waste of time and resources to use a system that will require the printing of a document from page 1 each time.

5. SUBSCRIPT AND SUPERSCRIPT.   An example of a subscript is H_2O and of a superscript is R^3. The system must have the capability of printing at these lower and raised positions.

6. SIMULTANEOUS PRINTOUT.   If your system configuration provides for more than one printer, you will want the capability to simultaneously print on every one of your printers.

OPTIONAL SOFTWARE FEATURES (3.5)

Depending on the situation, some of the previously described "required features" may be moved into the "optional features" as desired. The purpose of the optional section is to set forth in one place in the vendor's proposal those options that buyer or vendor feel may be of assistance, but usually at additional cost.

1. LIBRARY OF STANDARD PACKAGE PROGRAMS.   A "package program" is a fully operational software program that performs a particular series of functions, such as payroll, general ledger, or inventory. These programs usually have limitations in the amount of "customizing" that can be done to make the program reflect the particular operating methods of the customer. However, smaller computer/word processing operations usually use package programs because extensive customization of programs is generally too expensive for a small operation.

Learning about the complete library of programs and the associated cost of each will aid you in planning and in opening possible options to be incorporated into your operations. For the first purchaser, it is recommended to start with the basic software requirement, then to grow into optional packages as knowledge and experience in using the system are gained. You do not want to be in a situation where you will need to hire a programmer to support the software. Too many people have failed because they have attempted to run before they knew how to crawl!

2. AUTO FILE SORT.   The ability to sort documents by arranging them in alphabetical, numerical, or other order is a particularly useful feature in sorting address lists or sorting names in alphabetical order.

3. AUTO FILE SELECT.   The ability to make selections from documents based on characters that appear in a certain field or position; for example, using the ZIP Code field, the system can select all addresses with ZIP Code 07043 for one letter and type a different letter to those in ZIP Code 07110.

4. DEWEY DECIMAL.   The ability for the system to automatically number paragraphs by the Dewey Decimal numbering system.

5. AUTO CROSS REFERENCE.   The ability automatically to cause a cross reference to be stored when created. If the reference is moved within the text, the cross reference is appropriately moved in the table.

6. AUTOMATED MAILBOX.   This feature allows messages to be received at a terminal and causes an indicator to light that a message has been received, such as, a message in the mailbox. When the recipient is ready to look at the messages, he or she accesses the mailbox and reads the messages. A reply can be sent directly from this terminal. This feature also allows the same message to be sent simultaneously to multiple stations. Automated mailbox promises greater communication between offices and a substantial reduction in paperwork.

7. ABILITY TO COMMUNICATE WITH MAJOR DATA BASE. Ability to communicate with major data bases is a significant advantage. An office is able to access, through telephone lines or even microwave circuits, major data bases located around the country. This allows a small office computer to access a major library of automated information instantaneously. Such systems now operate for law libraries where small offices with terminals can access a major law library and do extensive legal research in a fraction of the time, without leaving the office. This capability may also be needed by branch offices of large corporations so that access can be gained to the corporate data base for many management and business questions.

8. OCR INPUT CAPABILITY.   Optical character recognition (OCR) is the machine ability to read characters made directly by people or machines. Examples are the bar symbols on groceries referred to as universal product code, or, more practical for word processing, the ability to read special typewriter font, and, in some cases, even being able to read handwritten numbers. The technology is this area is advancing particularly fast, and you may be interested in seeing the vendor's plan and capabilities.

9. DISTRIBUTED DATA PROCESSING (DDP).   DDP is defined as a network of small computers connected through a communications system to a large central computer and where each remote computer has full range of input and output devices plus a limited amount of computational power. DDP is usually found in organizations that have a large

central computer and geographically dispersed smaller offices. Each small computer has a full array of functions for limited amounts of processing. Then at periodic times during the day, the small computers communicate with the central computer to update master files, provide input, and receive output from the central site. Some DDP networks are established by communicating with remote locations throughout the world.

Hardware Features

In this section the emphasis shifts from the software and system operation to hardware and features.

REQUIRED DISPLAY FEATURES (3.6)

"Display" refers to the terminal generally known as a cathode ray tube (CRT). This is the video screen display and typewriter keyboard used by the operator to key in instructions and text.

1. MINIMUM DISPLAY.   Eighty character columns across and 24 lines down the screen are somewhat of a standard in the industry; however, unless you specify your requirement, you may not get what you want. Display capacities can vary greatly. Many businesses may require more data or fewer data (with large characters) per screen.

2. HORIZONTAL SCROLLING.   You may frequently have reports requiring data to be shown on the page horizontally or "lengthwise." The physical capacity of the screen, as stated above, will be only 80 characters; thus you want to be able "to scroll," or to move the screen from the left to the right to accommodate a report of up to 158 characters wide. Not all data can be seen at once, but you can verify the relative position of data with this feature.

3. DISPLAY HIGHLIGHTING.   The capacity to "highlight"— show brighter on the screen, either with higher intensity or inverse video—any text to be moved or deleted will ease eye strain on the operator and speed the work flow. Highlighting permits the operator to easily verify that the correct word or phrase will be moved or deleted.

OPTIONAL DISPLAY FEATURE (3.7)

In many areas, you will not know what may be available for optional display features. If so, leave sufficient space in the RFP so that the vendor may suggest any features that might be desirable. Again, the box is provided so you can easily compare one vendor's optional features with another's.

REQUIRED STORAGE MEDIA AND CAPACITY (3.8)

Storage media refers to the disk drives and diskettes. A disk is a flat, hard rotating plate that stores data and text on magnetic tracks on the surface of the disk, much like the grooves on long-playing records.

A diskette is a small (about 8 inches) flexible (floppy), plastic disk, about the size of a 45 rpm record. The diskette has less capacity than the hard disk, but it is much less expensive. Diskettes are ideally suited for recording text and data and then filing the diskette in an office cabinet or desk to use as the need arises. A diskette normally can store from 100 to 500 pages of typed material. Floppy disks can be purchased for less than $10 each.

It is important to realize the distinction among the various magnetic storage devices. The most frequent problem, however, comes up with regard to disks, both hard and floppy. Floppies are almost always removable; hard disks are sometimes not.

Most systems with any substantial capacity (five million characters or more) will usually consist of some type of hard disk, either fixed of removable. If only a fixed hard disk is available in a system, there must also be a floppy disk drive or two; otherwise, there is no way to back up files or transfer data from one system to another. Even if removable disks are provided, it is still common to include diskettes.

As discussed earlier, a byte is a unit of storage space. It can be thought of as equivalent to a character of text. Thus, a diskette that holds 250,000 (250K) bytes would hold about 250,000 characters. Remember, however, the vendors sometimes disguise the actual *usable* capacity by ignoring the fact that there must be some formatting and overhead data on each disk. This unusable amount generally is about 5–10 percent of a disk's total capacity.

1. FIVE-TO-TEN MEGABYTE HARD DISK ON-LINE STORAGE.   It is important to point out that your requirement is phrased as "five-to-10-megabytes." Again, this places the burden on the vendor to recommend which configuration would best fit your needs. You completed the requirements study and reported your work load to the vendor in terms of letters prepared, bills sent, and so on. Now it is up to the vendor to configure storage capabilities as best as possible. You must evaluate the options and reasons behind them and then choose which option is most appropriate.

2. FLOPPY DISKETTE UNITS.   As stated above, the use of floppy disks can add unlimited off-line storage capability to a system. In fact, many times the data "backed up" on a floppy is stored off-site or in a fireproof safe to prevent loss of important archival data.

OPTIONAL STORAGE MEDIA (3.9.)

Any new capabilities or features regarding storage can be found in this section. The vendor may also be able to offer suggestions not considered here.

REQUIRED PRINTER FEATURES (3.10.)

Word processing has advanced significantly with the introduction of high-speed printers that produce work of typewriter quality. The printing speed and quality can be compared; these printers exceed 40 cps (characters per second) and more!

1. BIDIRECTIONAL, LETTER QUALITY, IMPACT PRINTER WITH 40 CPS SPEED. Bidirectional means from left to right, then from right to left, and so on. This capability eliminates the delay in a normal typewriter caused by the return of the print heads to the left margin. It allows continual print action. Impact printer means that the letters are formed by the impact of a key with the paper. There are other techniques of printing, for example, ink jet, thermal, dot matrix, and even laser, but for the general office you would probably elect to have letter-quality printing that is achieved by the impact style printer. This will allow the printing of carbons if required; some of the other types of printers will only print one copy.

2. ABLE TO PRINT

• Single sheet (manual and auto feed). The option for the operator to feed each single sheet individually or to have single sheets fed automatically from a paper tray feeder.
• Continuous paper. Requires tractors to feed the continuous paper with each sheet separated by perforation. Continuous paper is used to print draft documents since it is much faster than having one sheet at a time go through the printer. A final copy can later be printed on single sheets.
• Envelopes. To position the print automatically in the proper place on the envelope.
• Mailing labels. Must be able to use continuous label forms fed by tractors for high-speed label printing.
• Preprinted forms. Must be able to manipulate various sized forms.
• Seven-part carbon forms. The ability to strike the paper with sufficient force to create seven readable carbon copies.

3. WRITING WIDTH.   To allow the use of paper up to a width of 15 inches. This is usually the "132" column paper at 10 characters per

inch or "156" column at 12 characters per inch. The wider carriage will also allow the use of irregular forms.

4. SHEET FEEDER.   The special apparatus to allow for continuous single page feeding.

5. TRACTOR FEEDING.   The special apparatus that pulls fanfolded continuous paper through the printer.

6. ACOUSTIC SUPPRESSING NOISE TO 40 DECIBELS.   The high-speed forceful striking of the print heads creates an intolerable noise level for an office environment and can do harm to the operator. A noise suppression cover is needed to reduce the noise to 40 decibels.

ORIGINAL PRINTER FEATURES (3.11)

1. INTERCHANGEABLE TYPE STYLES.   It may be of interest to match the type styles of the word processing printer to the type styles of the other typewriters in the office.

2. OTHER FEATURES.   The vendor presents any options in this section.

Services

As already mentioned, the success or failure of a computer/word processing installation will be contingent in large part on the amount and quality of the services that are obtained by the customer. We have discussed the software and hardware, but the service and maintainability of these elements are what is important. Too frequently, first-time users think that they are buying merely the equipment and the programming, and they give little or no attention to critical service needs.

The hardware breaks down and the customer must wait days for repair. A serious software "bug" is created and no one seems to know how to fix it; in fact, every attempt makes the problem worse. A customer buys a system, but no one is around to train him or her in how to operate it, so the system remains in the corner gathering dust. The reports generated by the package programs need only a minor programming change, but no one from the vendor is available. And to top it off, the customer never received the quantity of manuals that were promised.

Impossible? No, these types of problems are all quite common when attention has not been placed on obtaining the proper and necessary type and quality of services.

Services Are Negotiable

It is important to note that services such as training, maintenance, programming support, documentation, and report customizing are frequently more negotiable with the local vendor's branch office representatives than is the selling price of the hardware and software. The latter is usually established by corporate offices and is negotiable, but usually within ranges and depending on the size of the equipment order and the prestige of the account. Services, however, frequently fall more within the jurisdiction of the local branch manager or computer store owner; who can parcel out resources according to circumstances. Training is a good example. If a customer knows enough to insist on thorough and competent training, the branch manager can merely assign personnel to provide extra training to that particular account.

TRAINING REQUIREMENTS (3.12)

1. EIGHTY HOURS PER OPERATOR. "No training needed" says the advertisement, which should make you immediately suspicious of the entire company because training is critically important to the first-time user. In fact, you should require 80 hours of training over a 30-day period to ensure that your personnel have an opportunity to assimilate the "computerese" to which they will be subject. Training should not be too intense over a short period simply because people generally cannot digest and really understand the full capabilities of the system over such a short period of time. A training plan is a useful way of having the vendor document when and where and to whom the classes will be given. Training does not mean formal classroom instruction. It most frequently should mean "hands on" time for the operator to get a feel of the system, to become acquainted with new procedures, to experiment, to make mistakes, and above all, to ask questions.

It is not enough simply to be familiar with the operations of the terminal. One or two of the staff must be knowledgeable about the principles of data processing and how and what goes on inside the box. This training, usually for a supervisor and/or lead person, is very important so that when simple problems occur, some corrective action can be taken immediately rather than always having to wait for repairs from outside.

It is also important that one or two backup people be trained for each terminal and/or operator. The demand for experienced word processing operators has never been higher and retaining excellent people is a difficult task. Backup training is valuable in the event that a lead operator seeks employment elsewhere or must be absent for an extended period.

Many corporations and government agencies have created the position of "word processing operator" so that experienced operators may be paid more than comparable secretarial positions.

2. MANAGERIAL TRAINING.   Usually the training of the managerial staff is overlooked while the operators receive the attention. This is a mistake because the implementation of systems that so directly affect standard operations is something that needs complete managerial support and involvement. Earlier we noted the serious and common mistake of keeping management out of the decision-making process, either by neglect or by delegating the responsibility to a consultant. By requiring the vendor to provide managerial training, you ensure managerial support and involvement, plus managerial input on the efficient usage of the system now and in the future.

3. FIVE COPIES OF TRAINING MATERIALS.   The specific number of copies will vary, but it is important to have training materials on hand to answer questions and to train new employees. Again, if you do not ask, you may find that you are short.

4. DOCUMENTATION UPDATES.   Just as hardware and software are constantly changing, training materials and operation manuals are also updated periodically. You want to ensure that the vendor passes these updates along to you.

OPTIONAL TRAINING (3.13)

Some vendors provide self-study books and programs that are learned at the terminal. Such optional features can be presented in this box on the form.

MAINTENANCE REQUIREMENTS (3.14)

Maintenance here means equipment maintenance and is usually referred to in either of two categories:

1. Preventative maintenance (PM), or routine maintenance, accomplished during regularly scheduled time periods. PM is like the six-month tuneup for your car; it helps to prevent failures.
2. Emergency maintenance, or remedial maintenance, accomplished by an emergency call from the customer in the event of equipment failure that is causing serious impact on processing. The key is to ensure that if a failure occurs that is an emergency, you will not have to wait days for someone to repair the system.

1. FOUR-HOUR RESPONSE DURING PRIME SHIFT.   A four-hour response to an emergency call means that a repairperson (called a customer engineer) will arrive at your installation within four hours. Geographic location, of course, will be a factor because travel time is included. Additionally, your requirement will be conditioned on the call being placed during prime shift, which is usually 8 a.m. to 5 p.m., and the time the vendor's staff is working at full strength.

You evaluate the vendor's capability to satisfy your requirement based on the number of similar systems installed, the number and quality of engineers servicing the region, and on checking with other customers to ensure that the vendor is responsive.

2. RESPONSE TIMES FOR EMERGENCIES AND COSTS.   If a failure occurs outside of the prime shift, you will want to know what to expect in response time and how much it will cost. If the failure can wait until the prime shift of the next day, you may elect to have the maintenance performed at that time.

OPTIONAL MAINTENANCE (3.15)

Any other plan or service the vendor may offer can be presented in this box, such as extended prime shift, dial-up diagnostic processing at the vendor's central computer, telephone access to an expert prior to dispatch of an engineer, or even a set of diagnostic disks.

REQUIRED SYSTEM SERVICES (3.16)

This section is for all requirements that deal with the computer/word processing system in general. These requirements are placed under services, again to recognize that the overall success of your installation will be based on the services provided by the vendor in support of the system. Each of the following requirements relates to areas where the vendor's timeliness and support of your account will be critical. These requirements pertain to all aspects of the system from supplies to compatibility, availability, and expandability, each of which needs to be defined.

1. SUPPLIES.   The vendor will set forth the costs for paper, forms, ribbons, spare parts, carbon forms, multipart forms, and any other expendable supplies. The vendor should also indicate alternate sources for these supplies.

2. COMPATIBILITY.   Frequently, individual units of equipment will be manufactured by different companies and brought together to form a consolidated system. You must ensure that all units are "plug

compatible" and can be moved from place to place and be reconnected.

3. PRODUCTS CURRENTLY IN USE.   One phenomenon of the computer industry is that because the technology is changing so rapidly, vendors will bid their newest products almost before they are off the assembly line and without adequate field testing. The customer then discovers that he or she is the only one in the country with this advanced model and also finds—even worse—that he or she is a "trailblazer" with this product without even being informed.

You can protect yourself from this practice by requiring that only standard products currently in use are to be bid. One option frequently used is to require the products to have been in use for six months or one year to ensure that someone else has done the "trailblazing." As a general rule in computers and automobiles, the first models have "bugs" that do not become apparent until after customer use. The trick is to let someone else suffer those bugs.

4. AVAILABILITY OF EQUIPMENT.   Another phenomenon of the industry is to discover after the agreement is signed that delivery cannot be made for nine months or longer (and in some unusual circumstances, two years). The demand for these systems is great and by the mid-1980s will be enormous. The manufacturing capability thus becomes the limiting factor as to when your system can be installed.

You face this problem in the RFP by specifying a required delivery date. If the vendor cannot satisfy the time frame, you can evaluate that response with all the other factors.

5. EXPANDABILITY.   Earlier we discussed the critical importance of being able to upgrade to higher capability systems. Expandability is related. With "expandability," you are asking for the total number of peripheral devices and terminals that can be attached to the computer/word processor. How many terminals, printers, disk drives, or diskettes can be attached to the computer/word processor or CPU (central processing unit) without the performance of the machine being slowed to an unacceptable level? Performance is often measured in the time it takes for the machine to accomplish required processing. The term is called "response time," which is measured from the time the operator presses the key to begin the process until the time the process is completed. The more units that are attached, the slower the response time. Vendor's will, therefore, specify a maximum number of peripherals that can be attached and still provide for an acceptable response time.

Remember, you want to select a configuration that will allow

you to add peripherals—more terminals, more printers, and so on—
without upgrading to a new computer. The amount of expandability of
the system bid will be set forth in this box.

6. BACKUP.   Every computer, like every car, will surely at
some time break down. Computers can fail for a number of extraordi-
nary reasons, like fire, flood, earthquake. In such an event, you want a
plan for a backup system if possible. Sometimes vendors may provide
their own demonstration system as backup. Or a vendor may arrange
the use of another customer's facility for backup processing during off-
shift hours. This section asks the vendor to bid such capability.

7. ENVIRONMENT.   Normally the modern office computer/
word processor should not require special air conditioning, humidity, or
temperature controls as long as a normal office environment is maintained. However, special power requirements, electrical grounds, car-
pets, power fluctuations, dust, and so on can all cause intermittent and
frustrating "downtime" (the time the machine is not operational). This
requirement will provide the standard tolerances for the system bid and,
if possible, should be reviewed by an electrical technician if there are
any questions about a vendor's response.

OPTIONAL SYSTEM SERVICES (3.17)
The possibilities for optional features are unlimited based on the
vendor's creativity and capabilities and space is reserved so the vendor
can describe these features.

REQUIRED PROGRAMMING SUPPORT (3.18)
This section pertains to application programming support,
which relates to the vendor providing trained computer programmers to
consult, design, write programs, or "debug" programs as your need
arises or at an hourly rate. Application programs generally refer to the
particular job that is processed on the computer, for example, payroll,
accounts payable, accounts receivable, and data base management.
Application programs may be of two types: (1) package programs,
which are prewritten, tested, operational, and usually do not lend themselves to extensive amounts of customizing, and (2) custom application
programs, which are written from scratch or package programs modified for your application by computer programmers. Custom application programs are very expensive and have substantial risks that are not
considered within the scope of this book.
This section of the RFP pertains to the amount and cost associated with having the vendor's computer programmers modify package

programs, usually to a limited degree, to make the package programs fit into your normal style of processing. Examples may be adding the firm name to headings or having the vendor's programmers review and analyze your operation periodically to determine if your procedures and programs are as efficient as possible.

1. APPLICATION PERSONNEL WITHIN 40 MILES.   This requirement will provide information about the availability of programmers within commuting distance. Travel expenses, hotels, and such can be eliminated if qualified personnel are available within commuting distance.

2. PERSONNEL PER INSTALLED SYSTEM.   Some vendors provide support based on the number of systems that are installed per customer. Others bid support based on revenue received. Frequently, vendors will bid a certain number of man-weeks or man-hours of support based on the value of the system and the anticipated expansion value in the future.

3. INSTALLATION SUPPORT.   It is important to understand precisely how much technical software support will be provided during the weeks (and months) that the system is being installed. This is an important criterion because your people, who are unfamiliar with the new operating procedures and software capabilities will be in an intensive learning phase. The on-site (or at least available by phone) software specialists should be able to answer any questions, solve any problems, and make any suggestions necessary to get your firm up and running as soon as possible. If they do not have immediate answers, at least they should have a contact in their factory, somebody you would not necessarily have access to, who should be able to help. Consider the case where the payroll program will not accept the necessary input or generates incorrect checks; where do you go for help?

4. ON-GOING APPLICATION SUPPORT.   The same arguments apply here as at installation time, except that you cannot expect a specialist on-site all the time. You do need to know who is available and how you can reach that person in a reasonable time frame.

5. SCHEDULED APPLICATION REVIEWS.   At least once a year, the vendor's technical personnel should visit your installation to review whether your programs and procedures are utilizing the system to the best of its capabilities. New products will become available and newer technology will be announced, and you will want to know about those options on a scheduled basis.

OPTIONAL PROGRAMMING SUPPORT (3.19)

The vendor can utilize this section to present other options for you to obtain programming support, for example, at an hourly rate, or estimates for custom application services.

REQUIRED DOCUMENTATION SUPPORT (3.20)

After the vendor has delivered the system and the support team has left, you need to have access to adequate documentation in order to use the equipment effectively and to train others in its use. Manual titles should be self-explanatory so you can get to the correct manual quickly, and they should be well indexed so you can find the right page or section without a telephone call. Take time to review the vendor's documentation prior to purchasing the equipment. Remember that a vendor's demo usually presents what the vendor wants and almost always ignores the documentation. Also, make sure that an adequate number of copies will be available for the various users; everyone will want his or her own copy, even if that isn't necessary.

1. LIST OF MANUALS.   Vendors are asked to list the documentation manuals by titles included at no cost and what the cost of additional copies will be.

2. MANAGEMENT AND ACCOUNTING MANUALS.   Because you may be interested in the documentation regarding a specialized area, you may request a special list for the specialized subject.

OPTIONAL DOCUMENTATION SUPPORT (3.21)

There might be tutorials for self-learning or pocket summaries of some of the more useful operating commands. You want to review the materials prior to making a choice of suppliers.

MISCELLANEOUS OPTIONAL FEATURES (3.22)

This section is a catchall area for the vendor's offerings that do not fit into any other category. It is desirable for you to leave a place in the RFP for items that you have never even thought of. The computer industry is just the place to have this section replete with all sorts of surprises!

ACCOUNTING SYSTEM REQUIREMENTS (3.23)

In the model RFP are listed a number of required accounting features. This section can be treated just like the previous word processing features. (These requirements are analyzed and sample reports provided in Chapter 3. Refer to that chapter to review the accounting and management reports.) Just as with the other sections of the RFP, you need to list requirements and give the vendor an option to include extras to enhance the offered package.

Many of the newer small business computers support some of the best word processing programs available. It is entirely possible that all of the features required could be supported on an office computer. Just remember that the RFP is supposed to let the vendors know what you need, and the model RFP should help to formulate those needs.

Vendor Capabilities (Section 4)

This section is required so that you have an opportunity to see, in writing, what the vendor has been telling you. This is not a question of distrusting the sales rep, but of wanting some verification.

1. CORPORATE FINANCIAL REPORT

You want to deal with a reputable firm, of course, and preferably one that has been in business for several years. You also want to know that people are going to be around when you need help and when you want to upgrade the system. The annual report, while no guarantee, will give some indication of these facts.

2. AVAILABILITY OF STAFF

In the RFP, you are also asking the vendor to substantiate the claim that "there will be someone on call to help you." A list of some of your contacts along with some background information should help you to decide whether this vendor has the qualified personnel to support your future needs.

3. REFERENCES

You would like the opportunity to discuss the proposed system and applicable support with someone who has already gone through the frustration of purchasing a new system. As mentioned previously, you do not want to get the first such model; being able to talk with someone who already has a system you plan on purchasing will help to convince you that you will not get stuck. You can also get ideas on how to optimize the system performance and the vendor support. Do not be afraid to call the references and even visit their sites to see what the system really looks like. Their names should not be on the list if they are not willing to talk to you.

Cost Sheets (Attachments 1 and 2)

There are two different types of cost sheets appended to the model RFP. The first is the "required" cost sheet wherein the vendor would complete the information based on the minimum requirements. The second is the "optional" cost sheet wherein the vendor could present the costs associated with the optional products, the "bells and whistles." Otherwise, the price sheets are identical. All costs must be shown, including transportation, installation, and taxes. The form provides space for the vendor to offer discounts, and thus shows what the grand total will be.

Use of the form is helpful because it requires the vendor to reveal all costs on one sheet so that they can be compared easily during the evaluation phase.

Conclusion

The use of an RFP has many advantages and can be as detailed as circumstances require. Microcomputers may be procured through the use of an RFQ. The RFP contains your requirements, and the more you understand your requirements, the more the vendors will be able to make a responsible bid.

In Chapter 5, we discuss some of the marketing practices you will probably experience during the next phase of the procurement procedure.

5

SERVICES: JOYS AND TRIBULATIONS

Henry Ford once asked a new auto dealer to change his sign from "Sales and Service" to "Service and Sales." Ford explained that "if you don't give customers good service, you'll have a tough time making sales."

As we have stressed, the success or failure of any computer/word processing installation is based in large measure on the continuing service provided by the vendor. Thus, the quality of service and personnel representing the vendor is of fundamental importance to the buyer.

This chapter analyzes the importance of personal services—maintenance, technical, marketing, training, and others—to identify the importance of the people-oriented basis of the computer/word processing industry. It looks at the human nature involved in many of the mistakes, tips, and trends that are prevalent. So armed, you can better identify, control, and react to many of the forces at work.

One common notion of the beginner is that what he or she is buying is a machine. What the beginner should learn is that what is really being bought is a service.

TYPES OF SERVICES

The monthly expenditure for personnel and maintenance service can be substantial. However, there are many very good reasons that justify the expense.

EQUIPMENT MAINTENANCE

This, as noted briefly in the previous chapter, is usually divided into two types:

1. Regularly scheduled maintenance, usually varying from once per month to once every few months, and referred to as preventative maintenance. This is similar to the normal maintenance program a car would need. "An ounce of prevention is worth a pound of cure" says the old expression. This is just as true for sophisticated computer equipment.

2. Emergency maintenance means that in the event of a failure of your computer system, a repair technician would come to your installation within an agreed-upon time limit, varying between four and 24 hours to repair and return the equipment to operating condition. This is referred to as remedial maintenance. This service is essential for a successful computer/word processing system. In the event of a major failure, "the system is down," all production frequently must stop immediately. All employees using the system must sit idly, obtaining full salary and benefits, but not contributing anything to the business or office. The "bug" that has caused the problem may take hours, weeks, or in some cases months to be resolved. Some of these bugs present themselves only irregularly and defy determining a failure pattern. The end result to your installation could be intermittent and serious failure of your computer/word processing system. The only solution in this intolerable situation, which unfortunately occurs too frequently, is to deal with a company that commits to and is capable of providing timely and qualified emergency maintenance. Quality remedial maintenance is an essential people-oriented service.

Fixing "Bugs"

A "bug" is a defect in the programming. Essentially, the program produces the wrong result. Usually a bug will be somewhat less than a major defect and will happen when unusual but valid data conditions occur. However, correcting bugs is an on-going service that must be provided by a vendor and must be done well for a successful installation. Because technology is growing at a tremendous pace, the software provided by a vendor is under constant revision and improvement. As new revisions or releases of software are provided, you will want to take advantage of the increased capabilities. However, each new release will have new bugs, which may or may not seriously affect your operation. The vendor must have a sufficient service organization to fix the bugs in a timely fashion.

Training

For all users, but particularly for the first-time purchaser, thorough and complete training is essential. With the smaller systems, buyers often overlook requiring in-depth training and consequently waste valuable time in attempting their own "on-the-job training." This usually results in very little success and a tremendous loss of time. A vendor must have capabilities to provide these services both on initial installation and continuously as the need arises.

Sales and Technical Support

As your work load increases and as more requirements are placed on the computer system, you should be supported by being kept alert for new products, new software, and technical improvements in the vendor's system. Vendors must have the service organization to keep a list of a customer's requirements and periodically visit the customer to analyze the work load and to suggest improvements. The small, fledgling vendor will rarely have this type of service capability.

These general categories of service make the corporation and the quality of personnel servicing your account of utmost importance to your success. However, as we will see, people are frequently the root of many problems.

THE GOOD, THE BAD, THE UGLY

Computer people are no different from the rest of the human race. There are conscientious, knowledgeable professionals who are a joy to work with (the good). Good salespeople put their customers first and ensure that the installation and continuing operation are successful, or they will take whatever steps are necessary to ensure success.

There are also the inexperienced, the untrained (the bad) abounding in this field, perhaps more than in other industries. Computer technology requires an in-depth understanding of data processing principles, which usually takes about two to four years of practical experience mixed with a fair amount of formal education.

The technology also is changing so rapidly that it is a significant effort to keep pace with the latest improvements and capabilities. Thus, an experienced and knowledgeable salesperson is very difficult to find and retain. Inexperienced salespeople are the rule rather than the exception. You should attempt to evaluate the knowledge and experience of the sales representative servicing your business, and if not satisfied, request or even demand a replacement.

Also, as in every group, there are the few dishonest people (the ugly). Some salespeople intentionally deceive customers as well as their own corporations to obtain commissions. Fortunately, there are relatively few of these types of individuals in the computer industry and no more than in any other area. However, you should be vigilant in your dealings to ensure that everything is straightforward and by the book. When a salesperson begins to try to influence your decision based on factors outside the computer and its services, anything from fancy dinners to trips to gifts, be suspicious and be cautious.

The most important point to remember is that the computer industry has grown so fast and requires such knowledge and experience that many neophytes now sell and service customer accounts. Rarely are improper motives at the root of the problem. Most frequently, it is just plain lack of knowledge and failure of communications. Unfortunately, too many people, both vendors and buyers, are reluctant to acknowledge their ignorance. Keep in mind the words of Somerset Maugham: "It wasn't until quite late in life that I discovered how easy it is to say, I don't know." Many of the following mistakes are caused by the failure to admit a simple lack of knowledge.

TYPICAL MISTAKES

Let us recap, expand, and emphasize some of the mistakes frequently made during the selling phase of the procurement. If you are aware of and understand the mistakes and the causes for them, you will be better able to avoid them.

Trust Me

An old lesson states that "we cannot really be for something that we don't understand." You should not have to trust other people exclusively. You should opt to gain your own understanding instead. The sales representative will want you to trust that the equipment has the capability and the capacity that you need. The technical consultant may want you to trust that you really need a new feature. You may be inclined to trust the judgment of friends, neighbors, or competitors in buying a similar system they have used.

But the key to success in this industry is to trust yourself. Understanding in the computer industry does take hard work. A wise person once said, "There's few things as uncommon as common sense," but that is where success lies. The procedure described here is not particularly easy. However, you must make the commitment to trust your common sense and to do your homework. Remember:

> You do not want a computer system unless it will fulfill your own specific, identifiable needs.
>
> You do not want a system just because a friend, competitor, or relative has one.
>
> You do not want a system unless you understand how it will work, what it will do, and how much it will cost.
>
> Be watchful of salespeople who play on your susceptibilities in this area and speak about personal relationships as the key to a successful installation. Trust is not the basis for a wise decision. Rather, misplaced trust can be the seed of disaster. Trust ultimately yourself and your own common sense.

Vendor's Oral Statement

It would seem obvious to say that any verbal statements made by the vendor and not written into the contract are not enforceable. Most people generally are aware of this, but the rule is broken too frequently in the computer industry.

The typical scenario, as noted earlier, occurs after the agreement has been signed and problems arise during the installation phase, as is to be expected. Frequently, the original sales rep has been transferred to a new account or new position and the customer tries to enforce something that the sales rep said months previously. The buyer is in an impossible position because there is no one to listen to his or her side of the story.

The solution, of course, is to take notes of all meetings and phone calls if possible. As statements are made, ask for a simple letter from the vendor to record the statement or commitment. At contract time, the letters can be incorporated into the contract as exhibits, so that nine months later the buyer can insist on performance by the vendor of the commitments made in the letters. If the vendor refuses to document the statements, negotiations can be terminated until the letter is forthcoming.

A general rule to remember is that if it is not written, it does not exist!

Bait and Switch

Because success in the computer industry largely depends on the quality of service representatives that the vendors supply, you must beware of the "bait and switch" mistake. This occurs when a vendor brings the best technical person to the customer to make a sales call. The technical person is, in fact, highly qualified and very polished in making the presentation and answering questions. You are impressed with the individual and move to complete the contract. You then learn to your surprise that this particular technical person will not be working on your account; instead, you will have a junior, less experienced, less knowledgeable person. The entire support level thus changes dramatically. One way to prevent this "bait and switch" mistake is to provide in the contract the name of the technical personnel whom you want to service your account. Require that as long as that particular individual is employed by the vendor, that person will be responsible to your account unless you desire a change. If the individual leaves the employ of the vendor, you cannot prevent that, but you may insist on a replacement person of comparable skills and experience.

Hardware Only

This type of mistake is probably the most frequently made today. Buyers become overly concerned with what the equipment alone can do and lose sight of the software and service requirements. The purchaser selects a system that appears to have the best hardware for the money, and buys it. No thought goes into training, for example, so the prospective users are kept in the dark and become uncomfortable and even disgruntled about the new machine. They then frequently find ways to avoid using it. The machine starts "gaining dust" and the monetary investment plus the potential savings and increased productivity are all lost.

The system software, for example, may have a programming problem, a software bug, and the problem remains unsolved for days or weeks due to the inadequacy of the service portions of the contract. Users then become exhausted with the effort needed to resolve each problem, and they look for ways to go back to the old system where the problems could be corrected with less effort.

This type of error, hardware only, will be corrected in the procedure to be described later in that you will base your selection on many weighted factors. The hardware is only one factor that will have relative importance compared to many other factors, such as service, training, and programming.

Vendor Demonstration

A vendor demonstration should be a learning experience, not necessarily a decision-making one. An important mistake to avoid is becoming emotionally enthused about a vendor demonstration. Usually, vendors have rehearsed their demonstrations many, many times; thus the presentations are extremely polished, fast, and usually impressive. The knowledge and capabilities of the persons making the presentation are also impressive. Most people naturally become enthusiastic about the product at a vendor's demonstration. Such demonstrations are designed to stimulate interest and whet the appetite. The computer routines and capabilities are designed to highlight the system's good points and avoid the weaknesses. Sometimes there may be slide shows, movies, equipment demonstrations, beautiful glossy sales brochures, and usually attractive, well-dressed, articulate sales representatives.

It is quite natural for the potential buyer to become emotionally enthusiastic about the product at this demonstration, particularly in view of the fact that shopping around among so many other vendors will take so much work, effort, and time. Why not simply choose the vendor who has demonstrated an apparently superlative system and end the selection process right there?

Remember that your emotions may get too much involved and that emotion can mislead you. We will describe here an objective, nonemotional method of making a selection, which is based on the facts of the system's capabilities as well as the service capabilities of the vendor's company. But for now, remember to avoid the emotional draw of the vendor's demonstration.

Cost Only

It is natural to shop for the product with the lowest possible price. However, this can be a serious mistake with computers/word processors. In this industry as many others, you get what you pay for. The cost of the hardware has been dropping dramatically since the beginning of the industry and will continue to drop. Price reductions for equipment are due to the reduced cost associated with improved circuitry and miniaturization of the components. The overall cost of data and word processing has come down; however, the percentage of expenditure allocated for the service side of the business has actually been steadily increasing.

The uniqueness of your particular office or business cannot be overlooked either. Thus, cost must be addressed as just one factor to be considered along with many others. The relative weight of cost in your overall decision may vary depending on your available budget, but it would be a mistake to make price the only factor to be considered.

If you discover that to meet your requirements you need a computer/word processor that exceeds your initial budget, the proper course would be to exert your energy and attention on procuring the needed money, not on buying the wrong system.

Overdelegation

The corollary of the "trust me" mistake is the overdelegation error. The manager, owner, or principal partner may not want to get involved in the nitty-gritty of making the decision about the system. He or she may be inclined to delegate it to a middle manager or consultant. The damage that can be done to the organization due to this mistake can be serious. Normally, without top management involvement, middle managers will not have the resources available that they may need to do the job correctly. Also, without top management support, first-level operators will be less motivated to support the new system and the many other organizational changes associated with the computer. Last, without top management involvement, the vendor may be less inclined to render the support that can be provided. Vendor personnel want to deal with the top managerial echelons of an organization to ensure that the key decision-maker is involved with the procurement. It is reasonable also to expect that the experienced manager will have greater expertise in dealing with vendors and exacting concessions. Gaining top management support is essential.

Selecting the Wrong Software

The market is replete with thousands of software programs that claim to do a myriad of functions. Much of the software, however, is inefficient, awkward, and of limited functionality or versatility. Be cautious in buying software based on the description in a catalogue. Your office or shop may have unique requirements that may need flexibility in the software to allow your business to grow and respond to changes.

This procedure will show how to purchase software based on your requirements and needs. You should not have to completely reorganize your internal methods to accommodate the vendor's software.

Instead, it should mold itself into your organization. As with other aspects of equipment procurement and programming, you place the burden on the vendor to satisfy your software requirements. Then you will ensure, based on rigorous testing, that the software actually performs as promised. The mistake to avoid is selecting software that does not let you grow.

Shopper's Syndrome

The mistake of the shopper's syndrome is to approach buying a computer or word processor by wasting a great amount of time shopping from place to place without definite requirements in mind. In the previous chapter, we described the requirements study, which identifies your work load and how much equipment and software will be needed.

In this procedure, you incorporate the findings of the requirements study into the RFP. Vendors then will bid to fulfill your requirements at the lowest possible price. You will not waste valuable time shopping aimlessly around the computer marketplace.

Over-the-Counter Mistake

With the emergence of computer stores around the country and usually around the corner, a typical buyer mistake is to believe that store owners do not negotiate with customers. The reverse is true. One can make a case that today it is a "buyer's market" for computer/word processing equipment merely by the number of vendors in the marketplace. Thus, do not be deceived by the appearance of the store. Negotiated deals can be made at computer stores on everything from systems to software to chips.

This procedure, however, eliminates the need for the buyer to go from vendor to vendor or store to store. Rather, the RFP document mailed to various qualified vendors reduces the work that the purchaser is required to do. The proposals received from the vendors can be evaluated without the time and effort it would take to visit various computer stores or vendor facilities. Once the selection is limited to the top few vendors, your time can be spent on vendor demonstrations and negotiations. You will negotiate the best deal possible even if you are dealing with a computer store.

Games People Play

One word about games and small computers. There is a tendency to be overly distracted by the mesmerization that can occur with the games available for these computers. Many people have and will purchase these systems thinking that their usefulness can occur in the future, but in the meantime, the games will suffice. This attitude is fine if the buyer recognizes that in all likelihood he or she is buying no more than a very expensive toy.

The key to success with automation is to identify the business requirements and to satisfy them at the least possible expense. Games have no place in the business decision.

To summarize: be aware of all the key mistakes discussed in this section; they can get you if you don't pay attention.

SURVIVING THE MARKETING MAZE

Most first-time users and even experienced pros are constantly faced with a barrage of marketing people and product options that usually defy any measure of consistency or coherency. Therefore, a few key tips are in order to assist you in handling the confusion.

Competitive Buying

As discussed earlier, competitive buying is the number one rule for selecting the right computer system, improving your negotiating leverage, and just plain saving money. Competitive buying simply means that you prepare your requirements in a written document, the RFP, which is mailed to several qualified vendors, and the vendors then compete against each other by proposing their best products to satisfy your needs at their lowest possible prices.

Then you evaluate and compare the respective proposals to select what you consider to be the best-qualified vendor. You negotiate with that vendor, and if not satisfied with the answers, you may then begin negotiating with the next ranked bidder.

One key element of competitive buying is that the layperson, or even the expert, may begin with essentially no knowledge about the various products and services available, but upon comparing the various proposals, becomes very knowledgeable about the state-of-the-art. This knowledge may be either technical, concerning product capabilities, or financial, concerning the going market prices for the particular products.

For example, how much should you pay for your new system? Assume the proposals indicate figures of: $5,000, $9,000, $11,600, $14,000, $25,000, and $60,000. You can easily see that the $5,000 system will probably not satisfy all your technical requirements, and the $60,000 system will probably be more than you need. You could eliminate the extremes and start to understand what type of budget you will need to make the right choice.

To eliminate this competitive procurement approach is to forego all the additional facts that can be learned; to forego the negotiating position among vendors that is so critical; and to limit your choice to one vendor. To deal with one vendor that you choose based on only limited knowledge of this industry is to hamper yourself needlessly.

Even if you are interested in a personal computer in the $4,000 to $8,000 range and you are sure which model you want, you should still write a Request for Quotation (RFQ) for the machine and mail it to several computer stores or vendors for pricing. Substantial dollars can be saved because computer store owners are ready to "deal" on prices for this type of machine. Computer stores will compete against each other in the buyer's market that exists.

The last point is that even if you are generally considering a computer sometime in the future, the preparation and issuance of an RFP or RFQ will provide a vast amount of data that you can use in your planning. The time and effort associated with the preparation of the RFP or RFQ are repaid thousands of times over in terms of savings on the purchase price and the freedom from an excessive amount of agony, stress, and disillusionment that goes along with selecting the wrong system.

Financial Leverage

This topic is discussed in detail in Chapter 8, but on any list of "tips," financial leverage must be included at the top. Financial leverage simply means not paying for anything until it is demonstrated and working at your own site. If required, you can agree to pay some percentage of money down when the contract is signed. However, there may be problems that involve the manufacturer's assembly line, shipping, electrical hookups in your facility, software bugs, hardware failures, and a host of other problems. To protect yourself from these typical problems, insist on a rigorous test and acceptance of all hardware components and software at your site over an extended period, usually from two weeks to one month, before you pay for the system. During the test period, the hardware must perform without material failure at an acceptable level, usually 90 to 95 percent of the total available hours that the machine is in use. The software must be tested during this period such that all the necessary functions are operational and working. During the period, the training and documentation deliveries should be accomplished.

Once the work is done, under your watchful eye, you pay the bill. If there are a number of deliverables that the vendor must provide over an extended period, you can agree to make partial payments for the items when delivered and accepted by you, but you should insist on holding back 10 to 20 percent of the entire contract value until the entire job is completed and working at your site.

This is financial leverage, and it is absolutely critical in this industry. To pay your money first would leave you without any kind of "clout" over a vendor, who may turn out to be too busy to get around to your problems. Financial leverage gives you that clout, and most assuredly, you will need it.

Start Small

There is a tendency to look at one's business or office and say: "Let's automate; this will be a real showplace!" Resist this temptation. As in other human endeavors, learn to crawl before you walk. Some of the greatest failures in this business have occurred because people make the giant leap without adequate experience, personnel, or capital. There is clearly an advantage with automation and, as described, the 1980s will witness an all-time high in businesses and offices using automation. But nothing takes the place of experience, and this is particularly true with the complexities and computerese language associated with data and word processing. So start or grow as the case may be, but do so realistically and with the required experience. If you are a small firm and just beginning, start with a small system and gain your experience with it. If you are a large organization but new to computers, start with a small system and gain your experience without impacting your central productive activity. You will know when you have obtained the needed experience. It will be when you feel confident in making your own decisions.

Consultants, Lawyers, and Friends

The corollary of making your own decisions is to weigh carefully the advice received from consultants, lawyers, and friends.

Consultants can be extremely valuable and necessary, but they may be inclined to feel that the computer can do everything. Proceed at your own pace, not the pace of the consultant.

Lawyers can also be extremely important in reviewing the vendor's boiler plate contracts and assisting in negotiations. However, practices in the computer industry are relatively new and unfamiliar to many lawyers. Thus, the typical attorney may be inclined to be cautious to the point of preventing action, and thus may hinder the procurement. Attorneys are trained to avoid risks when possible and to address all identifiable risks in the contract. Unfortunately, there will always be risks associated with computer systems. Your task is to learn sufficient information to recognize the legitimate risks and select a system that will minimize them.

To litigate a computer contract is extremely expensive and time-consuming, and in major metropolitan areas it can take four to five years before a trial can be started. You certainly need to work with your attorney to minimize risks, but it is up to you to select the right system for the right price. The contract will record your agreement. It will not protect you from a fundamentally bad selection on your part. There rarely is a real winner when a computer contract is litigated.

Friends can be loosely defined as people who like us and have our welfare at heart. Notice that there are no qualifications to be a friend. A friend need not be knowledgeable in computers or word processing. A friend does not have to know about finances or law or even your business. So the advice given by friends, relatives, or business competitors must be taken in the correct perspective.

Imitating another's use of a computer system must also be questioned because the key to the successful use of a system is based on the unique requirements of each business or office. If another's requirements are different than yours, then that computer/word processing system could simply be all wrong for you.

Gain knowledge through the competitive buying procedures, gain experience through starting small, and protect your investment of time and money through financial leverage and a fair and reasonable contract.

VENDOR'S COMMISSION PLAN

An understanding of a vendor's commission plan frequently may help in making sense out of a vendor's behavior, but not always. Commissions are the percentage of the selling price or lease amount paid to the sales representative based on the dollar volume of the sale. The other source of income for a sales representative is the weekly or monthly salary. What can be particularly enlightening for the buyer is to understand the relationship between the sales rep's commissions and salary.

Sales representatives who are heavily compensated by commissions rather than salary will be more inclined to make the sale and move on to another sale rather than ensure continuing service. If a sales rep's financial livelihood is based on making sales, clearly that is where he or she will be motivated. Many companies operate in this manner. The sales representatives operate in the capacity of independent contractors rather than employees of the vendor. Compensations for sales are usually very lucrative and are designed that way to retain salespeople in this capacity. Smaller firms may not even offer salaries, so the sales rep operates as an independent broker and must rely on the sale for his or her exclusive financial livelihood.

Sales representatives operating under this type of financial reimbursement plan usually will not be available for post-installation problems. After the system is installed, they will be off working on another sale. There will be a support organization available for your problems, but not the individual sales rep who sold you the system. The disadvantage of this situation is that the customer must deal with new people from the vendor's organization. Frequently, the customer can get lost within the vendor's organization when trying to resolve a problem because he or she will not know where to turn for help.

The other type of compensation is where the sales rep is reimbursed predominantly from salary, and any particular sale is important but does not jeopardize the sales rep's financial livelihood. This arrangement encourages more of a service orientation and an on-going relationship between the sales representative who sold the account and the customer. From a customer's point of view, this method is preferable because on-going support is the secret of success with computers/word processors. A prospective purchaser might be wise to determine what sort of compensation plan the sales rep is operating under to anticipate the service support that might be forthcoming after the contract is signed.

EFFECT OF VENDOR'S QUOTAS

What will be the impact on you of the sales representative's marketing quotas for the year? Making quota may be the difference between holding and losing the job. In some companies, if a salesperson fails to make quota for two years in a row, it is time to look for another job. In most cases, the sales manager, branch manager, and all higher ups in the organization operate with a yearly quota of required sales.

Aside from the job dangers to the sales rep, many companies attempt to motivate their people by holding out special rewards for those who make or exceed their quotas. Such rewards range from trips to Hawaii or Europe, special recognition gifts like pens or plaques, trophies or watches. The use of these incentives has a definite effect on the sales staff.

A sales rep motivated by all of the above becomes committed to meeting the quota. In some cases, the rep starts to believe that meeting the personal sales quota is more important than meeting the requirements of the customer. Particularly as the end of the vendor's fiscal year approaches, a salesperson can become desperate to achieve the quota. In some cases, quarterly quotas can be almost as important as yearly quotas. What can be done from the customer's point of view in light of this knowledge?

Bargain! The almost frantic need for the sales rep to make the quota can be used effectively in negotiating important concessions from the vendor. As the end of the vendor's year approaches, vendors become more willing to offer extra to motivate the customer to sign up before the deadline. This point can be important and should be remembered.

EFFECT OF THE CORPORATION

Corporations are human organizations and vary in technology, service, and honesty as widely as do human beings themselves. The people who represent the company will be controlled greatly by the corporate policies and practices.

The larger the corporation, the greater resources in terms of marketing, technology, and service. Large corporations have the ability to declare certain accounts as "alert" accounts and to redirect additional corporate resources from around the region or around the country to solve a particular customer's problem.

Smaller corporations obviously will have smaller resources, which usually cannot be redirected as easily. Additionally, smaller companies may not be geographically located in proximity to your installations; thus travel time and expense must be considered.

One point that needs to be emphasized: you cannot generalize about the effectiveness of a company in relation to its size. Large as well as small companies overextend their resources. The nature of the computer industry, like all other industries, requires that machines or software must be sold to make the vendor a profit. To encourage sales, corporations of all sizes frequently make commitment that they doubt can be fulfilled with the current employee staff. However, rather than lose the opportunity for the sale, promises are made and, more frequently than not, are broken.

Remember that vendors may overextend their resources. Be sensitive to this and avoid vendors who operate in an overextended fashion as a matter of normal business.

THE SQUEAKY WHEEL

You might say that the only way to protect yourself against a vendor who is overextended is to write an airtight contract. That certainly is one way, which we will discuss in detail in a later chapter, but it is not the only way.

The other method to ensure compliance is to complain loud and long if the vendor does not deliver on promises. If the sales representative is no help, go to the rep's boss, and to that person's boss, and so on until you receive the service that you paid and contracted for. It is amazing how frequently the best course in this business is to take an irate and demanding approach until you receive what you are entitled to.

THE CUSTOMER RULES

There is no rule in picking out companies. However, there are a few items to look for. A wise businessman once said that "a company is known by the people it keeps."

The knowledge, both technical and financial, possessed by service representatives will give you an indication of what kind of company he or she represents. Solid corporations invest significant amounts of money and time in training their representatives. Experienced vendor employees should be paired with inexperienced reps, which is beneficial both to the customer and the vendor. We will discuss different methods to evaluate companies in a later chapter, but for now remember to avoid dealing with a vendor who is spread too thin and does not possess a corporate commitment to provide high quality and reliable service.

You are the customer and you deserve quality service in a timely manner. Anything less should not be tolerated.

ANALYSIS OF VENDOR'S PROPOSAL

Appendix B contains a model vendor proposal (B1), which will be evaluated and scored in the next chapter. Many of the responses in the proposal have been taken from actual proposals prepared by actual vendors who participated in my various college courses and seminars. Most vendor responses have been created to illustrate certain points.

Before evaluating the proposal, let us review the responses from Vendor A shown in Appendix B.

VENDOR COVER LETTER (B2)

PUFFING.   The superlatives used by the vendor in the cover letter need some explanation. One would think that words and phrases such as "A-plus," "most advanced and reliable system available," "most versatile and dependable" would protect the buyer from any mediocre performance by the vendor.

Unfortunately, this is not the case. The law has always recognized something referred to as "puffing" when dealing with marketing people. The theory is simply that in dealing with salespeople in a marketing environment, a reasonable buyer should be able to recognize when a sales rep is "puffing" his or her product. Such terms as "most advanced" and "most versatile" are not subject to objective measurement and would normally be considered to be puffing, and unenforceable.

Thus, in reviewing the vendor's cover letter, you can determine that there is very little that represents concrete, objective standards that can be incorporated into the contract and enforceable at a later time. The letter is a classic case of effective puffing.

TRUST ME.   The letter also illustrates the "trust me" mistake wherein the vendor attempts to develop a personal relationship with the buyer.

"I will personally assure you that the entire resources available within our organization will be standing ready." This is an effective technique to gain your confidence, but, unfortunately, it is not enforceable. If the vendor is transferred to another site, the customer is left with only the contract, not the promise.

HISTORY DISCUSSION (B3)

As in the cover letter, there is a large amount of puffing in these sections also. You should identify the puffing right away and eliminate those comments from your discussion.

You should notice the absence of concrete and objective numbers. How many sites does the vendor actually have in operation? How large a support staff actually exists? How many sites and references are available?

SYSTEMS DISCUSSION (B4)

Again, you witness a large degree of puffing (in this case, regarding the BD123 system): "The system will run without material failure for an extensive amount of time." What is needed in this section of a vendor's proposal are detailed specifications about the technical capabilities of the equipment. You specifically require a response by the use of your RFP format so that puffing can be kept to a minimum. (Chapter 6 discusses in detail how these technical specifications will be evaluated.)

WORD PROCESSING AND BUSINESS PROGRAMS DISCUSSION (B5, B6)

The puffing continues regarding the "most complete and versatile package of its kind." The vendor has acknowledged that the software is under constant improvement; however, the vendor has not been specific regarding updates or the years that the programs have been in actual use.

PRICE DISCUSSION (B7)

The "lowest possible prices" is another example of puffing and is not legally enforceable. It is important to recognize that prices are effective for 90 days. The selection, negotiations and contracting must be completed within three months or the prices may be raised.

REVIEW OF PROPOSAL

A general observation is that one proposal by itself (although it provides a great amount of detailed information) is less than adequate until you compare the proposals received from the other vendors. The fact that a particular system has certain features and does not have other capabilities only has meaning when compared to the technical features of the other systems.

GLOSSIES

"Glossies" are those attractive flyers on glossy paper that show pretty pictures of professional models smiling and standing around computers trying to look busy. Glossies normally contain certain specifications about the equipment and its capabilities. The problem with them is that unless the specifications are expressly incorporated into the contract, data contained on the glossy are not enforceable. Some data found on glossies are simply not true.

You can enjoy how beautiful and handsome the people and equipment seem to be, but do not rely on the information presented.

SUMMARY

Due to the service orientation of the computer/word processing industry, your marketing representative becomes extremely important to your long-range success. Many marketing people are excellent individuals with the highest professional goals. Many are, unfortunately, untrained neophytes trying to do the best possible job but lacking the experience to be considered effective. There are a few crooks in every field, and you must be alert to these persons.

Keep in mind these four important tips: competitive buying, financial leverage, starting small, and guidance on the advice-givers—consultants, lawyers, and friends. And remember that the marketing commission plans and quotas and the overall corporation may have significant impact on your particular circumstances.

The customer rules; do not forget your role in this buyer's market.

In Chapter 6, we demonstrate how to evaluate between competing vendors.

6

EVALUATION
AND SELECTION

Selecting a computer system by evaluating proposals might be compared to deciding on a new car by reading the automobile road tests published in such magazines as *Road and Track* and *Car and Driver*. These road tests are very uniform, and they rate cars as to handling, performance, quality, and esthetic factors. They also rank similar models based on mileage, performance, price, stopping distance, noise level, and maintainability. By reading these road tests and evaluation reports, the potential car buyer can get a "feel" for the car he or she prefers in terms of performance and mileage and can determine which cars he or she can afford.

One big difference with computer buying, however, is that there are too few similar "road tests" published for the computer industry. Any such reports are usually heavily technical and make comparisons based on engineering details and specifications of electronic capacities. These reports also use "computer language," which is not as familiar to people generally as is "car language."

Bookstores carry numerous books and publications that have extensive statistical information about computers. The problem with so much of this material is that the information is not presented in a meaningful way. To know that one machine can execute one and one-half times faster than another does not necessarily indicate which of the

98

two would fit your particular need. The fact that one machine has five million characters of storage is not very significant unless you know whether your requirement is for three million characters or 15 million characters.

This problem can be solved by sending out RFPs to several qualified computer vendors, which will require them to devise a system to meet your requirements. Sending out an RFP is the equivalent of writing to all the car manufacturers and giving them your requirements for a car (passenger capacity, mileage, top speed, and so on). Their response would be to propose one or several of their cars that may meet your requirements, and they would quote a price. You would then pick the best car at the best price. Car dealers do not do this, but computer vendors typically will sell their systems by responding with written proposals. A computer system is far more complex than a car, and there is much more work in evaluating and ranking systems. This chapter discusses effective and efficient procedures for evaluating computer systems.

By sending out RFPs, you hope to narrow the field of potential systems down to the few that will do your work at the best price. A quick glance through the proposals will tell you what the prices are and how complete the proposals are, which may give you a "gut" feeling as to which computer you would rank as one, two, or three. However, a computer is too complex to be selected in such a fashion. Systematic selection and evaluation techniques must be used. Even if you do not follow the procedures described here, it is highly recommended that some objective procedure be used to select your computer.

You probably wish to reach a quick decision and have a natural desire to rely on your instincts and gut feeling. However, it may be helpful to remember that tremendous risk is involved in making the wrong decision. The cost of the machine and software is only the tip of the iceberg. The greatest risk is associated with transferring your current systems (which presumably work to some degree) to a new computer system that just plain does not work. The impact in terms of lost bookkeeping records, extensive delays in delivering products or services, negative effect on employees, and low employee morale are the stakes involved. The cost of the computer is, in reality, a very small part of the risk.

The mental procedure for evaluating and selecting a computer is similar to what would be involved in making any complex decision. The difference is that these procedures recommend that the evaluations be written and that more than one person be involved, if possible.

The evaluation and selection procedure consists of the following general steps:

Preparing an evaluation document.
Forming an evaluation team to do the actual evaluations.
Evaluating and scoring the proposals.
Selecting a vendor.

This procedure is expanded and explained in detail in the following pages.

The entire selection process can be painless and almost automatic if the organization and preparation are done ahead of time. The RFP requires vendors to respond by a particular date. All the preparations should, therefore, be completed by that date to allow for an easy and rapid selection. Selecting the evaluation criteria should be done at the RFP stage. This allows you to list your general selection criteria in the RFP so the vendors will know what areas you are most interested in. This selection document can be as detailed as necessary and will usually correspond to the RFP. In a straightforward RFP, the document itself may be used as a checklist for the evaluation document.

Appendix C shows a RFP page that is modified to illustrate its use as an evaluation form. You could adapt the RFP in Appendix B to this purpose by covering the vendor's response column, photocopying, and ruling as necessary to create an evaluation form. The possible points to be awarded for each requirement are listed for ease of reference in a separate column. When the vendors return the completed RFP, the evaluator can score the points in the column and annotate comments or reasons for the particular score.

Normally, the evaluation form will have several columns to list the scores of the respective vendors. In this example, we list only three columns for Vendor A, B, and C, so that several difference responses can be shown.

THE EVALUATION FORM

Because you will be dealing with so many factors in evaluating the proposed computer systems, it is necessary to have a form that you can use to score them. This form is easy to use and is similar to a checklist. The evaluation form will have a list of the requirements you want the computer to meet and a list of vendor performance responses. The form will correspond to the RFP and the vendor's proposal, so it is easy to go from item to item on the evaluation form and award points. As an example, some items that might be contained in an evaluation form are: full-sized screen, 5 points; numerical keypad, 3 points; contractor's years in business, more than five years, 10 points. You would be able to read the vendor's response and find that the computer has a full screen, so you would award 5 points. The computer may not have a numerical keypad, so that vendor would be scored 0 points for that item. The vendor may only have been in business for two years, so you might award 4 points for being close to your three-year requirement, or 0 points for failing to meet the requirement. The way you award points depends on the particular emphasis you decide to place on a particular requirement. If you absolutely require a minimum of a numerical keyboard, then it is appropriate to award 0 points for failing to meet this requirement.

EVALUATION CRITERIA

Although the details for selecting evaluation criteria can be extracted almost intact from the RFP, the evaluation criteria tend to fall into the following general categories and sample percentages of the total decision which is equal to 100%.

Technical discussion	40 percent
Vendor capabilities	30 percent
Price	20 percent
Vendor support	10 percent

These percentages are offered only as a guide; your actual percentages are very much a part of your unique circumstances. You may have a specialized scientific application so that the technical capabilities of the computer system may need to be weighted 50 percent or higher of the total score. If, on the other hand, your office is small and cannot afford a large expenditure, the price category may be as much as 30 percent. There are no concrete rules; however, these guidelines may help. The following sections give an overview of each general category.

Technical Discussion

The technical discussions may be the most important part of the proposal and should be evaluated thoroughly and in as much detail as feasible. The RFP represents a substantial effort to define your requirements and put into writing what the computer has to be able to do. Now you have the vendor's proposals, which are recommending computers that may or may not actually do what you asked for. It is important to read the proposals carefully since vendors may be proposing responses that are "close" or "similar" to your technical requirements. They may also submit an alternate proposal and recommend a computer that is different from what you requested. The vendor may believe in the alternate proposal as a credible solution to your requirements. An alternate proposal will often be based on a vendor's re-evaluation of your requirements.

The technical discussion is the part where you work down your list in the evaluation document and check that the vendor's system contains all the software features and hardware capabilities you require, such as: full screen, standard keyboard, programming, certain types of printers, software availability, and others. Full points are awarded for having satisfied a requirement, and no points for not having a particular requirement. Partial points may also be awarded for partial or substantial compliance with the requirements.

Vendor Capabilities

You evaluate the vendor's capabilities of providing and implementing a reliable computer system and for performing other obligations such as training and maintenance. Under vendor capabilities, the vendor would be evaluated on ability in areas such as: being in business a minimum number of years (three or more), having a certain size staff with training and maintenance specialists, whether the vendor is located nearby, the quality of the staff assigned to your installation, having a strong financial record, having successfully installed similar systems, and having good references.

Vendor capabilities are frequently overlooked and not fully understood by many would-be purchasers. Remember that there are over 140 companies providing these types of products and services. The computer industry has already witnessed the withdrawal of a few corporate giants. You want to ensure that any company you elect to do business with will be around for many years. Therefore, you assign 30 percent of your total evaluation score to vendor capabilities (see section 4 of the RFP.)

If a vendor has been in business for less than three years, there is always the possibility of business failure, which could leave you with a worthless computer system. If a relatively new vendor is selected, make sure that the system you select is available through other local dealers, with parts and maintenance readily available on short notice. Requiring a strong financial position is another method for helping to ensure that your vendor will not go under, but will remain accountable for the computer system for many years.

It is a good idea to determine that the vendor has a sufficient number of maintenance personnel to service all customers. With the industry growing so fast, some companies are making and selling computers faster than they can train qualified personnel to service them. When the machine fails, the customer can be stranded for many days without competent maintenance support.

Although it may seem obvious, it is very important to check references and call or visit similar installations. This will provide good information, particularly if the vendor has performed poorly before. A poor performance usually leaves frustrated users who are very willing to discuss complaints. It is also important to remember that good references do not guarantee that you will be free of problems. A vendor can be rated outstanding and prior users may think that the vendor can do no wrong, but a company can have excellent references and still fail to provide a qualified representative for your particular business. References have value, but they are not foolproof.

Price

Price is also an important factor in ranking vendors. The price may be a simple purchase price, or it may be made up of several lease or lease-purchase options over a varying number of years, such as a three-year lease, five-year lease, or seven-year lease. The various finance plans should be awarded points based on various considerations. The simplest technique is to award the full amoint of points for the lowest (best) price and fewer points for successively higher prices. The point spread between the lowest and highest price may be up to you. It is important to treat price like the other factors because the lowest price may not be for a complete system, or the lowest priced computer may not have all the required features.

Vendor Support

Vendor support is also very important for the continued success of a computer operation. Areas to consider are vendor training and the quantity and availability of training. Also important are vendor maintenance and response time for service.

Vendor support is concerned with the specific commitments that the vendor will make to your particular business. Here you are not concerned with the capability to perform (that area is covered in vendor capability, discussed earlier), but rather with the quantity and quality of the services to be committed to and to be incorporated into the contract.

THE SCORING SYSTEM

The human mind can make distinctions between items and rank them in order of preference. However, there are significant problems with this intuitive method. The ability to rank proposals reliably disappears when a person tries to sort through three, four, or more. As the number of proposals increases, some sort of system has to be used to score, record, and rank the proposals. This same problem arises when the proposals become more technical and detailed. It soon becomes impossible to keep track of all the details that have to be compared in each proposal.

Another problem in scoring proposals is subjectiveness. Three different people can score the same proposals and select three different vendors as the winner. Using a scoring system that is applied uniformly, objectively, and mathematically will reduce this problem.

The most practical scoring system is one that is straight-forward and awards points for various predetermined requirements. Most scoring systems are based on 100 points. If there is a good deal of detail to be scored, the total can be raised to 1,000 points.

Earlier in this chapter some sample areas for evaluation were given as: technical, 40 percent; vendor capabilities, 30 percent; price, 20 percent; and vendor support, 10 percent. Using the 100-point scoring system, it is easy to convert these percentages into points, so that the technical evaluation would be awarded a maximum of 40 points, the price a maximum of 20 points, and so on. Within each group of criteria, the points would be allocated among the various items in that group. The scorer has to make an evaluation of whether the requirement is met by the proposal before awarding any points or partial points. As the points are scored, comments should also be made for each requirement, indicating where the proposal discussed that particular requirement and why points or no points were awarded. This will leave an audit trail and allow for verification in case of problems or discrepancies between the various scores.

Use of comments become important later in discussions with other members of the evaluation team because a comment can trigger a reason for a particular score being given, or it will raise a question to be discussed or a point to be researched. Comments also can become important in preparation for negotiations. The comments section will show where a vendor is weak and what the vendor must do to address that weakness. Comments are invaluable and well worth the time it takes to jot down your reasons for a particular score.

If possible, several people should independently evaluate and score the proposals. Their scores can then be averaged for each proposal. This will even out individual variations in the scores. For example, if one evaluator gives higher scores than the others and another gives scores that are much lower, the averaging process levels off the extremes, provided that all proposals are scored by each member of the committee.

PROCEDURE

As shown in Appendix C, each proposal should be scored on a standard form that lists all the categories, maximum points to be awarded, and has space for comments. Each evaluator will fill out a form scoring sheet for each proposal.

The procedure involves a prescoring meeting with the evaluators. The purpose is to hand out the proposals and scoring forms and to "synchronize" all the scorers by describing what the evaluators should look for, how they should score, and to answer any questions.

The evaluation team will then evaluate the proposals individually. Although the proposals are considered separately, it is a good idea to have the evaluators discuss the evaluation as a group. This ensures that the appropriate concentration and time are spent on this project, and any questions or problems can be solved immediately.

Discussion as a group is also important so that the individual evaluators can ask questions of other team members in their respective areas of expertise. The computer expert, for example, can ask questions about the functional requirements from a person in that area. Discussion allows individuals to adjust their scores in light of new knowledge gained during the team talk.

After all the proposals are evaluated and scored, the team will regroup. The scores for each proposal will be averaged and the proposals ranked, based on average scores. The evaluation committee will also make note of the superior qualities of a vendor's product, as well as any deficiencies. The deficiencies will be addressed during negotiations.

SCORING OPTIONAL SECTIONS

The primary purpose of the optional sections is to provide information about enhancements to the basic system and to identify any additional costs. As discussed earlier, the detailed evaluation pertains to the limited scope of basic requirements. The optional sections then allow you to consider additional features for either the current procurement or for some time in the future. The basic evaluation, however, does not include a mathematical scoring of the optional features. To do so would mean to "mix apples and oranges." It is better to complete the basic evaluation using "apples" only, that is, the basic requirements. After this exercise is completed, optional considerations can be added to your basic requirements.

For example, the automatic mailbox feature is a desirable capability (see under 3.5 Optional Software Features). However, there may be an additional cost. If you have decided that you do not absolutely need this feature at the present time, you do not want to analyze and score it as part of your basic evaluation. However, through the optional sections, by learning of cost and availability of this feature, you may elect to begin planning its use in the future. Additionally, you may want to give 10–20 bonus points to the particular vendors who have this product. The bonus points can be given at the discretion of the team members and as the individual deems appropriate.

Bonus points can influence the ultimate selection and should be used only on a limited basis.

THE EVALUATION TEAM

Whenever possible, several people should comprise the evaluation team to look over the proposals and select a vendor. By using a team, personal biases will be balanced out and the vendor selection will be more objective than if a single individual were selecting the vendor. Using an evaluation team also has the advantage of providing different areas of expertise. Rather than having three technical people evaluate proposals, it is important to utilize people experienced in different areas, such as financial, management, and technical. Sometimes a data processing consultant who may be familiar with the company's requirements can be used as one of the members of the evaluation team.

By using people with various backgrounds, the probability of doing an effective evaluation and selecting the best-qualified vendor increases. A financial person will ensure a correct interpretation of the vendor's price section and can determine what financial benefits may accrue to the business from each proposal. The management and/or executive person will be able to determine how well a vendor's proposal meets the overall requirements of the company. The technical person will be able to evaluate the technical portions of each proposal. Two or more of these functions may be performed by a single individual, so that the evaluation team should not have to be any larger than three or four people.

In addition to evaluating the proposals, the team may decide to validate the claims made in the proposals. Validating the proposal may involve having vendors give oral presentations, demonstrations of their computers, or actually visiting the vendors to determine what facilities and personnel are available for service.

VENDOR DEMONSTRATIONS, SITE VISITS, AND THE LIKE

A reminder about vendor demonstrations; asking for a demonstration of the various features described in the vendor's proposal may be very helpful at this point. Questions raised in discussions can be answered by requiring the vendor to demonstrate any questionable features. Visiting the vendor's site or another customer's site to see the feature or function in use are very valuable at this phase of the deliberations. Requesting the vendor to make a verbal presentation to the evaluation team may also help in completing the scoring process.

The key point to remember is that the buyer can use any method within his or her power to ascertain facts about the vendor's company and product. Stockbrokers, newspapers, trade magazines are other sources of facts to be considered. It is hard work, but worth the effort.

VENDOR SELECTION

The vendor with the highest average score will usually be selected as the supplier. The selected vendor will not always have the lowest price because there are many other requirements to be considered in an RFP. Picking the lowest priced vendor will not ensure getting the best product. As stated before, a low priced computer with inadequate maintenance support can be essentially worthless if a serious equipment problem occurs.

After the vendor is selected, the vendor's rep should be notified and invited to make arrangements for negotiating the contract. This vendor should also be informed that if a successful contract is not agreed upon, the next ranked vendor will be selected. This creates a strong bargaining position for the buyer.

EVALUATING AND SCORING PROPOSALS USING THE MODEL RFP

Even if you can appreciate the advantages in using a formal evaluation procedure, it still can be difficult to translate theory into practice. Creating an RFP can be easily accomplished with the directions previously provided and using the sample in Appendix B. The sample can be used by any size company simply by scaling the requirements up or down and by adding or deleting requirements based on individual needs.

The RFP could be a two-or three-page document requesting proposals for a single, simple terminal, or it could be a very large document requesting a large system capable of supporting hundreds of terminals and printers. As your requirements grow more complex, the RFP will expand in detail to describe your needs to the vendors.

It is important that the evaluation document and ranking of vendors be used correctly. Vendor evaluations should be considered a tool that helps make the "best" decision; they are not a "straightjacket" that forces an unwanted decision. Even if your organization decides on a vendor other than the top ranked one, you will have the benefit of knowing specifically how the chosen vendor compared with all others. Your organization will have comparable information from all the vendors so that the final decision will be made with all useful information available.

You will have acquired, without an excessive amount of work, the comparable information provided by *Road and Track* magazine for the car buyer. Better yet, the information will all be understandable and related to your "unique" business or office.

There are many precedents to this kind of practical decision-making. As an example, colleges require some sort of test scores from applicants. They can then evaluate and rank applicants on the basis of their test scores, high school grades, and other achievements or activities. A committee will usually evaluate applicants, using a worksheet. Although some colleges are very objective and set selection cutoff points based entirely on the applicant's overall ranking, others may admit a number of students for subjective reasons or future potentials. Here, as in computer vendor evaluations, the students are evaluated and ranked, but the final selection does not always pick only the top ranked students.

The academic committee will usually meet and discuss the prospective student, and the committee's vote is final. Selecting a computer is quite similar to many other decisions in life . . . only more complicated.

EVALUATION EXAMPLES

Let us get into the actual machinery of evaluating proposals. The 1,000 points assigned to the sample RFP (Appendix B) were allocated to seven main areas with the following values:

Proposal content	50 points	⎫
Business programs	100 points	⎬ Technical 40 percent
Word processing capabilities	150 points	⎪
Hardware features	100 points	⎭
Vendor services and support	100 points	} Services 10 percent
Vendor capabilities	300 points	} Capabilities 30 percent
Price quotations	200 points	} Price 20 percent
Total points	1,000 points	

This table shows that heavy emphasis has been placed on the vendor's capability and service. The reasoning is that computer equipment can be very similar from vendor to vendor and may all perform similar functions for similar prices, but if the vendor does not provide sufficient services, or is unable to maintain and keep the system up and running, your business may be jeopardized. In such a competitive, high technology market, the level and reliability of the vendor's service are the crucial distinctions between vendors. In this example, the combined 400 points for vendor services and support and vendor capabilities are a significant 40 percent of the total evaluation. This point can be illustrated even more convincingly when you consider buying a car. Would anyone buy a car that did not have dealer service, parts, or personnel? No, for if it cannot be maintained, a machine has little value.

Price is given 200 points, for 20 percent of the evaluation. This can be increased if price is a more important part of your selection. A point range of between 200 to 400 points (20 to 40 percent) would be within a standard range commonly used in evaluating price. Price could easily be made 100 percent of the proposal; in that case, the lowest price would be selected. This is not recommended in an RFP procurement. If your organization's resources are so limited as to allow consideration of only the lowest priced systems, it might be advisable to delay obtaining a computer system until sufficient financial resources are acquired, which would enable your organization to procure the system that best meets your needs, regardless of the price.

The proposal content is given 50 points, or 5 percent. This awards points if the vendor responded in the correct format with a complete proposal. It is important that all proposals be uniform so that the evaluation can be completed easily and accurately. This section is usually in the 5 percent range, and at the most may be increased to 10 percent.

The remaining 350 points, or 35 percent are allocated to the technical requirements of the hardware and software. This includes 100 points set aside for the business programs, such as accounting, manufacturing, or office.

The application of business programs, whether for lawyers, doctors, small business accounting, manufacturers, and so on is not discussed in detail in this section because the products that are, or soon will be, available defy accurate description since the rate of change is so great. The reader should develop and score the special business programs for his or her own business or profession. Model reports and forms in Appendix A may help.

The evaluation document sets forth the format to be used to state the required functions of the software and illustrates how these programs can be described in the RFP.

SUBJECTIVE NATURE OF SCORING

Scoring proposals will involve some subjective decision-making on the part of the evaluator. Each requirement has a maximum number of points that may be awarded to a proposer. These points may be 1 or 25. If the number of points available is only 1, evaluating is very straightforward because the vendor either meets the requirement or does not. With 1 point, halfway meeting a requirement or substantial compliance will be of no avail and will receive 0 points.

When more points are available, the question is more difficult. For example, you ask for an on-line storage capacity of 11 megabytes, and a vendor states the availability of 10 megabytes. If there are 4 points available for this requirement, the award must be made on a predetermined basis, which is derived from your requirements. The options are to aware some points for partial credit, or 0 points for failing to meet the requirement. Obviously, full credit cannot be awarded for being close (such as the vendor who has 10 megabytes) since that score must be reserved for the response that meets or exceeds your requirements. To do otherwise would devalue your comparison.

The decision on how to award these points has to be made for each requirement based on your needs. For example, if 11 megabytes is an absolute requirement, such that you cannot function with or accept 10 megabytes or any less figure, then 0 points must be awarded that proposal for failing to meet that absolute requirement. On the other hand, if your acceptable range is 11 megabytes down to four megabytes, you can award partial credit since there is a range of acceptable responses. The requested response of 11 megabytes of on-line storage would receive the full 4 points, nine megabytes to 10 megabytes might be awarded 3 points, seven megabytes to eight megabytes might be awarded 2 points, and a response of four megabytes to six megabytes might be awarded 1 point. The remaining responses of three megabytes or less can be awarded 0 points. A wide variety of vendor responses can be objectively handled in this manner. It is important when receiving your evaluation form to determine your company's absolute and variable requirements. The evaluation team can discuss these points prior to the final proposal evaluations being completed so as to synchronize scoring methodology.

In scoring the proposal for content, 25 points have been assigned for format and sequence, and 25 points for completeness of the proposal. This is fairly easy to score and is also more subjective than other sections. If it is obvious that the proposal followed the required formats, 25 points are awarded. If there are deviations, lesser points can be awarded all the way down to 0 points, depending on the severity of the deviations. Again, if a specific format is an absolute requirement, you can award 0 points if there is any deviation at all. The same is true for the completeness of the proposal. Proposals that do not follow the required formats or are incomplete will also lose points.

Although a full response is requested for each requirement, vendors may answer anywhere from a simple "yes" to a detailed paragraph. If the requirement is auto page numbering, then acceptable answers could be:

SOFTWARE PRINTING FEATURES	MAX. PTS.	VENDOR RESPONSE
Auto page numbering	5	*Yes—see operator Guide, page 6* *Yes—see attached sales brochure*
Auto pagination	5	Yes

An answer that refers you back to a clearly identified and readily obtainable document is acceptable in this type of question. For auto pagination a similar answer would be desirable, but auto pagination is such an industry standard that "yes" can be considered a complete and acceptable response. Five points can be awarded to each of these answers.

Clearly, if a vendor responded in the negative, as in this example:

SOFTWARE PRINTING FEATURES	MAX. PTS.	VENDOR RESPONSE
Auto decimal tab	5	*No auto decimal tab*

then 0 points would be awarded. The problem arises when the vendor fails to respond at all. If there is no response to a requirement, the assumption has to be made that the vendor failed to meet those requirements, and 0 points should be awarded. A vendor who cannot meet a requirement can be expected not to respond in the negative; after all, the vendor has nothing more to lose by not responding to such a requirement.

Another example of a vendor partially meeting the requirements is illustrated below.

SOFTWARE PRINTING FEATURES	MAX. PTS.	VENDOR RESPONSE
Able to edit 400-page documents	10	**60 page only**

There will be a variety of vendor responses in this area. If a 400-page edit capability is an absolute requirement, the 60-page proposal response must be given 0 points. If anything is acceptable, with 400 pages being preferred, partial credit may be awarded. A further review of this requirement might indicate that a 400-page edit capability is unreasonable from a vendor's, as well as from the organization's, point of view. The operative question is "how many 400-page documents are ever processed?" Or, "how many 200-page documents, or even 50-page documents?" It may be that 40 percent of the time your organization uses one-to-three page letters with occasional 15-to-20-page reports. If so, this excessive requirement should be evaluated accordingly.

Sometimes the proposal responds with information that was not considered.

SOFTWARE PRINTING FEATURES	MAX. PTS.	VENDOR RESPONSE
Global search and replace.	10	**Automatic only** **or** **manual only**

Since the requirement did not request anything more specific than the global search and replace, both answers appear to meet the requirement for the full 10 points. If the organization can determine a preference or advantage for one answer over the other, points may be awarded accordingly. More examples of this kind of response are:

SOFTWARE PRINTING FEATURES	MAX. PTS.	VENDOR RESPONSE
System security that prevents document access.	4	**File password is available** **or** **each user holds own diskette**
System can restrict unauthorized users.	4	**Log on password only** **or** **actual key** **or** **magnetic card**

On the restricted document access, both answers meet the requirements, although each user holding his or her own diskette may not have been a contemplated alternative. But if it is acceptable, either answer would receive the full 4 points. In the question on unauthorized users, all three answers would receive 4 points as being acceptable technological solutions to the user's requirements.

Sometimes a response to a requirement can have varied responses from the different vendors.

SOFTWARE PRINTING FEATURES	MAX. PTS.	VENDOR RESPONSE
Able to search in three seconds or less from menu to any document, via automatic file/document select, when diskettes are full	4	*Cannot guarantee any response time* *or* *depends on unique factors* *or* *5 seconds only*

For this requirement, the first two answers can be considered as nonresponsive and awarded 0 points. The response of five seconds again comes down to what the absolute requirements are. If three seconds is an absolute necessity, the last response should be awarded 0 points also. If it is acceptable, it should be awarded 2–3 points.

Sometimes a vendor's response will be affirmative, yet impose other requirements.

SOFTWARE PRINTING FEATURES	MAX. PTS.	VENDOR RESPONSE
Word processing software updates must be available	4	*At additional charge*

The vendor has answered that word processing software updates will be available, but the vendor is going to charge extra for the updates. Is that a valid response? Yes, because the requirement was only that the vendor make available any updates, which will be done. It is not unusual for vendors to charge for such things as software updates. So, 4 points should be awarded. You may want to negotiate for free software updates if they are released three to six months from the time you purchase the system, or you should ensure that these additional charges are included in your cost considerations.

Some technical requirements can produce different types of responses that make evaluation more difficult.

SOFTWARE PRINTING FEATURES	MAX. PTS.	VENDOR RESPONSE
Bidirectional, letter quality, impact printer with approximately 40 characters per second print speed	15	*Centronix (plug compatible)* *or* *ink jet printer* *or* *50 cps*

The Centronix printer response indicates that the vendor does not manufacture his or her own printer and relies on another manufacturer's product. Plug compatible means that the printer can be plugged into the vendor's hardware without any extra interfaces. This response would be awarded 15 points as the Centronix printer is readily identifiable. The vendor who responds with an ink jet printer should get partial credit, unless an impact printer is an absolute requirement. The vendor responding with 50 cps (characters per second) clearly meets the requirements and is awarded 15 points.

Another type of requirement elicits responses that have to be categorized to determine what points to award. Some typical requirements and sample point awards might be the following:

SOFTWARE PRINTING FEATURES	MAX. PTS.	SAMPLE POINT AWARDS
Specify response time for emergency requests outside of prime shift and costs	5	More than 16 hours. = 0 pts. 10–15 hrs. = 1 5–9 hrs. = 3 0–4 hrs. = 5

Here an acceptable range (and industry standard) of four hours response time is awarded the full 5 points. A similar type of category can be created for other types of responses.

SOFTWARE PRINTING FEATURES	MAX. PTS.	SAMPLE POINT AWARDS
Number of application support personnel within a 20-mile radius	5	1–3 personnel = 1 pts. 4–10 personnel = 2 21–30 personnel = 3 31–100 personnel = 5

These are just samples of ranges that might be considered as adequate responses. Based on each user's requirements, these standards may be lowered or raised.

A sample of the evaluation documents filled in with scores from three vendors is illustrated below. The columns can be expanded to accommodate as many vendors as submit proposals. All the subtotals will be marked in the section subtotals, and then totalled. The vendors are then ranked based on their totals, with the selected vendor having the highest score.

SOFTWARE PRINTING FEATURES	MAX PTS.	VENDORS A	B	C	EVALUATORS COMMENTS
1. Printed queuing—8 documents.	4	3	1	4	A—only 6 documents, not 8 B—only 1 document at a time C—10 documents

2. Each CRT can direct output to any selected printer.	4	4	0	4	A—*meets reqm't* B—*prints to only one printer* C—*meets reqm't*
3. Operator can make priority print assignments.	4	0	0	4	A—*not available* B—*not available* C—*meets reqm't*
4. Operator can print beginning desired page.	4	4	4	4	A—*meets reqm't* B—*meets reqm't* C—*meets reqm't*
5. Sub and superscript printout.	3	0	2	3	A—*not available* B—*superscript only* C—*meets reqm't*
6. Simultaneous printout.	3	3	0	3	A—*meets reqm't* B—*not available* C—*meets reqm't*
Subtotals	22	15	7	21	

VENDOR CAPABILITIES

We have emphasized that the computer and word processing industry is very much service-based, and the success or failure of an installation will frequently depend on the quality of the vendor's support. This fact makes your scoring of the vendor's ability (section 4) to provide the service and support of utmost importance.

> Does the vendor have backup for key employees?
> Does the vendor have extra resources that can be marshalled if the need arises?
> Does the vendor have a good reputation for the type of service that you need, or is the vendor trying to enter into new areas of technology?

Picking a good computer company is like picking a good doctor, lawyer, or mechanic. The size, location, quality of employees, and references are all important. Try to learn as much about the company as you learn about the products. Obtaining this information is not easy. But the difficulty, stress, and agony associated with selecting the wrong company far exceed the minimum work that is needed. If the service organization is poor, a minor problem can become catastrophic. Do not underestimate this point. It is well worth the 30 percent of the evaluation criteria and 100 percent worth of your time in making your selection.

Annual Financial Report (4.1)

An annual financial report will aid you in scoring. Is the vendor a corporation, subsidiary, partnership, or sole practitioner? Does the vendor even have an annual financial report that you can see? Some companies are reluctant to show their reports. Who are the officers of the company?

An annual financial report is not requested to determine the overall financial value of the corporation. Rather, it is requested to provide fundamental background data to inform you as to who and what you are dealing with. So often, there is a tendency to judge a company strictly on the looks and personality of the sales representatives. You need concrete facts and figures, however, to make an objective evaluation of the company that can best support you in your unique circumstances. The annual financial report assists in providing this information.

Another source of this type of data is the Dun and Bradstreet reports, which contain additional data on a vendor's credit history and past payment record. The more information to consider in this area the more accurate your score will be.

Location and Names (4.2.1)

If possible, you would like to know the names, titles, and addresses of the people who will be assigned to your account. You want to lock the vendor into supplying certain people to work on your account. This requirement protects you from the "bait and switch" routine discussed earlier, when an experienced technician goes on sales visits but a trainee or beginner is actually sent to work on your account.

Resumes (4.2.2)

By requesting the resumés, you can score the quality and experience of personnel who will service your account. Another advantage is that in the event a designated person leaves the employ of the vendor or is otherwise unavailable, the resumé will represent a standard of experience that must be satisfied in the replacement personnel. If a particular person is unavailable, you can require that an equally experienced person be assigned to your account (not a trainee or beginner).

References (4.3)

References are difficult to trust unless the individual providing the reference is a friend or personal acquaintance. However, references are additional data points that must be scored in making your selection. This section requires the vendor to provide the names and phone numbers of references. You should definitely make the phone calls. Frequently vendors provide references that give extremely poor reports or references with little similarity to your particular business. References may provide valuable insight about the vendor. As said earlier, a site visit to current vendor installations can also provide valuable information. All available information is valuable and used in your score.

Price Calculations

The price quotation can be handled by again setting up categories and awarding points for low prices in the following illustration:

Lowest price	A.	$_____	200 pts.
	B.	$_____	150 pts.
	C.	$_____	100 pts.
	D.	$_____	50 pts.
Highest price	E.	$_____	25 pts.

These categories can be expanded to accommodate as many vendors as necessary, and the points can be spread in any manner desired.

Summary

The evaluation procedure is intended to utilize a selection form that allows the buyer to choose the best system for his or her particular requirement at the lowest possible price. In order to reach this goal, it is necessary to follow a systematic approach. By following the techniques outlined in this book, any potential computer buyer can assure that he or she selected a system considering all the important information.

The sample documents in this text can be streamlined or expanded depending on the particular circumstances of each case. To underestimate the importance of conducting an objective evaluation is simply to invite disaster. The education alone in respect to the products, services, and capabilities of the respective vendors will go far in ensuring the success of your installation. If you would like to experience doing an objective evaluation, photocopy Appendix B adding the evaluation criteria from Appendix C to each sheet. Create your own distribution of points to the various categories. Evaluate for yourself the vendor responses in the right-hand column of Appendix B.

7

NEGOTIATIONS

Vince Lombardi, the great coach of the Green Bay Packers, once said: "Practice doesn't make perfect; perfect practice makes perfect."

By completing the requirements study, the RFP, and the evaluation, you have prepared yourself to begin the negotiation process. Your preparation will come to fruition during this phase.

NUMBER ONE
NEGOTIATING STRATEGY

The number one negotiating strategy is to have one or two backup vendors who can do the job. You should go into the negotiations *not* wanting to complete the contract as badly as the vendor does! You can be insistent when necessary and refuse to yield on important points. You can be aggressive in your requests for concessions, knowing full well that you are not bluffing. You can maintain confidence in knowing which options are available. You are attempting to select from the "best" options at the time. This is where you want to be; you worked for it.

Creating this negotiating relationship and keeping your options open to use other vendors works with remarkable success. Vendors who would not normally consider reducing their prices often do so, and sometimes more than once until the dollars bid reach an acceptable level. Maintenance service can be improved, additional training and documentation can be obtained, and even custom software can be written at no cost. All this from a vendor who does not want to lose the sale. Vendor deficiencies can be addressed and in many cases corrected, as long as the selected vendor believes that the sale can be lost to a competitor.

The computer/word processor business is, in fact, no different than most other competitive businesses. It is a give-and-take proposition. The smart buyer will recognize and understand that his or her purchasing dollar places the buyer in command. Too frequently, the purchaser of a computer system feels helpless in the face of the options, products, technologies, and costs. However, when armed with the technical knowledge obtained from the evaluation procedure and the business alternatives offered by the top ranked vendors, the purchaser commands the situation. The key is not to lose sight of this power during the negotiation sessions.

EACH NEGOTIATION IS UNIQUE

You must remember that each negotiation is unique. There are no golden rules of "how to negotiate" that guarantee success. A number of books do exist on how to negotiate and some seminars try to formulate various negotiation arts. Some of these theories are discussed later in this chapter, but keep in mind that the fundamental, underlying key relationship between the purchaser and the vendor is that the purchaser, if unhappy with the selected vendor's responses, can terminate negotiations and move to the next qualified bidder. Don't let the vendor forget it!

COMMUNICATIONS

Invariably there will be issues that separate the parties. One side, either buyer or seller, will have a "communications breakdown," which is an emotional reaction to an apparent bad motive or apparent deception or obvious rudeness on the part of the other side. No doubt this type of behavior does occur at times, but the more usual case is simply a lack of understanding of technical, legal, or business principles. As described earlier, the amount of information that must be understood in computer negotiations is enormous, and confusion, simple error, or frequent mistakes should not be construed as dishonesty, rudeness, or bad motives.

The remedy for lack of understanding is "communications," also referred to as "negotiations." Negotiating does not mean "let's get the other side." It means meeting to communicate and to learn from each side what are the other's policies, procedures, practices, and so on. Fundamentally, negotiations is the process of identifying the problems for each side and creatively finding ways around them.

WHAT IS THE PROBLEM?

What may seem a simplistic goal of identifying and resolving problems is not simplistic at all. The most important questions to ask are: *what is the problem and what is the reason or rationale behind the problem?* For example, a response from the vendor such as "this is against corporate policy" is not acceptable. The background reasons for the policy form a legitimate basis for a buyer's question. If the vendor's rep does not know the answer, he or she should be expected to find out and report back at a later meeting. If it turns out that the basis for the policy is reasonable and fair from the vendor's perspective, then the buyer would be expected to agree to the policy. If, on the other hand, the practice is not reasonable either in terms of the practice in the industry, or just because plain common sense says otherwise, the vendor's rep should be directed to seek a change from normal corporate practice. To do this will require that the purchaser explain the reasons that would justify the deviation.

The purchaser must be willing to abide by the same rules that the vendor is expected to follow. If the buyer wants a change from corporate practices, the buyer must explain the basis of such a request in terms of either the practice in the industry and/or the "unique circumstances" of the purchaser.

The unique circumstances of the purchaser thus become very important in this phase. Vendors are aware that individual customers will have special needs and that based on the explanation of those needs, vendors can and will change policies and practices. It is up to the customer to articulate his or her needs. Communications in a straightforward, honest manner can accomplish a great deal. There is no magic in this approach, no tricks, must plain honest communication.

I WIN, YOU WIN

Another key lesson to remember is that for your installation to succeed, the vendor must also succeed. Many failures in the computer business have resulted from the selection of a company that did not have the equipment or staff to support the job and from a customer who demanded impossible tasks to be accomplished by the vendor. Negotiations should take place with a vendor who has been selected after an exhaustive evaluation process. Therefore, there may not be any major issues that need to be discussed.

On the other hand, you may find great discrepancies between the offerings of various vendors, or major issues may separate you and the highest ranked bidder. There may be policy issues that are important to either side and cannot be compromised. What to do? Break off negotiations and begin with the next ranked vendor.

Each company can only go so far in negotiations. To try to push a company beyond its capabilities is to invite disaster. It is much wiser to find a "good fit" between your requirements and price and the vendor's products and services. The fit must be comfortable for both sides. Our goal is an "I win, you win" negotiations session.

NEGOTIATING MEMORANDUM

In preparation for the negotiation session, you should construct a list of negotiating points/concessions that you wish to discuss during negotiations. Many people have difficulty in creating such a list. They have to be prodded and encouraged to answer some of the following questions:

1. Is there anything I have forgotten to ask for in the RFP?
2. Is there anything I have learned from other vendor proposals that I would like the selected vendor to provide?
3. Is there anything I personally want to make my job easier?
4. Is there any response from the vendor that requires further clarification?
5. Are there any deficiencies that need to be addressed by the vendor?

The answers to these questions should be written in a negotiating memorandum, which will represent your requests to the selected vendor. Do not be timid in making the requests; you lose nothing by asking.

Frequently, points that you may consider to be tough, non-negotiable terms are agreed to without much vendor resistance. Other times, items about which you expect little trouble can prolong the negotiations. Appendix D shows a model negotiating memorandum. The points included represent deficiencies that have been identified from various sources.

The major source of deficiencies comes from the responses of the vendor contained in the proposal. By comparing the selected vendor's proposal with the other vendors, you can gain a large amount of information about what features or products are available. You can speak with authority about various features, armed with the knowledge gained during the evaluation.

You can also identify deficiencies from the vendor demonstrations that you attend. All of this information can be put to good use by including it in your negotiating memorandum and discussing the points with the selected vendor.

NEGOTIATING TECHNIQUES

The key to negotiating success is not so much in the style but in the ability to negotiate with the selected vendor against what the next ranked vendor is offering. If that basic relationship does not exist, no style in the world will help. However, there are a few techniques that may help in negotiations. At least, you should be aware that such a technique is being used against you.

Endurance

Frequently, negotiations can drag on for an extended amount of time, for example, 12 to 18 months or longer. The reasons for this delay are many, ranging from changing financial decisions to disputed technical capabilities. However, physical and emotional endurance can play a large role as time drags on. Negotiations can reach a point where one side caves in mainly because of the anxiety and uncertainty caused by the extended negotiations.

Endurance of the negotiators becomes very important, and you should be prepared to last if that kind of circumstance arises.

Use of the Magic Word—No

The most effective method of inducing a response from the other side is by simply saying "no." Each side is trying to convince the other. The vendor will chip away at the customer's resistance little by little, and the customer concedes the points, not knowing any better. Vendors will explain that for one reason or another a particular thing cannot be done. Your answer then may simply be "no," or "not acceptable," or "we'll take our business elsewhere."

Most frequently, the "no" will generate a more favorable response from the vendor.

Good Guy, Bad Guy

Particularly when there may be almost an adversary relationship between the parties, "good guy, bad guy" negotiating teams may be helpful. The bad guy plays the role of the short-tempered, abrupt, demanding one. The bad guy exudes the feeling that time is being wasted and attempts to intimidate the negotiators from the other side. Techniques like making the negotiator wait hours for a scheduled appointment or delaying until the last minute to negotiate an important point are the examples of this style. One "bad guy" character would explode from his seat, race around the table, and make a fist in the face of the other side's negotiator!

The good guy, on the other hand, plays the role of a compromiser between the bad guy and the other side. The good guy tries to structure agreement between the two sides, which, in theory, will ultimately result in a more favorable position overall.

Waiting to Make Additional Demands

If the negotiating memorandum is extensive, it may not be advisable to ask for all things at once. To do so would overwhelm the vendor. It may be more effective to begin work on a partial list, reserving the right to add to the list as additional items are needed. As work concludes on the initial list, the new items can be addressed.

This technique also intends to lock the vendor into the sale because of all the time that has already been spent.

Remember that until the final agreement is signed, either side may add issues to the negotiations. Often, the negotiator appears to have authority to bind the vendor, but that may not be so. The signature authority of the vendor may be the president or controller of the firm. The negotiator or salesperson works to develop the agreement and may believe that the terms will be acceptable to the company. However, when the agreement is submitted for final approval, the vendor's president or controller may turn it down.

The agreement is not final until it is signed by the authorized parties. At what appears to be the final hour, either side may bring up new issues or new demands. Remember to use this rule if necessary.

Aggressive Negotiations

It is up to the buyer to be aggressive in negotiations. The customer should come armed with a memorandum well prepared and thought through. The customer has one or two backup vendors in the wings, and should lead the discussions prepared with concessions that will be requested of the vendor.

The buyer should operate somewhat in this fashion: "This is what we need, this is why we need it; give us a good reason why we should not get it." Aggressive, informed, and prepared should be the attributes of the buyer's representatives.

But all too frequently, the leadership in negotiations comes from the vendor. The vendor is not looking to add to commitments so he or she will merely plan to talk a lot without saying much—a lot of "puffing" and "trust me" type of statements. Using the tools developed in the RFP and evaluation, you should have ample information to be aggressive in negotiations.

Switch Between
Major and Minor Points

It is frequently asked whether it is best to begin with all the major points and save the minor points for later. It is advisable to alternate between major and minor points. If all major points are addressed at once, the negotiations tend to get bogged down. Interspersing some minor points relieves the stress and allows breathing time so that solutions around the major problems may be found.

Recognizing "Hot Buttons"
from "Soft" Issues

In preparing your negotiating memorandum, identify which issues are the "hot buttons," the "stretch issues," the critical items, or the items that cannot be conceded. It is also important to recognize the items that are "soft," that can be given away. Determining which items are hot and which are soft should be done as a team so that all technical, managerial, and operational considerations can be given to the analysis. The lead negotiator for the customer must understand these distinctions because as the negotiations proceed, it may be necessary to make certain concessions. You want to make sure that if concessions are made, they are of minor importance.

Identify a Fallback Position

Aside from one or two fallback vendors, you should develop fallback positions wherever possible to the various stands you take. For example, if you ask for a certain amount of custom programming you should identify a fallback or minimum level that cannot be changed. You must prepare the negotiating memorandum in such a way as to identify what your initial position will be as well as your fallback position.

Concerning the tendency to ask for enormous deviations from what is the practice in the industry; it is usually not worth the time. Most experienced and reputable vendors know the industry practices and will not make major deviations, nor should they be expected to. Thus, for a customer to come in with a long list of demands that are not keeping with the industry will probably result in a big "no" from the vendor (which is a reasonable position to take). The customer must then scale down his or her demands to bring them generally within the practices in the industry. This process takes a great amount of time and by and large nothing is gained from such a strategy.

It is recommended that in taking your initial position, you should start from:

> Knowledge of the practices in the industry.
> Data gathered from other vendor's proposals.
> The unique requirements of your business.
> Your own common sense.

Use of Emotion

The image of the negotiator slamming a fist on the table and charging out of the session in an emotional outburst really has no place in a business environment. The reason is simple; it wastes time. If the parties are not interested in concluding the transaction, fine; there should be one or two backup vendors ready to initial negotiations. Emotional outbursts are time-consuming, distracting, and inject into the business arena factors that do not belong, such as personal attacks and insults.

Avoid the Overdelegation Mistake

Negotiations frequently take much time, and there is a tendency for top level management to say "go negotiate and when you're finished, I'll sign." Successful negotiations are a team effort. The owner, president, or executive need not attend every negotiation session, but it is important that the main issues be presented at the appropriate time to the "boss" for a resolution. If the negotiations have progressed as far as possible with staff personnel and have stalled, it may be necessary for the top executive or owner and the top representative of the vendor to meet to resolve the stalemate. As indicated earlier, top people must be involved in all stages of the procurement.

Take a Break

It is easy, of course, to write about the inappropriateness of emotion in negotiations, but in many cases emotions begin to rise or stalemates occur or just plain stress begins to overtake the session. At times like these, the best course is to take a break, either for a few minutes or until the following day. Give everyone time to relax, to put the issues into perspective, to create solutions. The ultimate objective of a negotiation is to reach an "I win, you win" situation.

I'll Trade You

Negotiations may come down to "I'll trade you this concession, if you concede on that." There is nothing wrong with this approach, but recognize which items are the "hot buttons" and "soft" issues and trade accordingly.

These techniques may help in an extended negotiation. But remember, if the evaluation process has been successful, you will have selected a qualified vendor at a competitive price, so there may be very little need for an extended negotiation.

ROLES OF VENDOR PERSONNEL

In the computer industry, a number of people may become involved in the sale, and it might be helpful to review the different roles played by each.

Sales Representative

Depending on the corporation, the sales rep can vary from an independent contractor selling the product strictly on commission to a straight salaried employee. In most cases, the sales rep will be paid a small salary and much of his or her income will be from commissions. As such, he or she will be highly motivated to make the sale. Watch out for the sales rep who seems to be singularly interested in getting a signature on the dotted line, rather than concentrating on customer problems and service. Sometimes a sales representative may even team up with the customer to convince the vendor's own company to give in to the concessions desired by the customer. The sales rep thus does not usually play a decision-making role in a negotiation. He or she frequently will act as a negotiator attempting to keep the procurement moving forward and endeavoring to make the sale

Realizing this limited role of the sales representative, it becomes clear that verbal representations made by a sales rep usually have little or no weight with his or her own company. A sales rep normally will not be given authority to sign the contract because the sales rep is not an agent of the company. Virtually all contracts provide that obligations between the parties must be in writing, which specifically preclude verbal statements made by the sales rep. In fact, as said earlier, the law recognizes a term called "puffing," which is not considered binding on the vendor.

Branch Manager

The branch manager is usually paid at a higher salary than the sales rep and receives a percentage of the sales rep's commission upon each sale. A branch manager is given a sales quota for the year and sometimes for quarters or for each month. The manager is also usually given a budget for limited resources placed at his or her disposal, such as for programmers, sales support activities, administrative costs.

Because of this position, the branch manager is considered the person in the middle between the corporation and the sale representative. The branch manager wants the sale because he or she must reach a quota to retain the job and make commissions. On the other hand, the branch manager will be held accountable for overextending resources and having customers terminate the contract or refuse to pay their bills. A good branch manager will balance these two competing forces if he or she has the needed skills and experience.

When the customer has a problem, it may be more effective to handle it through the branch manager, who has resources the sales rep does not. Plus, the manager has the ability to refer the problem directly to corporate headquarters for resolution. One other point is that developing a relationship with the branch manager is beneficial because he or she usually will not move from place to place as will a first-line sales rep.

The Corporate Attorney

If a corporate attorney gets involved in a negotiation, he or she will normally be the least willing to compromise. Lawyers try generally to prevent risks and increase the security factor of a contract. Unfortunately, the best way to accomplish their goals is to resist approving the negotiated contract.

One tactic to consider when faced with an unyielding corporate attorney is to get the marketing representatives (either the sales rep or the branch manager) to take your case to the corporate attorney. When a marketing person within the vendor's organization becomes the customer's spokesperson, the attorney may be more willing to concede.

The Computer Store Owner

With the growth of computer stores around the country, you may have to deal with the computer store owner. Computer stores vary greatly in products, prices, experience, and service. Normally, the systems and maintenance component of a store are much weaker than a manufacturer. However, most of the products offered at a store are at the low end of the cost spectrum and have less maintenance requirements (in theory).

The key to dealing with a store is to remember that the store will negotiate as well as or better than many manufacturers. Consider that one model of computer can be bought at computer stores around the city. Thus, for a store to stay in existence, it will have to negotiate everything from the prices to the services to be provided.

If you used an RFQ as described in Chapter 4, you will have received prices from various stores. You can the find the best price for the desired system and can negotiate for additional service and training if the need arises. Store owners are usually very creative in fashioning a solution to your needs. They have to be.

Conclusion

Negotiation is an essential phase in the procurement cycle. The strategy is to ensure that you have developed back-up vendors going into the negotiation. You do this by the RFP and evaluation phases. Remember the "I win, you win" objective of negotiations; otherwise, you may just be buying a disaster.

Prepare a negotiating memorandum, which addresses vendor deficiencies and sets forth your needs and the reasons for them. It also is a tool to identify which items are the "hot" issues and which can be conceded. There are various negotiating techniques that may be needed depending on the situation. They range from endurance to trading concessions.

Appendix D shows a sample negotiating memorandum for the model office, which may help illustrate the points that have been discussed.

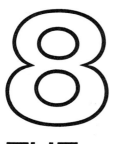

THE CONTRACT AND OBTAINING COMPLIANCE

This is a contract:

> One boat for a week rental at $500.

This is also a contract:

> Lessor will rent to Lessee upon payment of $500 cash and signatures below one 21-foot Starcraft sailboat, with all sails, all riggings, and standard equipment included from the 2nd of June to the 9th of June, beginning and returning at 9:00 a.m. from Dock A, Slip 23, provided Lessee has all appropriate licenses to sail the craft and there are no more than four passengers, and weather conditions on the date of departure are within acceptable tolerances. Lessor will maintain all required insurance coverage on boat, Lessee, and passengers; Lessee agrees that the boat is in good condition and agrees to indemnify Lessor for damage caused to the boat by Lessee's negligence.

The difference, of course, in these two contracts is that the second one has many more specifics; it sets forth who, what, where, when, and how much. Over and over it has been shown that thorough contracts, which include as much detail and planning as possible, result in successful computer installation. Without the detailed planning incorporated into the contract, the parties waffle as to whom the responsibility

129

for what and, consequently, the job does not get done and failure ensues.

Let us highlight some points and clauses from a somewhat standard word processing contract.

FORM CONTRACTS IN GENERAL

Generally, form contracts, also referred to as boiler plates, are pre-printed in small type by corporate attorneys who specialize in drafting language that is favorable to the vendor. The language is heavy legalese and the vendor's sales representative will say that the terms are pretty much nonnegotiable. It is generally a monumental effort even to read the document, let alone understand it due to its length and size of print.

Form contracts are designed by vendors to gain a psychological advantage over the buyer. What the buyer cannot understand due to the complexity of the language will end up favoring the vendor if there is a dispute. The theory goes that the customer will not hire legal counsel to review the details of the language, so will ultimately sign a document that he or she doesn't understand. Good for the vendor! But what can the buyer do?

HOW TO NEGOTIATE
CONTRACT CLAUSES

First, you must rely on your negotiating leverage by advising the marketing people that, unless the boiler plate language is explained in detail, you will begin to negotiate a contract with another bidder. Utilizing sales representatives to gain better explanations from the vendor is extremely worthwhile, for, as we have said, the marketing representative's commissions and quotas are based on making the sale. The sales rep may solicit contract expertise from the vendor's regional office or from the national office to explain the terms of the contract.

Second, you may want to use your own legal counsel who is experienced in contracting for computers. The measure of the need for legal counsel is not in the actual expenditure of money for the new system. Rather, it is the financial impact on the business if the new system fails. A $20,000 system can cause losses many times the initial investment if the system fails during operation.

There are attorneys around the country who have recognized the need to become knowledgeable in computers and word processing systems, both to aid their clients and to improve their own office operations. A Computer Law Association has many attorneys interested in representing both buyers and sellers of these systems. The assistance of a qualified attorney can be important in this phase.

Third, you have to "out think" the vendor! Most vendors use boiler plates to standardize their operations and to maintain corporate policies. Most recognize that the boiler-plate clauses do not fit all circumstances. Some vendors maintain a staff of contract specialists who are empowered to negotiate clauses on behalf of the vendor. The burden of the argument is on the customer. So it is the customer who must find any deficiencies in the boiler plate—and there may be many—and explain the reasons for the suggested change(s) to the vendor.

The method of negotiating contracts is to analyze the vendor's clauses, make suggested changes, and then provide the reasons why any change is required. Many times the boiler plate clause does not, in fact, fit the circumstances, and experienced vendors will make the changes accordingly.

Negotiation of clauses is a function of communication between the parties, and if reasons are communicated, appropriate changes to the boiler plate can be made.

A vendor who says "we can't change that" without providing a reason is not negotiating in a professional manner, and your response should be: "If you can't provide a reason for your wording or policy, there is no point in continuing the negotiations."

Let us look at an example: The vendor has a clause that establishes legal jurisdiction in the state where the equipment is manufactured. This type of clause would mean that you or your attorney would have to become knowledgeable in the laws of that state and cause additional expense in litigating any dispute that could arise.

You would explain to the vendor that the clause is unacceptable for those reasons and that the practice in the industry is to establish legal jurisdiction in the state of the customer.

There will, of course, be certain cases where it will be very difficult to give in on a certain position, from either side's viewpoint. Both sides will need to negotiate and discuss the reasons behind the conflicts. Once the reasons are understood, some compromise may be agreed upon. In many situations it is possible that, once the reason is understood, both sides can mutually construct an alternative position. If not, the customer can still maintain the option of negotiating with the next ranked bidder rather than giving in on something that is important.

CLAUSES THAT NEED EXPLANATION

Appendix E shows a standard computer or word processing rental agreement; it is selected because it is less complex than an outright purchase agreement and many first-time users will elect a rental arrangement prior to an outright purchase. The model is representative of a boiler plate for several of the largest word processing manufacturers. It is not conclusive. Also, the model does not demonstrate many of the other optional clauses that the customer can propose to protect his or her interests.

Each major clause in the rental contract shown in Appendix E is numbered and summarized below in understandable terms. A "comment" follows, in a layperson's language, which explains an alternative position, usually for the buyer's protection, with reasons for the proposed change.

Let us review each paragraph in the order shown in Appendix E and summarize the important points.

1. Acceptance

Acceptance is based on the customer credit report and the absence of mathematical error.

Comment: The relationship is backwards; it should be the customer who accepts the vendor's system, not the other way around.

2. Terms of Rental

The initial term is for 12 months and requires 30 days prior written notice to terminate, or the term continues automatically for a new 12-month period at the new prices, terms, and conditions. The new term also requires a 30-day notice of termination.

Comment: Automatic renewals at new prices and terms are risky; usually a few months into the new term, you discover that you owe four months of whatever price change occurred in the monthly rental rate!

3. Charges

1. Charges commence when the system is installed according to the vendor.
2. Payments are due in advance; deposits are held against early termination.
3. Charges in excess of one shift shall be 50 percent additional.
4. Taxes shall be extra.
5. There is a 1.5 percent late payment charge.

Comment: Note the absence of test and acceptance procedures.

1. Charges should commence upon acceptance of the entire system by the customer, not the vendor.
2. Payment should be due after the service is rendered to the customer, particularly if a deposit is being retained by the vendor.
3. The rationale for charging extra per shift may not be apparent. Ask.
4. Taxes currently are a legitimate expense for the customer to incur.
5. A late payment charge is not justifiable particularly because late payments are often due to administrative errors between clerical staff personnel. If the vendor requires a late payment fee, the customer should have a late service fee, in an equal amount, for poor service caused by the vendor.

4. Transportation

The customer pays all shipping charges plus crating and uncrating.

Comment: This clause is an open-ended obligation on the part of the customer to pay an uncertain amount. The vendor has access to the weights, destination, and all shipping information and should quote those costs as a fixed amount so that the customer may consider shipping costs in the overall evaluation and budget properly to pay for it.

5. Alterations and Attachments

No new gadgets or customer software can be attached or programmed into the system without the prior written consent of the vendor.

Comment: This is a fair and reasonable position that protects the customer as well as the vendor. Custom hardware attachments and programs can cause difficulties in maintaining and repairing the system: they make it harder to determine the source of the problem.

6. Maintenance

1. Vendor will provide "normal service."
2. Customer will give vendor complete access to the machine for maintenance.
3. Service outside normal business hours will be on a hourly rate.
4. Customer will be charged for other than normal use of machines.
5. Maintenance does not include costs for expendable supplies; making requested changes, or relocating the machine at customer's request.
6. Maintenance will not be provided outside a 50-mile radius.

7. Vendor is not responsible for failure to respond due to causes beyond vendor's control.

8. In remote locations, customer must deliver equipment to the service facility.

Comment:

1. "Normal service" is not defined; what will buyer be receiving in terms of maintenance—once a month? once a year?

2. It is unwise to allow the vendor to make the unilateral decision essentially to bring your operation to a halt so that the vendor can effect repairs. The customer may be able to work around the problem until after peak work hours and should have input into the decision as to when repair work will be done.

3. Service outside of normal business hours is generally on a hourly rate. The area of concern is to ensure that you have sufficient moneys in the budget for after-hours service and that you use it only when essential.

4. If customer's gadgets cause a delay, it is the practice in the industry to have the customer pay the higher hourly rate to effect repairs.

5. Expendable supplies are always the responsibility of the customer. Costs for customer-requested equipment changes, for example, vendor's accessories, attachments, and relocation of installed equipment, should be at the customer's expense provided the cost is not associated with the installation of additional new equipment supplied by the vendor. When the vendor is making a sale and upgrading equipment, the vendor should pay the moving costs.

6. For remote customer locations, it is fair and reasonable that the customer will have to make arrangements to deliver the equipment to the service facilities. Trained maintenance personnel should not be spending their time on the highway driving to remote locations. But the distance clause should be specific prior to signing the agreement; make it clear whether your location is or is not within the prescribed distance.

7. Vendor is excused from providing service due to causes beyond its control, which is a reasonable practice in the industry.

8. As described in paragraph 6 previously, the customer may need to bring equipment to the vendor from remote locations.

7. Supplies

Ribbons, paper, magnetic tapes, and such are not included in the rental price and may be purchased from any supplier provided they meet the specifications of the vendor.

Comment: This is a reasonable requirement. The vendor should know best the products that will allow the equipment to operate most efficiently.

8. Risk of Loss or Damage

1. Vendor accepts responsibility for risk of loss or damage.
2. Except as a result of nuclear causes.
3. Except for negligent or willful misconduct by customers or agents.
4. Other than in accordance with normal operations and manuals supplied by vendor.

Comment:

1. The vendor retains title to the equipment and thus maintains appropriate insurance for the property.
2. Nuclear and radiation effects are normally exempted by insurance companies so vendors must place the responsibility on the user rather than carrying the responsibility themselves.
3. Negligent conduct is a legal term that can be considered a simple act or omission when there is duty to do something. The vendor's insurance is a way to protect against simple negligent acts by the customer; thus this clause should be modified to require the customer to be "grossly" negligent or to engage in "willful misconduct" before the customer should be responsible for the loss.
4. It is reasonable to reqire the customer to use the machine in accordance with normal procedures, but these procedures must be clearly stated in the vendor documentation and not merely assumed.

9. Equipment

Equipment will be either new or "remanufactured," but, in any case, will meet specifications and be covered by warranty.

Comment: Electronic components frequently require a limited amount of "burn in" time to cause the components to stabilize for reliable use. Thus the fact that every component is not new and unused may not be a major deficiency. Computers are machines that wear out after extended use, and it is important to determine how old some of the components are and which ones have been refurbished, especially if the system reliability will be affected.

10. Warranty

1. Vendor warrants that the equipment will be in "normal operating order" and vendor will make "all necessary" equipment adjustments.
2. Provided that customer's account is current.
3. IN THE EVENT THAT VENDOR FAILS TO KEEP THE PROMISES,

CUSTOMER IS LIMITED TO VENDOR FIXING THE PROBLEM WHEN VENDOR AGREES THAT EQUIPMENT DOES NOT WORK.

4. VENDOR HAS NO RESPONSIBILITY FOR DAMAGES.

5. VENDOR DOES NOT PROMISE TO BE CLAIMING EXPERTISE IN SELLING THE RIGHT SYSTEM TO CUSTOMER.

6. VENDOR DOES NOT PROMISE THAT THE MACHINE WILL SAT-ISFY THE CUSTOMER'S PURPOSES.

Comment:

1. This clause regarding "normal operating order" is like baby cereal—soft to the point of being mushy! What are "normal operating order" and "all necessary adjustments"? The warranty does not have a penalty to the vendor if he or she fails to perform promises such as your money back or providing credits toward maintenance expenses for the hours that the machine is nonoperable, referred to as "downtime credits." The clause means essentially nothing.

2. Maintenance service on the condition of the customer's account being current should be agreed to only if the vendor will allow the customer to hold back or "off-set" payments for the vendor's failure to keep the machine in operating order. Vendors are loathe to agree to the customer's right to hold payments, and customers should be loathe to agree to a clause that allows vendors to hold back service until the account is current.

3. This warranty clause allowing the vendor to decide that the equipment does not conform to "normal operating mode" prior to fixing it is somewhat typical in that it does not specify details as to how fast the defect will be corrected, what type of maintenance service will be provided in the event of a failure, or even an escalation procedure to alleviate a problem quickly within the vendor's organization.

4. This clause regarding damages might seem a bit shocking because the vendor is disclaiming responsibility for the vendor's system. However, the clause is consistent with the practice in the industry and, generally, in legal cases to date. There are rare exceptions; however, for most business applications, *the customer is responsible for processing errors, not the vendor.* You control the environment in which the machine is used and the data input for processing. You have the responsibility for checking the output reports to ensure accuracy. Vendors could not remain in business if they were held responsible for processing errors.

5. This clause regarding "merchantability" (meaning that the vendor is holding him- or herself up as an expert in whom the customer can rely for the proper selection of the machine) is implied in many business transactions and must be specifically disclaimed or denied by the vendor or the vendor may be held responsible for the consequences. Such a disclaimer is valid in the computer industry because ultimately the customers are responsible for the proper selection of the equipment. *If the machine you select turns out to be completely wrong for the job, you can have no remedy against the vendor,* provided there is no fraud.

6. This clause regarding "fitness for purpose" is similar to the above point

in that, unless expressly disclaimed or denied, the vendor could be held to a standard that amounts to promising that the system will accomplish the particular purpose the customer intends. This is too broad a liability for the vendor to accept. It is the customer who decides which system is right to accomplish the customer's particular purpose. As a customer, you know the unique requirements of the job and the many varied demands placed on the system. The computer sales representative cannot be held accountable for that level of detail. The sales rep is just that: a seller of a system. *The buyer must face the responsibility in the selection of the right system.*

11. Default

1. If the customer defaults, the vendor,
2. in addition to other remedies,
3. may repossess without notice.
4. Customer agrees to pay repossession fees and attorney's fees.
5. The rental agreement will end if customer begins bankruptcy procceedings or similarly related acts.

Comment:

1. "Default" is too general to be meaningful. What constitutes a default? A late payment? Failure to install the electricity properly? Using a customer-written program on the machine without permission? The term is too all-inclusive and requires definition.
2. "Other remedies" allows the vendor to seek money damages in addition to those already stated. This is also too general; the specific remedies should be identified so that the customer knows what the vendor would be entitled to. The problem is "defaults," thus the succeeding language is also unacceptable.
3. Repossession of equipment without notice to the customer is unthinkable. Can you imagine going to work in the morning and finding your computer/word processor gone? This provision is totally unacceptable.
4. If the customer, in fact, is without merit in terminating a contract, just like all breaching parties to a contract, the expenses would be the responsibility of the customer, provided, of course, the customer is at fault.
5. The provision for the vendor terminating the rental agreement in the event that the customer files for bankruptcy or assigns the rental agreement for benefit of creditors is fair and consistent with the industry.

12. Other Provisions

1. This agreement supersedes all previous agreements.
2. The customer will not move the equipment without vendor's written consent.

3. Customer may not assign the agreement.
4. Customer will recognize vendor's right to assign.
5. Customer will not be entitled to set off against vendor's assignee.
6. Vendor will remain responsible for all obligations of performance.
7. Customer will acquire no ownership interest in the machine.
8. Vendor may remove equipment after its term has expired.
9. The agreement is governed by vendor's home state.
10. This agreement constitutes the entire agreement.
11. Customer's purchase orders will not modify the terms of this agreement.
12. Any "investment tax credits" will pass to the vendor and not the customer.

Comment:

1. It is in each party's best interest to incorporate all agreements into one document. Remember, verbal promises, the vendor's proposal, or correspondence, if not incorporated into the agreement, will have no force or effect.
2. Because the vendor is the legal owner of the equipment and also responsible to maintain the equipment, it is fair and reasonable that the vendor be made aware of any movement of the equipment.
3. The customer should have the right to assign (or transfer) the equipment provided the recipient is of equal financial responsibility as the customer and provided the customer obtains vendor's prior written permission. Business if often fluid and you may have to change your plans accordingly. Being unable to assign a contract and move the equipment to a qualified transferee is too great burden on you.
4. A vendor's assignment could change the person or place to whom the customer sends monthly payments and also could cause confusion concerning invoices coming from new financial institutions. Prior written permission by the customer because the vendor assigns the contract is a better method to handle this issue.
5. Regarding customer set-off, the vendor in most cases will assign the contract to a financial institution in exchange for cash. The financial institution insists that the customer will not withhold payments because of a dispute between customer and vendor. This clause could place the customer in the difficult position of being contractually obligated to continue monthly payments, yet at the same time being totally dissatisfied with the service provided by the vendor. Vendors, on the other hand, may refuse to conclude the contract without the clause because the contract would not qualify for a financial assignment. What to do? Negotiate the removal of the clause if at all possible.
6. This clause makes it clear that although the agreement may be assigned (transferred) to a financial institution, the vendor will remain 100 percent responsible for all commitments and promises under the contract.
7. As a customer, you may accumulate credits toward the purchase of the system. However, because this is a rental agreement, the customer will not receive any ownership interest in the system.

8. Vendor may remove equipment, but only after the rental period expires and the customer is informed which units are to be removed and on what date, in writing. Also, the customer must have concurred in writing. There must be complete communication and planning before equipment is added, deleted, or moved.

9. As previously discussed, the jurisdiction for the contract with the customer must be in the customer's home state. To do otherwise would place an unfair advantage in the vendor's favor. The customer's attorney would have to become knowledgeable in the laws of the vendor's home state. Most vendors will concur in this suggested change.

10. This entire agreement is needed for both sides and it repeats that all documents that constitute the agreement are incorporated herein. Again, you should ensure that the vendor's proposal, correspondence, and any verbal promises be transcribed into writings and incorporated into the agreement.

11. There has been a controversy for many years as to which takes precedence, the signed agreement or the customer's purchase order that has contradictory terms. This clause gives precedence to the agreement. The signed, formal agreement between the parties should take precedence over the purchase order, which normally relies heavily on preprinted forms and small print. If the parties have a disagreement about terms, it is desirable to negotiate all changes in one document, the signed agreement. If the terms of the purchase order contradict the agreement, the disagreement should be worked out in the overriding contract.

12. Where allowed, the customer should be entitled to claim the advantages of investment tax credits. The vendor should not be able to claim such tax advantage without a detailed explanation to the customer.

This review of a sample rental agreement only scratched the surface on many of these issues. As mentioned earlier, the assistance of qualified legal counsel is valuable at this stage.

OBTAINING VENDOR COMPLIANCE

Most vendors are truly interested in ensuring a client's success. This brings with it good references and more business for them. Most vendors abhor a dissatisfied customer. Dissatisfied customers become chronic complainers, absorb enormous amounts of time trying to resolve problems, and damage future sales by giving poor references to prospective customers.

Vendors are, for the most part, honest, forthright, and reasonable businesspeople who desire on-going business relationships. The problem, as described earlier, is that the technology is changing so rapidly with so many new products and features that to stay ahead of the changes is most difficult for all but the limited number of technically trained and experienced marketing representatives. To compound the problem, the vendor may attempt to limit obligations in the contract with a view toward reducing expenses associated with the sale, thus increasing vendor profit. The inexperienced vendor may shortchange the sizing and implementation of the system, which results, in many cases, in a dissatisfied customer, an incorrectly sized computer system, and the chronic complainer situation.

The experienced vendor will make the effort to size the system correctly, ensure that there is adequate training and system test and acceptance procedures, and look forward to a happy customer who will give good references to prospective customers (and pay the bills on time).

You must identify the requirements that must be fulfilled by the vendor and construct a reasonable procedure to ensure that the services are provided as promised.

Project Manager—Buyer

To make sure that your interests are protected and that the vendor knows with whom to deal in terms of problems and questions, you should designate a high level person within your organization to be the central point of contact.

For the small business, the project manager would normally be the owner. As the size of the business increases, the question of who will act as the project manager becomes more complicated. You will need someone who has a position of responsibility within your organization. The person should know a great deal about the internal workings of the operations and be able to solve problems as they occur. In a typical office one of the principals might act as project manager or perhaps the lead secretary or office manager would perform the duties.

The importance of having a high level person as project manager cannot be overestimated. Recall the problems associated with "over-delegation" of the decision to a lower level manager or subordinate.

Project Manager—Vendor

It is of equal importance to ensure that the vendor be required to designate one contact person with sufficient skill and experience to oversee the implementation of the system. This person may or may not be the sales representative. Sometimes sales reps are too busy selling new accounts or lack sufficient technical experience to ensure a successful implementation. Other times, the internal workings of the vendor's company can be so confusing that it is impossible to determine who within the organization can solve your particular problem. To address these recurring problems, insist on a qualified project manager representing the vendor. The vendor's representative should also be in a sufficient position within the vendor's firm so that he or she can solve problems and make decisions as the need arises.

Regularly Scheduled Meetings

Problems will occur, schedules will have to be changed, and there must be provisions in the contract that require the project managers on both sides to meet regularly and discuss progress and problems that need to be solved. Once the agreement is signed, there is a mad rush on the part of the vendor and the customer in all different directions—site preparation, delivery schedules, missing pieces, electrical problems, training, and so on.

Problems usually occur when the project managers fail to communicate regularly and a good working relationship does not materialize. One side starts criticizing the other, and the problem begins to grow. The typical results is that schedules slide, the customer begins to complain, and vendors end up incurring additional costs trying to correct errors.

The solution in part is to ensure that the project managers meet on a regularly scheduled basis and resolve problems as they occur.

Written Status Reports

Project managers may meet, but without a written document to record the progress and problems, verbal discussions generally prove unreliable. To cover yourself adequately and also cover the vendor, require a biweekly status report from the vendor's project manager. The report includes the following information for the reporting period:

> Progress toward milestones.
> Progress against dollars in budget.
> Problems encountered.

With a written report describing the vendor activity during the period and the expenditure of funds, you can closely monitor what is going on in the project. By recording the problems encountered by the vendor, you will be able to focus your attention on such problems and resolve them, if possible, before they erupt into crises.

The written report allows you to identify what has to be done in a timely fashion and lets you create remedies around the problem, adjust priorities, or change schedules as the need arises. The work involved by the vendor in preparing the status report is relatively minimal. The experienced vendor will cooperate because the status reports will record what work has been accomplished and will also document when the task is completed.

Vendors who fail to document their progress frequently have trouble with customers who attempt to change their requirements during the project. Thus, it is in the vendor's best interest to provide a status report also.

The status report is a valuable and essential tool for a successful installation. Appendix F is a model status report that you should review. In addition to the status reports, a strict test and acceptance are also needed.

EQUIPMENT—TEST AND ACCEPTANCE

A thorough and rigorous test and acceptance of both the hardware and software are absolutely critical to ensure a successful installation. The customer does not pay until after the test is successfully concluded (financial leverage). If the test lasts 30 days and is successfully completed, the vendor is entitled to payment, not beginning from the date the test is completed, but retroactively from the *first day* of the test period. The vendor also is protected because once the test and acceptance are completed, the customer must accept the system.

Let us use a typical example to illustrate how a test and acceptance can work.

The activity on day one to start the test is to install the equipment for operational use and to begin as much sample testing as possible. Logs are maintained to report on any equipment deficiencies. The equipment is expected to operate reliably for a 30-consecutive-day period at an operational effectiveness or "uptime" level of 90 percent. This figure in present-day contracts is frequently raised to 95 percent because the quality of modern products is continually improving and a 95 percent level of uptime is now reasonable. "Uptime" equals operational use time minus downtime divided by operational use time.

$$\text{uptime} = \frac{\text{operational use time} - (\text{downtime})}{\text{operational use time}}$$

"Operational use time" is the amount of time that the equipment should be available for work. There are certain times excluded from the operational use time calculation, for example, preventative maintenance (PM) time. PM time is where the engineer cleans, checks, and repairs the equipment on a regularly scheduled basis. While the repair technician is working, the customer may not perform normal productive work on the machine. Test and acceptance are illustrated as follows:

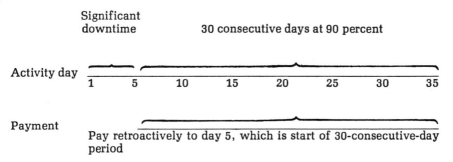

In this example, the first four days of the test period experienced significant downtime problems. On the fifth day, the system became stable and continued with acceptable performance (at 90 percent uptime) for the next 30 days. Since the equipment performed acceptably for 30 days, it must be accepted by the customer on the thirty-fifth day. Upon formal written acceptance, rent on the equipment for the previous 30-day period is due and payable at that time. The rental period is considered to begin on day five.

This type of test and acceptance of the equipment is very important to ensure that the initial use of the computer/word processor is without material defect. Frequently, the machine can be shaken during transportation and/or installation. In at least one case, the computer was dropped from the tailgate of the truck. An additional problem is that the electronic components frequently require a "burn in" period, which means, that until the components have been in use for an initial time period, they may be prone to failure.

A rigid test and acceptance procedure protects you against paying for equipment that is not operationally sound. When vendors are aware that the test and acceptance operation is required, they will make sure their technical representatives are available to address any problem quickly. We certainly benefit from this increased attention by the vendor. You benefit financially because you do not make any payments until the equipment is working satisfactorily and you benefit technically because greater attention is given to get the machine working.

Functional Test and Acceptance

In addition to the equipment, test and acceptance activities are a test of the functions of the software. Your requirement should be for the vendor to demonstrate the various functions and/or processing of the software on your particular machine after it has been installed in your office or plant. For example, a sample payroll processing cycle, a sample report, a demonstration of various word processing features, all should be demonstrated on your particular machine after it has been installed.

The functional test and acceptance should be conducted concurrently with the equipment test and acceptance so that you can increase your confidence that when the vendor leaves your site to go on to other sales, your hardware and software will have been tested and will run properly.

Response Time

As the requirements for the system increase due to the need for large data files and rapid response to inquiries, it may become important to conduct a "full load response time test." To do this, you require the vendor, as part of the acceptance procedure, to assist you in loading all of your data onto the computer/word processor. Once loaded you execute typical transactions and measure the time that elapses to complete them. You may even use a stop-watch to measure whether the response time of the system is between, for example, three to seven seconds. If you have a requirement for an response, within, for example, five seconds, you want to test and measure the response of the system before you accept it and begin paying for it.

Response times can become unacceptable when you have a large amount of data and the equipment is configured incorrectly. You may find yourself waiting 15 seconds for the computer to produce an answer. This response may be unacceptable. Again, the best time to ensure that the system will operate within acceptable time frames is to measure the response times during test and acceptance.

These three types of tests—equipment, function, and response time—are important and if accomplished prior to the start of payments will ensure your success in the initial phase of your operation.

Summary

In terms of obtaining vendor compliance to the specifics of the contract, we have identified several very important tools. The use of project managers, scheduled status meetings, and written status reports all aid a controlled transition to a new system or to upgrade to a large system. The use of rigorous test and acceptance procedures will aid in making your initial use of the new system less prone to major problems.

The last word, however, is to remember that when problems do occur in maintaining the system over the long term, and problems will occur, that the "squeaky wheel" does make a difference. If your vendor does not give the quality of service that is necessary for your smooth and successful operation, be prepared to demand, complain, and harass the vendors until the problem is corrected.

LEGAL ISSUES

PROPRIETARY RIGHTS

Proprietary rights deal with the ownership of ideas, programs, concepts, and techniques, for whose use people are willing to pay money. Consider a computer program. It could take several years and millions of dollars to create. Yet, through the power of technology, that same program could be copied and stolen in seconds!

The size of the software industry alone makes these issues very important. There are an estimated 500,000 computer programmers in the United States, many working as independent contractors or in small companies. The number of computer programs generated each year is estimated to exceed one million. The revenues from them are estimated at between $2 billion and $4 billion in the United States alone.

Even more remarkable is a finding by the International Data Corporation, which reports that in 1980 the software industry accounted for approximately $13 billion, or about half of the expenditures for equipment. However, software industry expectations by 1985 are approximately $33 billion, equivalent to about 60 percent of the expenditures for hardware. We are dealing with an enormous industry and the legal issues involved are crucial to the protection of these valuable assets. They need to be protected from the unscrupulous who would steal a program rather than make the substantial investment in time and money that is required.

It is the creative hard-working people who deserve personal recognition and reward for their creative efforts. As John Marshall, Chief Justice of the Supreme Court, said:

> A patent . . . is the reward stipulated for the advantages dervived by the public for the exertions of the individual, and is intended as a stimulus to those exertions.

Let us briefly review the forms of ownership protection available. The United States has always tried to stimulate inventions by rewarding the inventor for personal efforts and sacrifice. American law has recognized that effort by allowing the inventor to hold a legal patent, which gives exclusive rights to the invention/discovery (process, plant, machine, design) for 17 years. This means that if another person desires to use the invention, machine, or device, permission and a fee can be required by the owner of the patent. This method is a way of encouraging invention and "Yankee ingenuity."

One of our most famous inventors, Thomas Edison, is said to have had over 1,000 patents for his inventions.

We have also endeavored to protect literary and artistic work by the use of a legal copyright. A copyrighted document or work is registered with the government and protects the "actual expression" from being copied and being used by others. Traditional examples of copyrighted works are books, movies, and songs. The legal protection of the copyright lasts, under the present law, during the author's lifetime and for fifty years after his or her death.

The third major form of protection is the trade secret. Traditionally, when businesspeople have developed a "secret" that gives them an advantage over the competition, provided the business protects the secret from disclosure, the law will recognize the ownership rights in the secret if it is stolen by a competitor or sold by a thief to a competitor. Examples of trade secrets are confidential customer lists, secret recipes, or even confidental manufacturing procedures.

The difficulty with traditional legal remedies is that modern computer technology does not easily fit into any one of the three forms of ownership protection. What is a computer program—a machine, which is patentable, or an idea, which is not patentable? Is a computer program a "literary work," which should be copyrighted like a book and filed with the government for public notice? Or is it "a secret" to be kept under lock and key? Let us analyze these questions in more detail.

Patents

The Supreme Court heard several computer patents cases during the 1970s. Experts in the computer field even now have had difficulty in deciding conclusively whether a computer program is patentable. A patent was essentially designed to protect an "invention," a piece of equipment, a physical process, or a machine, but is not issued for an "idea" or a "mathematical formula." Patents are not for ideas or formulas, according to consistent law. So what is a computer program? An idea? A mathematical formula? An invention?

A program is defined as a series of instructions that direct the computer to perform certain steps. The Supreme Court has held that where a computer program is merely a mathematical formula that manipulates numbers, the program is not patentable (*Gottschalk v. Benson,* 409 U.S. 63; *Parker and Flook,* 437 U.S. 584). In the *Gottschalk* case, Benson had created a program that could automatically convert binary-coded decimal numerals into pure binary numerals. Essentially, this program could automatically convert one internal computer numbering system into another internal numbering system. An analogy might be a computer program that could automatically convert decimal mileage, such as 1 mile = 5280 feet, into metric distances, such as 1 mile = 1609.35 meters. The basic value does not change, but the method in which the value is presented is different based on the numbering scheme selected.

Benson wanted a patent on his particular computer program; however the Supreme Court held against him. The Court found that: An idea of itself is not patentable; and a principle which, in the abstract, is a fundamental truth, cannot be patented since no one can claim an exclusive right to it; mental processes are not patentable as they are the basic tools of scientific and technological work.

Benson's computer program was analyzed to be a mathematical formula, an algorithm, and it did not meet the test of a patentable "process" or "product." However, the Court made a point of expressly avoiding making a blanket statement about the patentability of all computer programs. It limited its finding to Benson's program exclusively. A later case was to expand our understanding of what is meant by a patentable "process."

Where a computer program merely controls a device for directing a new and useful machine "process," the mere fact that a computer is being used will not prevent a patent from being issued. A patent will be issued if the process considered as a whole is found to be a new, useful process or machine (*Diamond v. Diehr,* March 3, 1981).

In the *Diamond v. Diehr* case, Diehr had invented a machine press controlled by a computer that would constantly monitor the temperature and time that raw rubber products would be heated within a press. The computer, upon receiving the temperature data, would open the press at the proper moment in the curing process. Prior to that time, and without the use of the computer, the heating period was uncertain and many impurities occurred in the finished product. The mathematical formula used by Diehr was commonly known in the industry; it was the use of the computer and the press that was the basis for his request for patent.

The Supreme Court held that Diehr would qualify for a patent based on the "process" he had created. Essentially, the Court held that the combination of the equipment (the press) used in a new and constructive way (by control of the computer), which resulted in a new and productive "process," would qualify for the legal protection of the patent. The new and useful "process" was patentable, *not the computer program*. The mere fact that a computer program was used would not destroy the patent claim.

SUMMARY

What have these cases added to our knowledge about the patent as applied to computer programs? The Court has been consistent over the years in this respect. The Court will not patent the typical business progam based on the rationale that the program is a mathematical formula, an idea, a natural phenomenon. However, where a computer is used in a new and useful way in association with other machines or devices, a patent can be issued. There are other cases that will be heard by the Supreme Court over the next few years and they will further expand our understanding of these issues. But for now, we must look to these important Supreme Court cases to reveal the current state of the law.

Patent law will probably not affect the small to medium-sized business directly. However, the computer in the hands of a talented employee can raise these issues in the event that a new discovery or invention is found. We should be watchful for the new and creative processes that may qualify for legal protection. Particularly in the manufacturing industry, business managers should watch for a computer-controlled machine that is unique, new, and useful; it may be patentable.

Copyrights

Copyrights are used to protect a "particular expression" in a work, for example, the text of the book or the music of the song. The "particular expression," however, is *all* that is protected. For example, if a book is copied and condensed as a digest, there is no violation of the original copyright. There may be other forms of legal protection available, but the copyright does not help where the concept is copied as long as all the "particular expressions" are modified or changed.

The copyright law gives the owner of the work the exclusive right to copy it or transfer rights in it, including sale and leasing arrangements. Piracy by others of copyrighted material may be punished by fines, civil damages, or criminal penalties.

The important disadvantage of the copyright in respect to computer programs is that the "idea," "concept," or "algorithm" from which the computer program is based is not protected by the copyright law. Only the "actual expression," the individual program instructions, in machine language (lowest level computer language) or symbolic language (programmer's coding language) is protected. The key "idea" or "algorithm" of the computer program is not protected adequately by the copyright law alone.

Another disadvantage with a copyright is the notion that it is to encourage public distribution of the article that is copyrighted. Thus, if a copyright work is filed with the Copyright Office, it would be subject to public inspection. It is clear that permitting public inspection of the copyrighted work may jeopardize the confidentiality of the program.

If the rules behind copyright protection appear somewhat contradictory, that is, public inspection of a protected work, then we have correctly analyzed some of the weaknesses associated with copyright protection.

There is a provision that the first few beginning pages and the last few ending pages of a program listing can be filed, thus keeping confidential the main portion of the program, assuming that it is long enough.

The Computer Software Copyright Act of 1980 provided copyright protection for the first time to computer programs. Prior to that time, copyright protection for computer programs had been merely inferred from statements by Congressional committees. The difficulty had been in properly analyzing whether a computer program was an artistic expression or a machine. Copyrights had traditionally been thought to pertain to artistic works only. The Computer Software Act, however, clearly provided coverage for the computer program. The law also set forth that use or transference of copyrighted information from one computer medium to another can be a violation of the act. Thus, the instantaneous or computerized copying or transference of copyrighted material can be a violation at the instant the transference takes place. One authority described the law by saying that to input a copyrighted program into a computer is legally equivalent to copying the program statements by pen and paper or by photocopy machine. The ultimate use of the copyrighted data is not the violation; the transference itself is the violation.

Trade Secret

By definition, a trade secret may consist of any formula, pattern, device, or compilation of information that is used in one's business and that gives the owner a business advantage over competitors. Traditionally, trade secets have been thought of as lists of customer's names and addresses, a chemical compound, a recipe or process of manufacturing, treating or preserving materials. A trade secret must also be a process or device in continuous use in the operation of one's business. Under the traditional definition, a computer program could be protected by trade secret law.

The penalty for violating or misusing a trade secret varies from state to state; however, it may be equal to criminal penalties similar to grand larceny.

There are two major considerations involved in the use of trade secret protection:

1. The program must be treated as a secret and the secret protected from disclosure.
2. The trade secret can be lost by independent invention by another, accidental disclosure, or by "reverse engineering," that is, by starting from a known product and working backward until the process or secret for producing the known product is copied.

Treating Programs as Secrets

To retain trade secret rights in a program, one must demonstrate that, in fact, the program has been treated as a genuine secret. For example:

1. Employees should be required to sign nondisclosure agreements promising not to divulge the confidential information and to return all proprietary materials prior to their termination of employment.
2. Confidential programs must be so marked with a suitable stamp CONFIDENTIAL or PROPRIETARY DATA DO NOT DISCLOSE.
3. Confidential data or programs should be of restricted use so that only the persons who have clearances or a need-to-know have access to the program or data.
4. Confidential reports and listings should be numbered, accounted for, properly stored, and suitably destroyed.
5. Employees should be appropriately trained through formal or informal classes in their responsibilities with respect to the confidential information.

To protect your rights in a trade secret, you will have to prove that you have taken some or all of these steps to protect the "secret."

A wrongdoer will try to prove that the information was not, in fact, a secret; thus the data are not entitled to trade secret protection. If you properly protected yourself by following the above steps, you should be successful in protecting any trade secret rights.

How a Trade Secret Can Be Lost

1. Trade secret protection can be lost through independent invention by another. For example, if a competitor is offering a service or product that you feel is exclusively yours, you will not be able to restrain the competitor if he or she can prove that the service or product was independently invented, without using your secret. The law reasons that ideas are not protectable and that anyone who can create an idea should be able to profit from it.

2. Trade secret protection can be lost by accidental disclosure. For example, if you were to leave a trade secret on an employee's desk and it was accidentally discarded and later used by a third party, you could not claim secret protection because you caused the accidental disclosure.

3. Trade secret protection can also be lost by "reverse engineering." As mentioned earlier, a competitor becomes aware of a new service or feature that you have developed independently. The competitor then attempts to copy your product or service based on what he or she perceives as your product's capabilities. The competitor does not steal any of your plans or designs, but merely tries to duplicate the function. Trade secret law will not protect against this type of copying. As with other forms of protection, trade secret law also has limitations.

License Agreements for Programs

Questions frequently arise as to the relationship involved between a user and the owner of a "package," "prewritten," or "off-the-shelf" program, including such games as Space Invaders, Star Trek, and so on.

The rights of the user are referred to as a "license," which is an agreement by the owner for the mere "use" of the program subject to conditions established by the owner. The typical conditions are:

1. Restricts use of the program to the user's computer only.
2. Prohibits copying and providing copies of the program or documentation to others.
3. Requires return of the program upon the termination of the license or upon violation by the user of any of the conditions.

4. Prohibits changing the code of the program without prior permission.
5. Requires either a one-time charge or regular monthly payments.
6. Limits the program provided to the user to the object code (the machine language) and not the source code (that which can be read by the programmer). Thus the customer cannot decipher the program statements, but relies on the vendor for corrections, upgrades, and so on.

This is just a partial list of many of the restrictions imposed on users by the owners of software programs. Let us review some of the penalties associated with these agreements.

Penalties for Violation of License

The penalties for violation of the above conditions can be quite severe and are usually listed in detail in the license agreement. The penalties may include:

1. Immediate termination of the license agreement and immediate return of the program and documentation to the owner.
2. Payment of a penalty fee or liquidated damage as set forth in the agreement.
3. Payment of attorney's fees to restrain unlawful users who receive the program improperly.
4. Payment of the remaining payments under the lease agreement.

The penalties should be understood in detail at the time the license agreement is signed.

SUMMARY OF PROPRIETARY RIGHTS

First, the law is not clear in this entire area and the advice of a competent attorney is essential. Second, trade secret law is a desirable alternative to patent and copyright laws in protecting a computer program. The requirements of trade secret law are clear and must be followed in establishing "the secret."

Patent law does not appear to be a reasonable option for the typical business computer program. Computer programs in and of themselves have been considered to be mathematical formulas, or ideas that are not the subject of a patent. Patents have been thought of predominantly for machines or processes.

Copyright law protects the expression but not the "idea"; thus its protection is severely limited.

The rights and obligations of the user in respect to "off-the-shelf" software are set forth in the license agreement, which must be understood and adhered to or you may subject yourself to significant penalties.

COMPUTER CRIME:
HOW MUCH CRIME IS THERE?

The main computer terminal of the University Computer Center displayed the message: "If you don't give us a mixed assembly software program, we'll shut you down again." It was signed "System Cruncher" and "Vladimir," and it was no joke. The computer had just been disabled for two days during registration week, at a cost to the university of $22,252. This is an actual account of a situation experienced at DePaul University of Chicago.

The culprits turned out to be two high school juniors, "B" students, using a teletype terminal built in one of the boys' bedrooms.

Incidents such as these are on the rise. The Chamber of Commerce estimates a loss of $100 million every year; other estimates place the loss as high as $3.5 billion. In the cases reported annually, which run in the $100-million range, the annual loss equates to 20 times more than the annual take in the early 1970s.

The FBI reports a computerized white-collar crime rise to about 127 percent in 1981, about 1,770 incidents. That compares with 780 incidents reported over the prior 15 years.

Businesses are reacting to this obvious threat. Businesses annually spend $150 million for computer security systems—about 10 times what was spent in the late 1970s.

What makes computer crime so attractive to the thieves is the apparent size of the take. Consider that the average bank robbery nets about $3,000; the average computer bank theft nets about $1.5 million. The Wells Fargo computer fraud netted $21.3 million!

A few other examples illustrate the devastating effect of computer crime:

> Security Pacific—$10.3 million. Stanley Rifkin used an electronic funds transfer code and a public telephone to send money to a Swiss account. Out on bail, he pulled the same caper netting another $9 million!
>
> Union Dime—$1.2 million. A teller skimmed money merely by making simple computerized correction entries.
>
> Equity Funding—$27.5 million. The holding company used computers to create phony insurance policies that were later sold to reinsurers.

Crime and Punishment

The staggering truth is that every one of the computer terminals is essentially a portal for crime. Not only is the equipment itself fair game to criminal minds, but the potential for manipulation, pilferation, and abuse of data is almost beyond description.

"I'm too small," you say. "I don't have to worry." Such an attitude can be devastating. To overlook security precautions both for the equipment and the software is to invite disaster. Crime is ever-present; you must protect against it or be overwhelmed by it.

Computer Crime Statutes

One problem that has plagued prosecuters over the years has been the absence of statutes directly addressing computer crime. Prosecutors had to rely on antiquated wire-fraud statutes, which did not, in many cases, apply to the computer criminal. Modern jurisdictions have attempted to remedy this by enacting computer crime statutes, and a bill before Congress would make certain crimes a federal offense.

Suppose someone asks: "If I run our Snoopy calendar, is this a violation of the law?" The answer is, as usual, "it depends." It depends on the law in effect where the act occurs and it depends on the intent of the doer. It may even depend on the uses of the particular computer system. Let us analyze the act briefly. Does the employer consent to such petty acts? Where is the line to be drawn? What is the real cost of the calendar in terms of computer time and resources?

PENAL CODE SECTIONS

A brief analysis of *California Penal Code Section 502* may serve as a helpful example. The gist of Section 502 provides:

> (b) Any person who intentionally accesses or causes to be accessed any computer system or computer network for the purpose of (1) devising or executing any scheme or artifice to defraud or extort or (2) obtaining money, property, or services with false or fraudulent intent, representations, or promises shall be guilty of a public offense.
>
> (c) Any person who maliciously accesses, alters, deletes, damages or destroys any computer system, computer network, computer program, or data shall be guilty of a public offense.

The first two provisions of subsection (b) thus require a showing of intent to: (1) defraud or extort, or (2) to obtain valuables with false intent. This is a very important question because in our Snoopy example, we have to analyze the intent of the doer.

155

There are many legal tests available to determine an improper intent. However, note that the manifested intent to do wrong is the basis of the crime in conjunction with the unlawful act. Thus, we could conclude, without being a prosecutor, that the production of a Snoopy calendar for personal use would be insufficient to show a criminal intent, which is required under the criminal statute. Under subsection (c) pertaining to damage and alteration of computer systems, there must also be a showing of malice, which is the intent to do a wrongful act without justification or excuse.

In the earlier DePaul University example, we could conclude that a conviction could be obtained under the California statute. This type of statute is available in many modern jurisdictions and has filled a need to provide for the computer criminal. Now let us compare the proposed federal bill.

THE CONGRESSIONAL BILL

The federal bill is different from the California Code Section in several important ways. First, the jurisdiction of the federal bill would apply to:

> Any computer, computer system, computer network, or any part there-of which, *in whole or in part, operates in interstate commerce* or is owned by, under contract to, or in conjunction with, any financial institution, the U.S. government or any branch, department, or agency thereof, or *any entity operating in or affecting interstate commerce.*

Because so many computer systems cross state lines, the jurisdiction of the bill would be very significant and would probably be controlling in all cases where terminals are located across state boundaries.

Second, the language provides that:

> (a) Whoever *knowingly and willfully,* directly or indirectly accesses, causes to be accessed or attempts to access . . . for the purpose of
>
> (1) devising or executing any scheme or artifice to defraud or
>
> (2) obtaining money, property, or services for themselves or another, by means of false or fraudulent pretenses, representations or promises, representations or promises, shall be fined. . . .

Notice that the test is "knowingly and willfully" and not the "intent to defraud" as provided in California's Section 502.

What does all this mean? If you run your Snoopy calendar and willfully and knowingly (purposefully) did what you did, at least some experts claim that you could be guilty of a federal offense under the proposed law. That running a Snoopy calendar is to commit a federal offense is a bit absurd; however, the difference between the two statutes can be of importance.

The argument over the federal legislation will continue, but it is important to have a general understanding of the two different tests being applied and considered in this area.

WHAT CAN WE DO ABOUT CRIME?

As noted earlier, businesses are spending $150 million annually to protect themselves against computer crime. Here is a brief list of things that can be done at your installation:

1. Establish a physical security control system that prevents the access of *unauthorized* persons, such as door restrictions, color-coded badges, locks on the terminals, reducing the number of entries and exits from secured areas. It is interesting to note that Stanley Rifkin, who pulled the Security Pacific caper noted earlier, gained access to an unauthorized section of the bank to do the job.

2. Establish a valid security system for the data. This may mean establishing computerized passwords before a person can use the terminal; additional passwords before certain files can be accessed by the operator; password expiration dates, an alarm if an incorect password is entered three times in a row, procedures to control and store diskettes, and destruction of confidential files by complete erasure on the computer rather than merely erasing the heading on the file.

3. Carefully interview prospective employees with consideration to the security requirements of the job.

4. Conduct periodic meetings or classes for all employees to sensitize them to the dangers involved with computer crime and to solicit their help in reporting any unusual occurrences.

5. Separate job functions where practical. For example, separate the person who prepares the payroll from the person who operates the machine and prepares the check. This suggestion, of course, may not apply to the traditional small office.

6. Provide for continuous auditing and ensure that all transactions provide an audit trail. Computers and word processors can operate at enormous speeds, and the creation of an audit trail will normally not cause a substantial impact to processing speed. The audit trail will prove extremely valuable when a question arises.

7. Ensure, where possible, that computer programs provide for exception reports when data exceed acceptable ranges.

8. Periodically review records of losses, bad debts, and such to ensure that all entries are legitimate.

9. Establish certain limits on the amount of financial transaction permitted particular persons or job categories.

10. Establish written procedures wherever possible. The automation of an office or business represents a major departure from the old and a commitment to the new. The greater the detail of procedures to be followed, the greater the degree of reliability, accuracy, and timeliness of the output from the computer or word processor.

There are many steps that can be taken to protect yourself against computer crime. They take time and effort, but they are worth it because the effects of computer crime can be devastating on your business.

PRIVACY

Today the Internal Revenue Service has our tax returns.

The Social Security Administration keeps a running record on our jobs and our families.

The Veteran's Administration has the medical records of many of us, and the Pentagon has our records of military service. So in this diffusion of information lies our protection. But put everything in one place, computerize it and add to it without limit, and a thieving electronic blackmailer would have just one electronic safe to crack to get a victim's complete dossier, tough as that job would be.

And a malevolent Big Brother would not even have to do that: He could sit in his office, punch a few keys, and arm himself with all he needed to know to crush any citizen who threatened his power.

Therefore, along with the bugged olive in the martini, the psychological tests, and the spiked microphone, the critics have seen "data surveillance" as an ultimate destroyer of the individual citizen's right to privacy—his right to call his soul his own.

Thomas Watson

Think about it. How much information is stored in a computer about you? Aside from the federal computers we discussed, there are state computers for motor vehicle, welfare, tax, and criminal bureaus, and the county and city computers are used for everything from arboretums to zoos. The banks and savings and loan companies have computers; so do colleges and universities, as well as employers, hospital and insurance carriers, even stockbrokers.

The fearsome fact is that the technology is available to connect all of these computers! In some respects, and in terms of information, Orwell's *1984* technically does exist now.

What can be and is being done about this threat to our right of privacy?

Privacy Act of 1974

The Privacy Act of 1974, Public Law 93-579/93rd Congress, S.3418/ December 31, 1974, can be summarized by first identifying it as applying *only* to federal agencies and excepting law enforcement activities generally.

> The law requires federal agencies:
>
> To notify an individual on request if there is personal information about the individual contained in the agency's records,
>
> To permit the individual to examine and copy most of those records,
>
> Under designated procedures, to dispute the contents of the record and to place a statement of the dispute in the file.
>
> Agencies are required to publish notice of the existence of the files, to keep records of accesses and disclosure, and to refrain from disclosing information without the data subject's permission unless the disclosure is to one of the eleven excepted disclosees.
>
> Agencies are required to take reasonable precautions to protect the security of the records. Private companies that operate a record system for an agency are considered part of the agency, and their employees are subject to the same rules as federal employees.
>
> Willful failure to conform to the requirements of the Act results in civil liability of the agency for the individual's harm for actual damages of not less than $1,000. There is a criminal penalty of a $5,000 fine for an agency employee's willful failure to comply with the requirements of the Act. Unauthorized requests for and accesses to records under false pretenses are likewise punishable by a $5,000 fine.

The penalties associated with violation of the Privacy Act are quite substantial. However, there are many other computer systems that do not have similar restrictions. Each state and local jurisdiction may or may not have similar rules and regulations. If you are interested, inquire of your state attorney general, county or city attorney's office to determine what laws pertain to your personal data. You will find that there is a surprisingly limited number of laws at the local level to protect you against incorrect or misleading information contained in a computer.

Elements of Privacy

You may think that privacy is limited to current information about you. But it is much greater.

1. Accuracy. Obviously you are concerned about whether data are accurate. Computers do not generally make mistakes. However, the input to a computer is accomplished by human beings, who are very prone to error. For example, a credit limit of $10,000 vs. $100,000 is merely the difference of one keystroke.
2. Completeness. An incomplete file can lead to incorrect and misleading conclusions, and if that conclusion is about you, then you should be vitally concerned.
3. Currency. A computer fact can be 100 percent accurate and complete, but if it is 15–25 years old, it should be analyzed accordingly.

These are just a few of the concerns in this area that is so susceptible to abuse. As a manager or owner of confidential personal information, you must make sure that you and your employees protect the confidential nature of the data, just as you would demand comparable treatment by owners of data pertaining to you.

Summary

The legal issues involved with the computer and word processing industry are important and need to be generally understood. The proprietary rights and obligations associated with the computer software industry can result in a significant financial gain or loss if the ownership rights are not understand and followed. Computer crime is on the rise and people must be willing to take the required steps to protect themselves.

APPENDIX A: QUESTIONNAIRES AND FORMS

ORIGINATOR'S QUESTIONNAIRE (A1)

Date _____

NAME _____ TITLE _____ DEPT. _____

SECRETARY/TYPIST _____

Is current secretarial/clerical support sufficient? _____ If not, explain.

_____

_____

How many originators share your secretary/typist? _____

       Name(s)   ___Title___

   _____   _____

   _____   _____

   _____   _____

How many hours per day do you spend creating correspondence? _____

How is this work generated?

    Longhand _____%   Shorthand _____%   Machine dictation _____%

Do you create work outside the office? _____   Frequency? _____

    How created: longhand _____%   machine dictation? _____%

Do you request rough drafts? _____

    What percent of work? _____%   How often? _____   Why? _____

    _____

Do you occasionally revise correspondence sent to you by support staff? _____

    How often? _____   Why? _____

    _____

Do you create repetitive correspondence? _____

Do you create correspondence with fill-ins? _____

Do you use standard paragraphs to create correspondence? _____

Do you incorporate other text into your work? _____

Are you satisfied with present turnaround time? _____

Are there backlogs in typing? _____

    Frequently? _____   Occasionally? _____   Never? _____

Do you send work out due to lack of secretarial/typist time to complete? _____

Are you satisfied with the quality of documents leaving your office? _____

Are you performing any work your secretary/typists could do if time permitted?

_____

    Photocopying _____   Filing _____   Sorting _____

    Research _____   Composing _____   Posting/bookeeping _____

    Other _____

Do you have any work currently not being done? _____

    If yes, would this generate more typing? _____

List peak periods and approximate time they occur (i.e., weekly, monthly, etc.).

Description/Title of Work   When

_____   _____

_____   _____

_____   _____

Do you anticipate any personnel changes within the next six months?_____

What? _____

Please indicate any suggestions you would like to see implemented to improve your ability to perform your job and/or your department's functions.

_____

_____

_____

_____

_____

TYPIST'S QUESTIONNAIRE (A2)

Date _____

NAME _____ TITLE _____ DEPT. _____

SUPERVISOR _____ NUMBER & NAME OF OTHERS YOU SUPPORT _____

Present typing equipment _____

    Pitch 10 _____ 12 _____ Proportional spacing _____

How is work presented?

    Machine dictation _____% Shorthand _____% Longhand _____%

    Copytype _____%

How much is rough draft? _____%

Average number of revision cycles? _____

Average amount of revision? _____%

Average number of revisions due to author change? _____%

Average restarts due to typographical errors? _____%

Are you retyping and/or incorporating portions of previously typed documents in your work? _____

Are you allowed to cut and paste? _____

Are erasers prohibited on any of your work? _____

    If yes, on what?

    Explain _____

_____

Indicate the following information for each type of document:

	Average Length	Average # of Copies/Carbons Required
Straight text	_____	_____
Statistical	_____	_____
Forms/envelopes	_____	_____
Standard paragraphs/repetitive	_____	_____

Is a photocopy machine near your desk? _____

Average time per day away from your desk (i.e., photocopying, etc.)? _____

Maximum paper width required? _____

Do you have a need for special type styles and/or symbols? _____

    Specify _____

What is the average timeline requirement to complete:

	Hour(s)/Day(s)
General correspondence	_____
Statistical work	_____
Miscellaneous forms	_____

Reports   _____

Describe peak periods (daily, monthly, etc.)

Document Title	Period/Due Date	Average Length of Document
_____	_____	_____
_____	_____	_____
_____	_____	_____

How often are you backlogged and explain situation?
_____
_____

How do you handle overloads?
_____
_____

Estimate the average time you spend daily on the following activities:

	Hour(s) Per Day
Typing	_____
Proofreading	_____
Administrative functions:	
Sorting and handling mail	_____
Telephone calls	_____
Photocopying	_____
Posting/bookkeeping	_____
Filing	_____
Research	_____
Assisting others	_____
Reception duties	_____
Shorthand	_____
Special projects (describe)	
_____	_____
Other (describe)	
_____	
Waiting for work	_____
Personal time	_____
TOTAL HOURS PER DAY	_____

List nonroutine work, special projects, or assignments that occur on a sporadic basis (i.e., monthly reports):

Type of Project	Frequency	Amount of Time To Complete
_____	_____	_____
_____	_____	_____
_____	_____	_____

Please indicate any suggestions you would like to see implemented to improve your ability to perform your job and/or your department's functions.

_____
_____
_____
_____
_____
_____

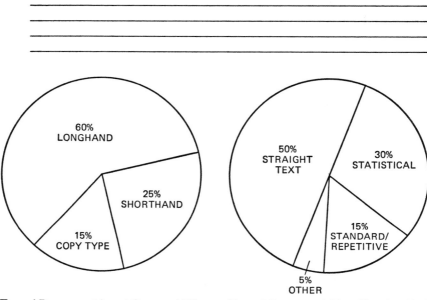

Typed Document Input Source (A3)   Typed Document Classification (A4)

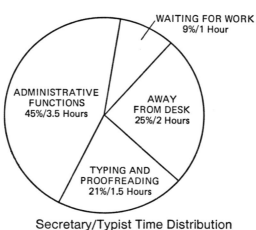

Secretary/Typist Time Distribution
(A5)

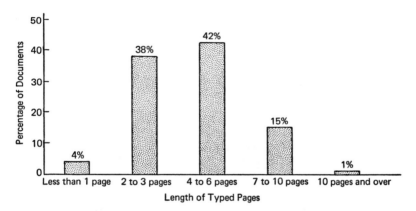

Length of Typed Documents (A6)

COMPUTER QUESTIONNAIRE (A7–A10)

ACCOUNTING FUNCTIONS

BILLING AND TIMEKEEPING (A7)

How many characters of data do you retain per customer for billing purposes? _____ (Attach sample form)

How many customers do you have at the current time? _____ How many in next three years? _____ (Attach sample report)

How many time entries are logged in each day? _____ Week? _____

How many characters of data are recorded per time entry? _____ (Attach sample form)

How much time is spent each day recording or correcting time entries? _____ Each week? _____

How many errors occur in recording or transferring time entries each week? _____ Each month? _____

Once a time entry is recorded, how many entries do you require to change or modify each week? _____ Month? _____

How many different types of bills do you use? _____ (Attach sample form)

Do you need fee structures stored in the computer and automatically generated on bills? _____ Or are bills prepared from manual input only? _____

Do you want dunning notices sent? _____

ACCOUNTING REPORTS (A8)

How much time do you spend on accounting reports each week? _____ Each month? _____

How many accounting reports are generated each month? _____ (Attach sample reports)

Do you need:
      a. Aged Accounts Receivable Report? _____
      b. Principal Earnings Report? _____
      c. Service Report by Matter? _____
      d. Activity Summary by Staff Member? _____
      e. Staff Productivity Report? _____

How many copies of accounting reports do you need? _____

CASH PROCESSING (A9)

How much time do you spend on cash disbursements each week? _____ Each month? _____

How many characters comprise an entry in your disbursement log? _____ (Attach sample form)

How many cash transactions do you have each week? _____   Each month? _____

PAYROLL (A10)

How much time per week is spent processing payroll? _____

How many characters of payroll data are filed on each employee? _____   (Attach sample form)

How many employees do you have now? _____   In next three years? _____

How many reports are produced on payroll? _____   (Attach sample reports)

Who handles payroll activity? _____   How much does it currently cost? _____

How frequently do errors occur in the current payroll system each week? _____   Each month? _____

Does payroll include year-to-date information? _____

Are yearly W-2 forms prepared manually? _____

New Business Memo (A11)

NEW BUSINESS MEMO

Firm No.	Client No.		□ New Client □ Client Change

Client Name (45 Characters)	Alpha Client Sort (20 Characters)

Client Address (Line 1) (30 Characters)	Client City (22 Characters)	State	Zip Code

Client Address (Line 2) (30 Characters) | Client Telephone Numbers (With Area Code) (2 Permitted)
#1 ( ) #2 ( )

Client Address (Line 3) (30 Characters) | Summary Billing
□ A = Statements & Summary
□ B = Invoice & Summary
□ Z = ELIMINATE DATES

Matter No.	Description (40 Characters)	□ New Matter □ Matter Change

Neg. Atty No.	Atty-In-Charge No.	Hourly Rate Over-ride	Case Type No.

Estimated Fee: | Statute of Limitations Date:

BILLING FORMAT

FEES

Frequency	Dollar Extensions	Time on Statement
□ Monthly (M)	□ No	□ No
□ Totals (T)	□ Yes - Each Line	□ Yes - Each Line
□ Contingent (C)		□ Total Only
□ Fixed (X)		

COSTS

Frequency	Dollar Extensions
□ Monthly (M)	□ No
□ Totals (T)	□ Yes - Each Line
□ Contingent (C)	
□ Fixed (X)	

TRUST ACCTNG

Print on Statement
□ No
□ Yes

DUNNING

Print Statement
□ No
□ Yes

Original – Yellow – Firm File Copy

CLIENT DIRECTORY (A12)

BY CLIENT ID
ENTIRE CLIENT FILE
OPEN + CLOSED CLIENTS

CLIENT ID/ CLIENT NAME/COMPANY NAME TELEPHONE (HOME/BUS.)	ADDRESS	BILLING ADDRESS	BILLING ATTORNEY/ ATTENTION LINE	REG. DATE/ CLOSING DT/ ALPHA SORT KEY
00001 WILLIAM BARKER ABC CO. (555-1234)	MAIN STREET SUITE 123 TOWN, STATE	SAME	JER JEFFREY MR. BARKER	12/31/8x
00002 DONALD JONES DEF CO. (555-5678)	FIRST STREET SUITE 456 TOWN, STATE	SAME	SB STEVEN M	12/31/8x
00003 MARY SMITH SMITH, INC. (555-9101)	ANY ROAD TOWN, STATE	P.O. Box 123	JER JEFFREY MARY	12/31/8x
NUMBER OF CLIENTS ON FILE 3				

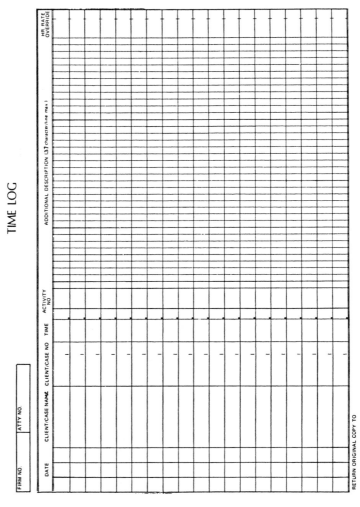

TIME LOG

Time Log (A13)

172

LEZIÉ, DUNAWAY, WOLSKI & DONOHUE
A LAW CORPORATION
1112 OCEAN DRIVE · SUITE 202
MANHATTAN BEACH, CALIFORNIA 90266

JAMES P. LEZIÉ
KATHRYN DUNAWAY
SYLVIA V. WOLSKI
BRIAN C. DONOHUE

AREA CODE 213
TELEPHONE 372-1167

Mr. John Smith
Central Computer, Inc.
123 Forrest Street
Anywhere, U.S.A.

FOR PROFESSIONAL SERVICES RENDERED - 198X

		Hours	Fees
5/7/8X	*Conference with Mr. Smith re: formation of Corporation, Central Computer Inc.; discussed pending contracts with Jones Distributors; reviewed lease agreements for new office space.	2.0	$ 200.00
5/8/8X	Prepared corporate documents and forwarded to Sec. of State	Agreed Fee	750.00
5/10/8X	Mr. Paralegal conducted research re: tax effect of distribution contracts.	10.0	30.00
5/21/8X	Prepared draft pension plan for 5 employees of Central Computer Inc.	1.4	140.00
5/21/8X	Prepared profit sharing plan and conducted research re: the impact of the Economic Recovery Tax Act of 1981.	3.0	300.00
	Total Hours	7.4	$ 670.00

For Professional Services $1,420.00

COSTS:

5/10/8X	Secretary of State	70.00
5/10/8X	Photocopying	3.20
TOTAL BALANCE DUE		$1,493.20

*With the timing device described in Section 3.23 of the RFP, the
description of services rendered can be of any length.

Computer-Generated Bill (A14)

AGED ACCOUNTS RECEIVABLE (A15)

CLIENT NUMBER	CLIENT NAME	INVOICE NUMBER	INVOICE DATE	FEES EXPENSES	0–10 DAYS	11–30 DAYS	31–60 DAYS	61–90 DAYS	91-ABOVE DAYS
00002	DONALD JONES	001013180	01/31/8X	0.00					0.00
				0.00					0.00
		001ONACC	03/01/8X	417.50–	0.00	0.00	0.00	0.00	417.50–
				0.00					0.00
		CLIENT FEE TOTALS		417.50–	0.00	0.00	0.00	0.00	417.50–
		CLIENT EXPENSE TOTALS		0.00	0.00	0.00	0.00	0.00	0.00
		CLIENT TOTALS		417.50–	0.00				417.50–*
00003	MARY SMITH	001013180	01/31/8X	100.00	0.00	0.00	0.00	0.00	100.00
				0.00					0.00
		CLIENT FEE TOTALS		100.00	0.00	0.00	0.00	0.00	100.00
		CLIENT EXPENSE TOTALS		0.00	0.00	0.00	0.00	0.00	0.00
		CLIENT TOTALS		100.00	0.00				100.00
00001	WILLIAM BARKER	002122879	12/28/8X	0.00	0.00	0.00	0.00	0.00	0.00
				0.00					0.00
		001013180	01/31/8X	280.00					280.00
				45.00					45.00
		001030580	03/05/8X	145.00					145.00
				8.70					8.70

CLIENT FEE TOTALS	425.00	0.00	0.00	0.00	0.00	425.00
CLIENT EXPENSE TOTALS	53.70	0.00	0.00	0.00	0.00	53.70
CLIENT TOTALS	478.70	0.00	0.00	0.00	0.00	478.70*
COMPANY FEE TOTALS	107.50	0.00	0.00	0.00	0.00	107.50
COMPANY EXPENSE TOTALS	53.70	0.00	0.00	0.00	0.00	53.70
COMPANY TOTALS	161.20	0.00	0.00	0.00	0.00	161.20**

ATTORNEY EARNINGS REPORT (A16)

ATTORNEY	--- CURRENT PERIOD ---		---- YEAR TO DATE ----	
	EARNINGS	% OF TOTAL	EARNINGS	% OF TOTAL
JER JEFFREY RYMER	3,789.01	51.00	10,675.90	51.00
SB STEVEN BARTOW	1,785.98	28.00	6,993.98	21.00
SM SUSAN MAZUR	989.43	21.00	4,939.42	28.00
** GRAND TOTAL **	6,564.42	100.00	22,609.30	100.00

175

STAFF SERVICE REPORT BY MATTER (A17)
FROM 05/01/8X to 05/31/8X

JER   JEFFREY RYMER

CASE   CLIENT   MATTER

00001.002 WILLIAM BARKER

SVC DATE	HOURS	CODE	SERVICE CATEGORY
05/01/8X	0.00	FILC	FILING FOR CORPORATE NAME
05/01/8X	1.00	PCOR	PREPARATION OF CORPORATE MINUTES
05/03/8X	0.20	TELI	TELEPHONE CALL TO
05/03/8X	0.10	TEL2	LONG DISTANCE TELEPHONE CHARGE
05/03/8X	1.20	TSEA	TITLE SEARCH

* TOTAL NUMBER OF TRANSACTIONS   5   HOURS   2.50
FOR MATTER

00005.002 JOHN COVINGTON

SVC DATE	HOURS	CODE	SERVICE CATEGORY
05/02/8X	0.00	DIVE	DIVORCE-ESTIMATED EXPENSES
05/06/8X	8.00	CONI	CONFERENCE WITH CLIENT
05/07/8X	0.00	ADP	AD PRE-PRITNTS
05/07/8X	3.00	CONA	CONFERENCE WITH OPPOSING ATTORNEY
05/16/8X	0.00	DEPI	DEPOSITION

* TOTAL NUMBER OF TRANSACTIONS   5   HOURS   11.00
FOR MATTER

00005.003 JOHN BACON

Date	Code	Value	Description
05/01/8X	CSEP	0.00	COLOR SEPARATIONS
05/13/81	DEPI	1.00	DEPOSITION
05/13/8X	DEPI	8.00	DEPOSITION
05/14/81	ILL	3.00	ILLUSTRATIONS
05/16/XI	ADP	0.00	AD PRE-PRITNTS
05/29/8X	FILI	0.00	FILING OF COMPLAINT

* TOTAL NUMBER OF TRANSACTIONS FOR MATTER   6   HOURS 12.00

** TOTAL NUMBER OF SERVICES FOR STAFF MEMBER   16   HOURS 24.50

***TOTAL NUMBER OF STAFF MEMBERS   1

ACTIVITY SUMMARY BY STAFF MEMBER (A18)
ACCOUNTING PERIOD 6

**FEES AND EXPENSES	OUTSTANDING TRANSACTIONS 04/01/8X — 06/06/8X				YEAR TO DATE 01/01/8X — 06/07/8X			
STAFF MEMBER	UNBILLED HOURS	UNBILLED DOLLARS	NON BILLABLE HOURS	NON BILLABLE DOLLARS	BILLED HOURS	BILLED DOLLARS	NON BILLABLE HOURS	NON BILLABLE DOLLARS
JEFFREY RYMER	131.33	12,954.09	4.00	400.00	106.67	3,913.25	0.00	0.00
SM SUSAN MAZUR	45.00	2,700.00	0.00	0.00	44.50	2,035.85	0.00	0.00
SB STEVEN BARTOW	0.00	0.00	0.00	0.00	0.00	0.00	0.00	0.00
** GRAND TOTALS **	176.33	15,654.09	4.00	400.00	151.17	5,949.10	0.00	0.00
PERCENTAGE OF CURRENT TOTALS	97.8%	97.5%	2.2%	2.5%	100.0%	100.0%	0.0%	0.0%
PERCENTAGE OF YTD TOTALS	97.8%	97.5%	2.2%	2.5%	100.0%	100.0%	0.0%	0.0%

STAFF PRODUCTIVITY REPORT (A19)
* ATTORNEY SUMMARY *
* FEES ONLY *

ATTORNEY		BILLABLE HOURS	AMOUNT	NON-BILLABLE HOURS	AMOUNT	TOTAL HOURS	AMOUNT	AVERAGE BILLING RATES BILLABLE	NON BILLABLE	TOTAL
JER JEFFREY RYMER	CURRENT MONTH	142.67	14,590.30	4.00	400.00	146.67	14,900.30	102.27	100.00	102.2
	%'S OF TOTAL	97.3	97.3	2.7	2.7					
	YEAR TO DATE	142.67	14,590.30	4.00	400.00	146.67	14,990.30	102.27	100.00	102.2
	%'S OF TOTAL	97.3	97.3	2.7	2.7					
	MONTHLY AVERAGE	23.78	2,431.72	0.67	66.67	24.45	2,498.38	102.27	100.00	102.
	%'S OF TOTAL	97.3	97.3	2.7	2.7					
SM SUSAN MAZUR	CURRENT MONTH	80.50	4,560.00	0.00	0.00	80.50	4,560.00	56.65	0.00	56.6
	%'S OF TOTAL	100.0	100.0	0.0	0.0					
	YEAR TO DATE	80.50	4,560.00	0.00	0.00	80.50	4,560.00	56.65	0.00	56.6
	%'S OF TOTAL	100.0	100.0	0.0	0.0					
	MONTHLY AVERAGE	13.42	760.00	0.00	0.00	13.42	760.00	56.65	0.00	56.6
	%'S OF TOTAL	100.0	100.0	0.0	0.0					
*** GRAND TOTAL	CURRENT MONTH	223.17	19,150.30	4.00	400.00	227.17	19,550.30	85.81	100.00	86.0
	%'S OF TOTAL	98.2	98.0	1.8	2.0					
	YEAR TO DATE	233.17	19,150.30	4.00	400.00	227.17	19,550.30	85.81	100.00	86.0
	%'S OF TOTAL	98.2	98.0	1.8	2.0					
	MONTHLY AVERAGE	37.20	3,191.72	0.67	66.67	37.86	3,258.38	85.81	100.00	86.0
	%'S OF TOTAL	98.2	98.0	1.8	2.0					

CASH FLOW APPLICATION ADJUSTMENTS

Firm No.
5

Date (Firm Use)

CLIENT CASE
(Blank for attorney level adjustment)

REMOVE AMOUNT FROM:

Closing Date of Case
(Blank for attorney level adjustment)
(All zero = use oldest uncleared month)

MM DD YY

Source
Attorney No.

AR = Accounts
COS = Costs
REC = Receipts

Amount $
$. ¢

APPLY AMOUNT TO:

Source
Attorney No.

AR = Accounts
COS = Costs
REC = Receipts
Blank = No Application

Closing Date of Case
(Blank for attorney level adjustment)
If case level adjustment
1) Blank = use same date
2) All zero = use oldest uncleared month

MM DD YY

COMMENT OR REFERENCE TO OTHER NARRATIVE
(30 Characters Maximum)

10   20   26   29   36   39   45

Cash Flow Application Adjustments (A20)

STAFF MASTER FILE (A21)

** COMPLETE STAFF/RATE FILE LISTING **

STAFF NAME ID	TITLE	EMPLOYMENT DT/ TERMINATION DT	YTD BILLED EXPENSES/ FEES/HOURS	YTD NONBILLABLE EXPENSES/ FEES/HOURS	RATE 1/ RATE 2/ RATE 3	RATE 4/ RATE 5/ RATE 6	RATE 7/ RATE 8/ RATE 9
DJ DAVID JORDAN	ASSOCIATE	03/30/8X	700.09	190.00	80.00	90.00	0.00
		00/00/0X	10.00	2.00	75.00	85.00	0.00
			160.00	27.00	70.00	100.00	0.00
JER JEFFREY RYMER	PARTNER	10/20/80	1.00	126.83	100.00	75.00	0.00
		00/00/0X	62.00	10.00	90.00	70.00	0.00
			688.00	112.00	80.00	65.00	0.00
PM PAULINE MASUCCI	ASSOCIATE	01/01/8X	1.00	248.66	80.00	65.00	0.00
		00/00/0X	34.00	14.00	75.00	60.00	0.00
			490.00	198.00	70.00	55.00	0.00
SY SUSAN YOUNG	PARA-LEGAL	11/09/80	0.00	97.50	60.00	35.00	0.00
		00/00/0X	15.00	3.00	50.00	30.00	0.00
			490.00	88.00	40.00	0.00	0.00

NUMBER OF STAFF MEMBERS ON FILE = 4

APPENDIX B: REQUEST FOR PROPOSAL AND VENDOR RESPONSE

OFFICE AUTOMATION SYSTEM (B1)
Request for Proposal (RFP)

TABLE OF CONTENTS

1. Introduction
2. Background
   2.1 Office Organization and Facilities
   2.2 System Objectives
   2.3 Workload
3. Requirements
   3.1 Scope
   3.2 Equipment Configuration
   3.3 Optional Hardware
   3.4 Required Word Processing Features
   3.5 Optional Software Features
   Hardware Features
   3.6 Required Display Features
   3.7 Optional CRT Display Features
   3.8 Required Storage Media and Capacity
   3.9 Optional Storage Media and Capacity
   3.10 Required Printer Features
   3.11 Optional Printer Features
   Services
   3.12 Training Requirements
   3.13 Optional Training
   3.14 Maintenance Requirements
   3.15 Optional Maintenance
   3.16 Required System Services
   3.17 Optional System Services
   3.18 Required Programming Support
   3.19 Optional Programming Support
   3.20 Required Documentation Support
   3.21 Optional Documentation Support
   3.22 Optional Miscellaneous Features
   3.23 Accounting System Requirements

4. Vendor Capabilities
   4.1 Corporate Financial Report
   4.2 Availability of Staff
   4.3 References

OFFICE AUTOMATION SYSTEM
REQUEST FOR PROPOSAL (RFP)

1. INTRODUCTION

The member firm of ABC conducted a requirements study of the firm's current office management, financial management, and secretarial support systems. This study established that a computer system could provide significant efficiencies in several areas:

> Management of the office can be made more effortless with a computer system to handle repetitious chores.
>
> Repetitious typing can be substantially reduced by means of the storage and retrieval capabilities of a word processing system.
>
> The amount of rework required can be substantially reduced by use of the text editing features of a word processing system.
>
> Efficient timekeeping and accurate, timely billing can improve cash flow and increase profits.
>
> Automated accounting reports can keep the firm constantly informed as to its financial status by customer and matter.

Therefore, ABC is writing interested vendors to bid on a word processing and computer system, as per the requirements stated herein. Although it is believed that a word processing and computer system that completely meets the RFP specifications will be the most cost effective solution for the requirements of ABC, alternate proposals will be considered if vendors wish to recommend an alternate system with comparable functional capabilities and cost effectiveness.

2. BACKGROUND

2.1 Office Organization and Facilities

ABC Firm has six principals, four secretaries, and two assistants. One or two part-time clerks are also on hand. Two secretaries may be assigned as full-time operators to the word processing functions if needed. All four secretaries will be responsible for entering the time, receipt, and disbursement logs and for creating required reports. The assistants may also perform word processing functions on a part-time basis and one full-time word processing operator may be added to the firm if the need develops.

The office has determined that the current overhead expense, particularly in salaries and benefits, is becoming too burdensome and is impacting the firm's profitability. Current overhead accounts for approximately 55 percent of gross revenues; thus the firm is looking for a way to reduce overhead and increase productivity of all staff personnel including the principals. Work load has steadily increased and the firm is just barely able to keep pace with the current work load. The firm has been experiencing a 10 percent increase in clerical work annually, which is expected to continue.

2.2 System Objectives

Although there is some variation in the firm's typing workload, a configuration is required that will enable any sort of work to be done at any work station. The firm's goal is a flexible system that can be responsive to changes in the amount, nature, and distribution of work without requiring training or retraining or shifting of staff or equipment.

The firm's objective is to ensure that office productivity is able to keep pace with the expected growth in administrative and clerical tasks and at the same time prevent any increase in the overhead expense to the firm.

2.3 Work Load

The current work volume is approximately 150 typing hours per week for the firm and the word processing system must be able to produce a preponderance of the typing work. The timekeeping, billing, accounting, and report generating require approximately 45 staff hours per week.

Following are details regarding the types of documents and lengths of the firm's weekly typing work load:

	Approximate
Correspondence	100–200 pages
Formal reports	130–160 pages
Time reports	75 pages
Draft reports	50–200 pages
Forms/contracts	50–400 pages
Client bills	150 pages
Bookkeeping reports	30 pages

Input Source	
Longhand	60%
Shorthand	25%
Copy type	15%
No machine dictation	

Typed Document Classification

Straight text	50%
Statistical	30%
Standard	15%
Other	5%

Length of Document

Less than 1 page	4%
2–3 pages	38%
4–6 pages	42%
7–10 pages	15%

3. REQUIREMENTS

3.1 Scope

The computer/word processing system required by the ABC Firm will be composed of items described in this section. Vendors should bid the following:

1. Unit cost and lease per item using Attachment 1.
2. Options available and cost per option using Attachment 2.

Vendors must propose a total configuration including services and bid the cost for the complete system using Attachment 1.

Vendors should propose a configuration that will meet the current need of ABC Firm and allow for future growth and system expansion.

3.2 Equipment Configuration

The following equipment should be proposed in a suitable configuration. Vendors should evaluate ABC Firm's requirements and propose the appropriate number of components using the attached chart (Attachment 1).

CPU/controller.
Hard disk unit.
Floppy diskette unit.
CRT terminal(s).
Letter quality printer(s).

3.3 Optional Hardware

Components may consist of the following, in addition to others that vendors may propose using the attached chart (Attachment 2).

OCR page reader.
Acoustic printer cover(s).
Single sheet feeder.
Continuous paper feeder.

INSTRUCTIONS ON COMPLETING
SPECIFICATION FORMS

The specifications are divided into two parts: a description of the required or optional feature on the left side of the form and the vendor's response on the right side of the form.

Each "required" section is followed by the associated "optional" section.

Completing the Form

Vendors are advised to make their responses as detailed as possible. To fail to complete a response or to fail to provide sufficient explanation in your response will result in substantial points being lost.

It is recommended that a page reference: (i.e., Technical Manual 123, page 12, paragraph 1) be used wherever possible so that ABC may analyze the response in detail. A response without detail (e.g., "Yes, we have that") may be considered a nonresponse, and substantial points will be lost.

Optional Sections

The optional sections are provided so that the vendor may present additional components, features, or services that may assist ABC in its work. The features should be described in as detailed a manner as possible and the cost for the options may be shown on Attachment 2.

MODEL COVER LETTER FROM VENDOR (B2)

VENDOR A
1000 Central Avenue
Metropolitan U.S.A.

ABC FIRM
123 Mainstreet
Anywhere, U.S.A.

Re: PROPOSAL FOR COMPUTER/WORD PROCESSING SYSTEM

Dear Manager, President, Owner:

It is our pleasure to submit this proposal to you for a BD123 Computer/Word Processing System to satisfy your requirements contained in your request for proposal.

The BD123 is the most advanced and reliable system available in the marketplace. Our programming software is the most versatile and dependable product of its kind anywhere. And, as you know, Vendor A retains one of the best-qualified and experienced staff of personnel in this region.

If you select Vendor A, I will personally assure you that the entire resources available within our organization will be standing ready to respond quickly to any call for service. Our training is of A+ quality and will more than meet your needs.

Please feel free to call me at any time if any question arises that needs further explanation. I will personally ensure that your installation will be successful.

Attached is background information about Vendor A plus our responses to your specifications.

We feel confident that you will determine that Vendor A has the superior product at the lowest possible price.

Sincerely,

I. M. Vendor

I.M. VENDOR
Sales Representative

HISTORY OF VENDOR A (B3)

VENDOR A is one of the fastest growing companies of its kind. Our reputation for service and quality is unparalleled in the industry. We believed that customer satisfaction is of utmost importance and are committed to providing A+ service at all times.

Vendor A was founded three years ago and has grown rapidly ever since. We have grown quickly because of our superior product and excellent staff of personnel. We now have satisfied accounts in many cities in our region.

Vendor A will remain a leading company in our region and will satisfy your requirements in the future.

THE BD123 SYSTEM (B4)

The BD123 System clearly is the state-of-the-art in terms of available hardware and software. The BD architecture is unique in the industry and provides the greatest transaction rate per cost compared with any other system of its kind. The BD123 will run without material failure for extensive periods of time.

THE WORD PROCESSING SOFTWARE (B5)

The word processing software is the most complete and versatile package of its kind. It contains all the major features that are needed in any office system and will guarantee a satisfied user. The software continues to be improved by our experienced programming staff and new releases and improvements are regularly made available.

THE BUSINESS PROGRAMS (B6)

The Vendor A business programs contain essentially every function that a typical business would ever need. The accounts receivable and accounts payable packages are the finest of their kind and have been tested and improved through years of actual use.

PRICE (B7)

The prices proposed in the pricing schedules are the lowest possible prices available for comparable equipment. The current prices will remain in effect for 90 days and are subject to increase after that time. We are confident that the ABC Firm will find that the prices proposed by Vendor A are consistent with your financial goals.

BUYER REQUIREMENTS (B8)
3.4 REQUIRED WORD PROCESSING
SOFTWARE PRINTING FEATURES

3.4.1 Text Input Features

1. Auto page numbering.	*Yes, see operator guide pg. Page numbering format is flexible and automatic.*
2. Auto pagination.	*Yes, regardless of reformatting.*
3. Auto word wraparound.	*Yes.*
4. Auto centering.	*Yes, on one keystroke.*
5. Auto decimal tab.	*Yes, column of figures will line up by decimal place.*
6. Table of contents/menu.	*Yes.*
7. Auto footnote.	*No auto footnote.*

3.4.2 Text Edit and Merge

1. Able to edit 400-page documents.	*Yes, single disk holds 150 to 175 pages of text.*
2. Paragraph and page block move and block copy within a document and to another document.	*Yes, instantaneous block move/copy/ delete.*
3. Global search and replace.	*Yes*
4. Column move/delete.	*Yes, instantaneous.*
5. Document assembly/merge that allows manual and automated combining of prerecorded text with keyboard text to form new document.	*Yes, no disk access required for adding text to document.*

3.4.3 Required Miscellaneous Software Features

1. Able to store multiple formats and space from field to field with a single action (keystroke).	*Yes, unlimited stored format and forms fill out capability.*
2. Able to search in three seconds or less from menu to any document, via automatic file/document select.	*Yes, response time depends on unique factors.*
3. Revision, status, and document production reporting.	*Yes, optional feature.*
4. Ability to save files/documents for backup purposes.	*Yes.*

5. Upgraded to higher capability word processing systems.	*We upgrade the software, not the hardware.*
6. System security that prevents document access.	*Best safety measure is putting data disks in a safe place.*
7. System can restrict unauthorized users.	*Yes, password or key lock.*
8. Passwords are not displayed.	*Not displayed.*
9. Disk erase.	*Yes.*
10. Word processing software updates must be available.	*Yes, all new software upgrades easily installed from diskettes. All systems share software compatibility. Updates usually at no charge.*
11. Machine dialog/menu prompt.	*Yes.*
12. Special key for section symbol (§).	*Yes, if requested.*

3.4.4 Software Printing Features

1. Printout queuing—eight documents.	*Yes, more than the required eight documents.*
2. Each CRT can direct output to any selected printer.	*Systems may share a printer, but cross-wiring of multiple systems with multiple printers is not recommended.*
3. Operator can make priority print assignments.	*No.*
4. Operator can print beginning at desired page.	*Yes.*
5. Sub and superscript printout.	*Yes, one keystroke command.*
6. Simultaneous printout.	*Yes.*

3.5 Optional Software Features

1. Complete library of standard package programs.	*Yes, see booklet "Software Programs" for description of programs.*
2. Auto file sort.	*Yes, via data management, see pg. 32 of manual.*
3. Auto file select.	*Yes, same as above.*
4. Dewey decimal.	*Yes, with optional programmable keys—additional $200.*
5. Auto cross reference.	*Yes, via data management, see pg. 32 of manual.*
6. Automated mail box.	*Yes, software available in one year.*

7. Ability to communicate over telephone lines with major data bases.	*Yes, requires modem and interface that lists at $2,000; software interface available at $80/month.*
8. OCR input capability.	*Yes, requires OCR reader that lists for $5,000; can be leased at monthly amount.*
9. Adaptability to distributed data processing.	

HARDWARE FEATURES

3.6 Required Display Features

1. Display a minimum of 24 lines of 80 characters.	*Yes, uses 24 × 80.*
2. Horizontal scrolling to 158 characters.	*Yes, up to 450 characters.*
3. Display highlighting of text to be moved or deleted.	*Yes, beginning and end of text marked visually by highlighting.*

3.7 Optional CRT Display Features	
	Graphics capability available in 10 different colors; cost is $200 extra per month.
	Five additional programmable functions keys available at no cost.

3.8 Required Storage Media and Capacity

1. Five-to-10 megabyte hard disk on-line storage.	*Yes, 5-meg currently, up to 80 meg next year.*
2. Floppy diskette units for archiving of permanent storage.	*Yes.*

3.9 Optional Storage Media and Capacity	

3.10 Required Printer Features	
1. Bidirectional, letter quality, impact printer with approximately 40 characters per second print speed.	*Yes, 60 CPS dot matrix; sample attached.*
2. Able to print: • single sheet (manual and auto feed) • continuous paper • envelopes • mailing labels • preprinted forms • seven-part carboned forms.	*Yes, to all. Single-sheet feeder optional.*

3. Writing width of 13 inches and carriage paper width of 15 inches.	*Yes, up to 16 inches.*
4. Sheet feeder.	*Optional for $1750.*
5. Tractor feeder.	*Optional for $170.*
6. Acoustic suppressing noise to 40 dbm.	*Optional, extra charge for $100.*

3.11 Optional Printer Features

1. Type styles similar to those available on IBM fonts.	*IBM fonts are available.*
2. Other features that the vendor desires to present may be placed in this section.	

3.12 Training Requirements

1. Provide no-cost training, 80 hours per operator, over a one-month period, to a minimum of two operators per terminal, prior to installation, or to four operators if only one terminal is installed.	*Forty hours total provided with cost of system, additional training at hourly rate.*
2. Provide no-cost managerial assistance.	*Provided as part of above 40 hours.*
3. Provide five copies of system documentation, user manuals, and training materials with the delivery of system.	*One copy at no charge. Pay additional for other copies.*
4. No-cost documentation updates.	*One copy, no charge.*

3.13 Optional Training

	Self-study books available at extra charge.

3.14 Maintenance Requirements

1. Provide four-hour response to requests for service during prime shift (i.e., maximum time between request and delivery of service).	*Yes, four-hour response in 25-mile radius.*
2. Specify response time for emergency requests and costs.	*Time and materials hourly rate if after 5 p.m. and weekends.*

3.15 Optional Maintenance

	Dial-in service to central maintenance facility available for $50/month.

3.16 Required System Features

1. Supplies: specify required supplies by type, volume, and cost.	*Supplies worth $600–$1,000 set up free, includes paper, ribbons, diskettes.*
2. System compatibility: all bid components must be compatible and interchangeable.	
3. Systems and components must be standard products currently in production systems.	
4. Availability: equipment should be installed within 60 days of signing contract.	*Within two weeks.*
5. Expandability: specify the number of CRTs, printers, and other peripherals the CPU can support efficiently.	*Depends on # of CRTs plus # of printers.*
6. Backup: describe standard and other backup features available or recommended. Indicate cost.	*Customer may use vendor's data center during second shift as backup.*
7. Environment: describe environmental conditions required for optimum CPU, terminal, and printer functioning.	*Temperature must not exceed 85 degrees F, dedicated electrical line required for CPU.*

3.17 Optional System Services

	Systems weigh less than 100 pounds and can be easily moved.

3.18 Required Programming Support

1. Number of application support personnel within a 40-mile radius.	*Six full time for Southern California.*
2. Number of application support personnel per installed system.	*Enough to comfortably handle all support calls.*
3. Nature and duration of no-cost application support available during equipment installation period.	*Included in the 40 hours supplied in training. Unlimited phone support.*
4. Nature and duration of no-cost on-going application support.	*On-going support at our offices or by phone unlimited.*
5. Frequency of scheduled application reviews.	*None established, but can be arranged.*

3.19 Optional Programming Support

3.20 Required Documentation Support

1. Documentation manuals by title at no cost.	*Word Processing User Manual* *Word Processing Training Manual* *System II Utility Manual* *System Installation Manual* *Accounting User Manual*
2. Documentation for management and accounting systems.	*Yes, all programs.*

3.21 Optional Documentation Support

3.22 Optional Miscellaneous Features

1. Vendors should indicate availability of report customizing.	*Custom programming is available at $50/hour.*

3.23 Accounting Systems Requirements

3.23.1 Timekeeping

1. Principal should have to fill out a simple time log or use biling device on telephone.	*Principal or secretary retains time log; see ch. 5 of Timekeeping booklet.*
2. System should automatically produce monthly billings.	*System automatically generates monthly bills.*
3. Should show by client how much is to be billed, how much work in progress is unbilled, and how long it is unbilled.	*Yes, all are available except work in progress.*
4. Variable statement formats: descriptive statements with one total fee; descriptive statement with itemized fees.	*Only one form of statement is available.*

3.23.2 Accounting

1. Creates accounting reports from initial input documents (time, receipt, and disbursement logs).	*Reports are available; see Accounting Systems booklet for details.*
2. Provide report on financial status of ABC Law Firm, as well as cash transaction reports.	*Cash management is available and described in Financial Systems booklet, pg. 150.*
3. Provide a trust accounting feature.	*Not available.*
4. Process payrolls.	*Customer must select which payroll system will be used.*

3.23.3 Management System Requirements

1. General ledger and profit/loss.	*Available at $50 per hour programming rate.*
2. Cost accounting.	*Yes, see pg. 52 of Timekeeping booklet.*
3. Inventory control.	*Not available until next month.*
4. Diskette library management.	*Not available.*
5. Sales management.	*Not available.*
6. Archival file storage and tracking.	*Available, see pg. 103 of Office Systems booklet.*
7. Management forms.	*Available through word processing software at no additional cost.*

3.23.4 Optional Packaged Reports

1. Other services the vendor wishes to present may be placed under this section.

4. VENDOR CAPABILITIES

In this section, the bidder should demonstrate specific capability to fulfill the requirements according to the following criteria:

4.1 Corporate Financial Report	
1. Supply current corporate annual financial report.	*Financial report not available.*

4.2 Availability of Staff	
1. Supply locations and number of employees by title who will service this account.	*Ralph Smith, Senior Programmer Analyst.* *Ed Jones, Engineering Specialist.*
2. Supply résumé of personal sufficiently qualified to execute the work described in this RFP.	*Résumés not available.*

4.3 References

| 1. Supply at least three references of previous or current accounts where similar systems are installed. Provide reference contact point and telephone number. | *1. Harry Anderson, Acme Corp. (312) 555-2100.*
2. Ruth Florence, Star Enterprises (416) 555-5431. |

REQUIRED
HARDWARE, SOFTWARE, AND SUPPORT PRICE SCHEDULE

Attachment 1

Qty.	Model	Description	Price Purchase	1-yr/Term Monthly Rental	3-yr/Term Monthly Rental	1-yr/Term Monthly Maint.	3-yr/Term Monthly Maint.
1	BD100	128K Memory CPU—2 floppy drives—standard CRT	$10,710.00	$528.30	$456.30	Included	
1	BD123	Letter-Quality, 40-character per second printer	3,600.00	173.70	148.50	Included	
1	BD125	24-megabyte hard-disk drive	6,948.00	377.10	329.40	Included	
1	BD300	Word processing software (one-time fee)	540.00	—	—	—	
1	OSP-1	Business system program (one-time fee)	4,000.00	—	—	—	
SUBTOTAL			25,798.00*	1,079.10	934.20		
TAXES			1,547.88	64.75	56.05		
INSTALLATION COSTS			250.00				
EST. TRANSPORTATION COSTS			300.00				
DISCOUNTS							
GRAND TOTAL			$27,895.88	$1,143.85	$990.25		

ALL PRICES MUST BE SHOWN ON THIS SCHEDULE WITHOUT EXCEPTION
*Includes $4,540 one-time costs.

Qty.	Model	Description	Price Purchase	1-yr/Term Monthly Rental	3-yr/Term Monthly Rental	1-yr/Term Monthly Maint.	3-yr/Term Monthly Maint.
1	OCR	Optical character reader	$12,150.00	Purchase	Only		
1	LP	High-speed line printer	3,096.00	$153.00	$133.20	Included	
1	AC	Acoustic cover	346.50	Purchase	Only		
1	SSF	Single sheet feeder	166.50	Purchase	Only		
SUBTOTAL			$15,759.00				
TAXES			945.54				
INSTALLATION COSTS			56.00				
EST. TRANSPORTATION COSTS			63.00				
DISCOUNTS							
GRAND TOTAL			$16,823.54				

ALL PRICES MUST BE SHOWN ON THIS SCHEDULE WITHOUT EXCEPTION

APPENDIX C: EVALUATION FORM

EVALUATOR'S FORM
(Adapted from RFP Appendix B)

3.4 REQUIRED WORD PROCESSING SOFTWARE FEATURES

3.4.1 Text Input Features	MAX. PTS.	VENDOR A	B	C	EVALUATOR'S COMMENTS
1. Auto page numbering.					
2. Auto pagination.					
3. Auto word wraparound.					
4. Auto centering.					
5. Auto decimal tab.					
6. Table of contents/menu.					
7. Auto footnote.					
3.4.2 Text Edit and Merge					
1. Able to edit 400-page documents.					
2. Paragraph and page block move and block copy within a document and to another document.					
3. Global search and replace.					
4. Column move/delete.					
5. Document assembly/merge that allows manual and automated combining of prerecorded text with keyboard text to form new document.					
3.4.3 Required Miscellaneous Software Features					
1. Able to store multiple formats and space from field to field with a single action (keystroke).					
2. Able to search in three seconds or less from menu to any document, via automatic file/document select.					

APPENDIX D: NEGOTIATING MEMORANDUM

The deficiencies listed here have been drawn from Vendor A's proposal (Appendix B) assuming that Vendor A has been ranked number one in the evaluation process. These points are merely illustrative of the types to be discussed in a negotiation.

Buyer wants:

Vendor responds:

Able to search in three seconds or less from menu to any document, via automatic file/document select.

Response time depends on unique factors.

Comment: *Unacceptable response. Try to pin down response time to three seconds; use test and acceptance to verify.*

Revision, status, and document production reporting.

Yes, optional feature.

Comment: *Unacceptable response. Obtain sample report to verify what data are reported.*

Ability to save files/documents for backup purposes.

Yes.

Comment: Unacceptable response. Have feature demonstrated and time backup operation.

Upgrade to higher capability word processing systems.

We upgrade the software, not the hardware.

Comment: *Answer does not make sense. Try and obtain software updates at no additional cost.*

Automated mail box.

Yes, software available in one year.

Comment: *Ask if you can test software in exchange for obtaining software at no additional cost.*

Provide 80 hours of training.

Forty hours total.

Comment: *Negotiate 40 additional hours of training at vendor's site; vendor may be more willing.*

System compatibility.

No answer.

Comment: *Unacceptable response. Demand additional material to ensure all systems are upward compatible; this is important (stretch the issue).*

Current production units.

No answer.

Comment: *Unacceptable response. Double check references to ensure that equipment in use at references is identical to equipment being bid. Get additional penalties if equipment bid is brand new.*

Application support during installation.   **Included in 40 hours supplied in training.**

Comment: *Unacceptable response. You need at least 20 hours of application support so that your people will understand how the computer programming works (stand pat on 20 hours).*

Report customizing.   **$50 per hour.**

Comment: *Too expensive; would cost you a lot of money. Ensure that all computer reports will at least have firm name in title; this should be at no additional cost.*

Annual financial report.   **Not available.**

Comment: *See if vendor can bring financial report to negotiation session.*

Provide five copies of system documentation.   **One copy at no charge.**

Comment: *Negotiate right to reproduce the publications for internal use only.*

APPENDIX E:
SAMPLE
RENTAL AGREEMENT

SAMPLE RENTAL AGREEMENT

1. ACCEPTANCE

This Agreement will be accepted by VENDOR A upon 1) Customer's credit report being approved and 2) the lack of any mathematical error from VENDOR A's published price list.

2. TERMS OF RENTAL

This Agreement shall become effective from the acceptance date at VENDOR A's office and shall be for a minimum rental period of 12 months and shall remain in effect until all the Equipment has been discontinued from rental. Said Equipment may be discontinued at the end of the period set forth hereof by either party provided notice is sent in writing to the other thirty (30) days in advance. The Agreement will automatically renew, if not discontinued, for successive 12-month periods subject to the then current price lists, terms and conditions, and such successive rental periods may be terminated upon thirty (30) days written notice by either party to the other, given prior to the end of any successive period.

3. CHARGES

*1) On the date that the unit of equipment is installed ready for use the rental charges for each unit of equipment will commence, which is referred to as the Ready for Use date.

*2) Payments for rent shall be due and payable monthly, in advance, on the Ready for Use date and monthly thereafter. Fractions of months will be based upon the monthly rental being multiplied by twelve (12) months and then divided by 365 days. Any payments held on deposit will be applied to the rental period after the notice of termination of the rental.

*3) The Monthly Charge includes the use of the Equipment during one shift only. An extra rental charge shall be made at a rate of 50% of the Monthly Charge when the Equipment is used more than the one shift.

*4) Taxes, however, designated, levied or based thereon or on this Agreement or the Equipment or its use, including state and local privilege or excise taxes based on gross revenue, personal property taxes, if any, and any taxes or amounts in lieu of any aforesaid obligation paid or payable by VENDOR A shall be added to the monthly charge paid by the Customer.

*5) Customer agrees that VENDOR A shall have the right to charge and the Customer will pay a late fee of 1.5% per month if the Customer fails to pay any charges when due and payable. Late charges shall not be in excess of the maximums permitted by law on the unpaid amount.

4. TRANSPORTATION

CUSTOMER WILL PAY ALL TRANSPORTATION CHARGES FOR MOVING THE EQUIPMENT BOTH TO AND FROM CUSTOMER'S LOCATION. Crating and uncrating costs will be paid by the Customer, except if it is performed at the VENDOR A factory.

5. ALTERATIONS AND ATTACHMENTS

Written consent of VENDOR A is required prior to making alterations in, attachments to or modifications of the Equipment or associated systems software provided by VENDOR A.

6. MAINTENANCE

*1) While the equipment is on rent, VENDOR A will provide normal maintenance service on the Equipment. Adjustment and repairs, cleaning and parts replacement will be included.

*2) To provide the service, VENDOR A will be given full and free access to the Equipment during normal business hours.

*3) If service is requested outside of VENDOR A's normal business hours, such service if available will be charged at the then current time and materials rate.

*4) If the Customer has a malfunction for

other than normal use or because of parts, attachments or devices not provided by VENDOR A, Customer will be charged at the then current time and materials rate.

*5) Service does not include: supplying or replacing platens, expendable supply items (magnetic media, type elements, ribbons, etc.) or accessories; making changes to the specifications requested by the Customer, painting or refinishing the Equipment or providing materials for that purpose; services associated with the relocation of the Equipment; or attaching or removing accessories, attachments or other foreign devices.

*6) A surcharge will be added for service or equipment located beyond a 50-mile radius from VENDOR A's service facility.

*7) VENDOR A will not be obliged to provide maintenance in the case of strikes, fire, flood and causes beyond its control.

*8) For equipment located in certain remote locations, VENDOR A may not provide service at the Customer's location. Customer, under these circumstances, will be required to provide two-way transportation of the Equipment to the nearest service center.

7. SUPPLIES

The rental charges do not cover ribbons, paper, magnetic media and other supplies used by the Customer to operate the Equipment. VENDOR A will provide these supplies for a separate charge or they may be obtained from any other supplier providing the supplies must satisfy VENDOR A's specifications for proper use of the Equipment.

8. RISK OF LOSS AND DAMAGE

*1) VENDOR A will relieve Customer of responsibility for risk of loss or damage to any unit of Equipment *2) except if loss is caused by nuclear reaction, nuclear radiation, radioactive contamination *3) negligent or willful misconduct of the Customer or his agents or employees, or use of the Equipment *4) other than in accordance with normal operations and the

operating instructions and manuals provided by VENDOR A.

9. EQUIPMENT

Newly manufactured Equipment or remanufactured after previous use will be supplied by VENDOR A. Newly manufactured and remanufactured equipment may contain components which have been remanufactured; however, all Equipment supplied will conform completely to the specifications for the operation of the Equipment and will also be covered by the warranty provisions set forth in Paragraph 10.

10. WARRANTY

*1) VENDOR A warrants that the Equipment, when installed, will be in normal operating order and all necessary Equipment adjustments, repairs and parts replacements will be made by VENDOR A without additional charge to maintain the Equipment in this condition, *2) provided Customer's account is current. All equipment provided by VENDOR A is subject to these warranties. *3) IN THE EVENT OF A BREACH OF ANY WARRANTY BY VENDOR A, CUSTOMER'S EXCLUSIVE REMEDY WILL BE THAT VENDOR A WILL MAKE ANY EQUIPMENT ADJUSTMENTS, REPAIRS OR PARTS REPLACEMENTS TO ANY EQUIPMENT WHEN IT DETERMINES THAT THE EQUIPMENT DOES NOT CONFORM TO THESE WARRANTIES. *4) IN NO EVENT WILL VENDOR A HAVE ANY OBLIGATIONS OR LIABILITY FOR DAMAGES, INCLUDING BUT NOT LIMITED TO CONSEQUENTIAL OR INCIDENTAL DAMAGES, ARISING OUT OF OR IN CONNECTION WITH THE USE OR PERFORMANCE OF EQUIPMENT. *5) NO OTHER WARRANTIES, EXPRESS OR IMPLIED, INCLUDING THE IMPLIED WARRANTIES OF MERCHANTABILITY AND *6) FITNESS FOR A PARTICULAR PURPOSE WILL APPLY TO THE EQUIPMENT.

11. DEFAULT

*1) Default by the Customer, *2) in addition to other remedies, *3) will allow VENDOR A to repossess the Equipment without notice, in which case *4) the Customer will pay all reasonable costs and expenses for collection and repossession which will include attorney's fees associated therewith.

*5) In the event that Customer assigns this Agreement for the benefit of creditors, or a voluntary or involuntary petition is filed by or against Customer under any law having its purpose the adjudication of the Customer a bankrupt, or the reorganization of Customer, this Agreement will terminate.

12. OTHER PROVISIONS

*1) This Agreement supersedes all previous agreements with respect to the rental Equipment. *2) Customer agrees not to remove the Equipment from the installed location without prior written consent. *3) Customer may not assign the Assignment, nor transfer to another location without prior written consent. *4) VENDOR A may assign its interest in the Equipment and *5) Customer upon request will furnish the assignee with written acknowledgment that this Agreement is in full force and effect, and that Customer is not entitled to any counterclaim or set-off, and that customer will not assert any counterclaim or right of set-off against the assignee. *6) If a covenant or condition is to be performed by VENDOR A, Customer agrees that no such assignee shall be obligated for the covenant or condition and that VENDOR A shall remain solely liable. *7) Customer shall not obtain any ownership rights except by purchase. *8) After termination of rental of the Agreement, any unit of equipment may be removed.

*9) The laws of the State of Vendor shall govern this Agreement and *10) constitutes the entire contract between the parties.

*11) This agreement shall govern over any order provided by the Customer.

*12) Any investment tax credits or other tax provision relating to the procurement and use of any time of Equipment shall pass to VENDOR A and VENDOR A shall not treat Customer as the owner of the Equipment.

APPENDIX F: STATUS REPORT

TO: Customer Project Manager
FROM: Vendor Project Manager
SUBJECT: Biweekly Status Report

I. PROGRESS TOWARD MILESTONE

Task	Projected Date	Status
Secretarial training on word processor	5/1–5/10	**Completed**
Installation of longer cable for master terminal		**Completed**
Data entry of boilerplate forms	5/3–6/15	**One-half completed as per schedule**
Training of principals on billing system	5/10–5/15	**One week delay due to sickness of instructor**
Resolve problem with power supply	5/10	**Unresolved due to fluctuation of power in building**
All equipment installed	5/15	**Still waiting for replacement for printer damaged in delivery; new date for replacement is 6/1**
Resolve programming problem with billing program	4/15–5/10	**Have expert from headquarters still working on problem**
Documentation delivery	6/1	**Order was placed on time but lost in mail; reorder took place 5/15**

II. PROGRESS AGAINST BUDGETED DOLLARS

A. Estimated expenditures for services to date $410.00
   Current expenditures of services to date $300.00 (−110.00)
B. Estimated expenditures for supplies to date $200.00
   Current expenditures for supplies to date $300.00 (+100.00)

III. PROBLEMS ENCOUNTERED

A. Tractor piece for printer missing.
B. One diskette drive requires calibration.
C. WP software gets hung in accounting program when year-end totals are requested.
D. One box of diskettes was left out in rain on shipping dock and must be replaced.
E. Cable to main power line is defective.

A.M. Vendor
I.M. Vendor

APPENDIX G: COURSE OUTLINE FOR INSTRUCTORS

EL CAMINO COLLEGE

I. COURSE DESCRIPTION
Complete Title: DP27—How to Buy a Computer or Word Processor
Prerequisite: None

Catalog Description: A comprehensive overview of all aspects of the selection and procurement of computers or word processors. Methods to analyze and to measure requirements are studied. Methods to permit vendors to bid their best products and prices are discussed as well as how to evaluate competing products. Form contracts are analyzed in lay terms.

II. COURSE OUTLINE PEPARED BY: Brian C. Donohue, J.D., M.B.A., Attorney and former Data Processing Contracts Manager.

III. COURSE OBJECTIVES:
The course objective is to provide students with "how to" knowledge to select and contract for computers or word processors. Additionally, legal rights and obligations are analyzed. Students participate in actual vendor selection.

CHAPTER	OBJECTIVE	
2	1.	The student will be able to explain the growth of the computer and word processing industry and the associated growth in technology.
2	2.	The student will be made aware of the problems associated with automation in terms of employee resistance, psychological impact, and "future shock."
2	3.	The student will be provided examples of successes and failures in the industry and some key "tips" for success and also common "mistakes" made in the procurement of these systems.
1	4.	The student will be able to explain a generalized procedure to follow in procurement: Requirement Study, Request For Proposal (RFP), Evaluations, Negotiations, and Contracting.
3	5.	The student will learn how to measure the current work flow in an office or business.
3	6.	The student will learn the proper use of consultants.
4	7.	The student will learn how to prepare a Request for Proposal document.

4	8.	The student will learn the advantages and disadvantages of an RFP versus a Request for Quotation.
4	9.	The student will learn the purposes and objectives of a Bidder's Conference.
4	10.	The student will analyze in detail a Model Office Automation RFP with special emphasis placed on word processing capabilities.
5	11.	The student will learn the practices involved with salespeople and marketing organizations to include the effect of commissions, quote, and corporate resources.
4	12.	The student will experience three (3) vendor demonstrations in the classroom with the use of a minicomputer and CRT terminal.
6	13.	The student will learn and experience how to evaluate the computer systems demonstrated in class.
6	14.	The student will learn the relative importance of the technical discussion, vendor capabilities, cost, and vendor support.
6	15.	The student will learn a scoring system, the use of an evaluation committee, and how to make a selection of the best-qualified vendor.
7	16.	The student will learn negotiations strategy, preparation of a negotiation memorandum, and the roles of the respective players in a negotiation.
8	17.	The student will learn how to interpret vendor's preprinted contracts and how to negotiate contract clauses.
8	18.	The student will learn how to ensure vendor compliance to the contract.
9	19.	The student will learn the legal theories and cases regarding patents, copyrights, trade secret law, computer crime, and privacy.

IV. TEST AND EVALUATION

Distribution of Final Grade

Term project notebook	30%
Written report of evaluation of vendors	30%
Class participation and homework	10%
Final exam or written analysis of vendor's contract	30%

V. OUTLINE OF SUBJECT MATTER

Week	Topic	Chapters Studied	Corresponding Objective
1	The Computer Age is upon Us People and Machines Overview of Procedures	1,2	1–4
2	Measuring Current Work Flow Use of Consultants Introduction to Case Study	3	5–6
3	Preparing Requirements Use of a Request for Proposal Request for Quotation Personal Computers	4	7–10
4	Salespeople—The Good, Bad, Ugly Mistakes Frequently Made Effect of Commissions, Quota, and Corporation	5	11
5	Analysis of Office Automation RFP	4	11
6	Analysis of Word Processing Requirements	4	11
7–9	Three Vendor Demonstrations in class using a minicomputer for use in business or office environment. Demonstrations are based on the RFP the students studied during previous classes.	4	12
10	Evaluation of Vendors Evaluation Document Evaluation Participants	6	13–15
11	Negotiations Strategy Negotiations Memorandum Negotiations Techniques Roles of Respective Players	7	16
12	Contract Clause Review Negotiating Contract Clauses Obtaining Vendor Compliance	8	17–18
13–15	Legal Issues Analyzed Patents, Copyrights, Trade Secrets, Computer Crime, Taxes, Privacy	9	19

VI. TEXT

How To Buy An Office Computer Or Word Processor
Brian C. Donohue
Prentice-Hall, 1983

VII. TERM PROJECT

There are three term projects:

1. Notebook of current periodicals relating to course material. Student must prepare a three-fourths page summary of article.
2. Preparation of written evaluation document that analyzes the products presented by the three vendors during the course.
3. Preparation of typed analysis of legal contract available from commercial vendors.

GLOSSARY

BUZZWORDS AND TECHNICAL TERMS

Address. A group of digits or characters that tells a computer where certain information is stored.

Algorithm. A set of step-by-step instructions for completing a given routine. A cook's recipe is roughly analogous. Computer programs are made up of algorithms.

Alphanumeric. Used to describe a set of characters containing single digit numbers and the letters of the alphabet, along with punctuation marks and symbols.

Analog. * The first computers were analog devices. They measure rather than count. They are used today mostly to measure physical variables, like voltages, pressures, and temperatures, and to measure production line operations. A household thermostat is a simple form of analog computer.

ANSI. * (American National Standard Institute). An agency concerned with setting up industrywide standards.

Applications Programs. * Designed to do specific jobs, like general ledger or inventory record keeping. Usually written by the user

*All starred definitions copyright © 1979, Datapoint Corporation. Reprinted by permission.

or computer consultant, although some widely used programs are available for purchase.

Architecture. * The way a computer or a computer system is put together. It can refer to the arrangement of components inside the cabinet or to the way a system is hooked up.

ASCII. * (American Standard Code for Information Interchange; often pronounced "Asky"). One of a number of industry standard computer codes for converting alphanumerics and punctuation into binary numbers.

Assembly Language. A programming language supplied by the computer manufacturer to enable programmers to write machine-oriented programs capable of performing binary level operations. Each manufacturer has a different assembler that works with that manufacturer's machines. They are not generally used to write business programs. (See *High Level Language.*)

Asynchronous. * A data transmission term meaning that a character must have a signal at the beginning and the end to tell the computer when to start and stop. Messages are not time limited. Each character thus becomes a complete message. Simple hardware like teletypes communicate this way.

Audit Trail. * A record detailing all of the activity that has taken place in an applications program. It is usually stored on a disk and can be used to recreate data in the event that files are lost due to machine failure or operator error.

Automated Office. * A business office where most standard office functions are carried out electronically by computers, word processing machines, magnetic file storage devices, automatic call distributors, electronic mail devices, and so on. Frequently referred to as the "Office of the Future," since some of the necessary electronic devices are yet to be put on the market. Be careful here; integration is the big problem. All the devices must be compatible in order to work together.

Backup. Copies of data files that can become useful for reconstructing lost data.

BASIC. * (Beginners All-purpose Symbolic Instruction Code). An easy-to-use, high level language that works best in solving equations, although it is often used in business data processing.

Batch Processing. * When information is saved up and put into the computer for processing all at one time. Once, it was usually done with punched cards, but batch-type jobs can be done with almost any kind of data input terminal today. Preparing W-2 forms for employees once a year is an ideal batch processing job. Order and inventory control are not. (See *Interactive.*)

*Baud.** A measure of speed in data transmission; 500 baud means 500 bits of data per second can be transmitted (500 can be equated roughly to 50 characters per second).

Belt Printer. A rugged, medium-speed printer that uses a rotating belt to transfer characters to paper.

Bidirectional. Refers to the ability to communicate in both sending and receiving directions. Also, in reference to a printer, indicates that it can print both from left to right and right to left.

*Binary.** The base-two number system digital computers use. It uses only 1's and 0's to form all numbers and letters.

Bit. A single digit in binary math. It can be either a 1 or a 0.

*BPI.** (bits per inch). The density with which digital data can be packed onto magnetic tape or other recording devices.

*Buffer.** A part of a computer's memory where data can be stored temporarily until the computer is ready to do something with it. Some peripherals also have buffers.

*Business Computer Systems.** Nearly every modern business computer is made up of the same components. They often vary in size and speed, and also in some of the details of their operation, but the similarities are more significant than the differences.

*Byte.** Eight bits (see *Data Storage* in Components sections of Glossary).

Canned Programs. Commonly used in most businesses; available for purchase from manufacturers or other users of the same type of system.

Cassette. See *Data Storage.*

*CPU (central processing unit).** Technically, the logic and arithmetic circuitry inside a computer; the place where data actually gets processed. In jargon, sometimes used to describe a big computer. The term originated when manufacturers started incorporating processing capabilities into peripherals like printers so they would not slow down the central computer. CPU differentiates between the computer and these peripheral devices.

*Character.** A single digit, letter, or symbol that a computer can recognize. Ordinarily represented in a one-byte combination of 1's and 0's.

Character Printer. A printer that prints one character at a time.

*Chip.** A tiny bit of silicon, the size of a fingernail or smaller, some containing as much electronic circuitry as some room-sized computers of 20 years ago. Chips make microcomputers possible. Also refers to the integrated circuit.

*COBOL.** (COmmon Business Oriented Language). A programming language that simplifies business data processing programs. Its instructions are very similar to ordinary English.

Code.* Jargon for a computer program. The symbols and characters that mean something to a computer. Programs are written in code.

Command. An instruction in code that tells the computer what to do next.

Compatibility.* The ability of a computer from one manufacturer to work with different models from the same manufacturer or with computers from other manufacturers. Also, a computer's ability to work with other devices such as printers, data storage units, and such.

Compiler.* A computer program that translates instructions written in a specific high level programming language into machine language the computer can understand. If the program is in COBOL, you would need a COBOL compiler. (See *High Level Language.*)

Configuration.* The design or layout of a particular computer or dispersed data processing system with all its peripherals.

CPS (characters per second). One way to express the speed of printers, or anything that produces text.

CRT (cathode ray tube).* CRTs are the TV screens that sit on the typewriters, and their capabilities, particularly with graphics, are great. The screen itself can instantaneously and silently generate hundreds of characters, usually on a display field of 24 lines by 80 characters. There are two types of CRT display terminals. The lower cost units can only display alphanumeric information (numbers or letters). The more sophisticated type can project graphs, charts, and designs. The display can be altered, corrected, and modified as fast as the operator can work and, with an attached printer (see below), the output can be printed right away.

Daisy Wheel.* A wheel with characters around the rim used on some types of printers to transfer characters to paper. They provide the closest to typewriter-quality text of all the mechanical printing methods.

Database. All the information stored in a computer system.

Data Storage.* Devices that store information outside the computer come in a wide variety of styles, including disks, diskettes, cassettes, and reel-to-reel magnetic tape. Each style has advantages and disadvantages, although all store information magnetically in about the same way that a tape recorder stores sound.

Disks provide a lot of storage in a relatively small space. *Diskettes,* sometimes called "floppy (because they are flexible) disks," are a smaller, less expensive version of the disk. The primary advantage of disk storage devices is in their ability to retrieve information as it is needed, no matter where it happens to be stored. This "random access" capability allows the disk to go directly to the one-hundredth item recorded without first reading the 99 items that precede it. The speed of data retrieval that results from random access is the key virtue of disks.

Cassettes and reel-to-reel magnetic tape storage devices provide only sequential access, meaning that the first 99 items must be read before the one-hundreth can be retrieved. Reel-to-reel devices are generally used to store massive amounts of data that are not needed on a day-to-day basis; a company's archives, for example. Cassette tape devices are normally associated with the transfer of small amounts of data between systems, such as daily accounting transactions from a remote office being sent to the home office for further processing.

The major factor in evaluating data storage is capacity, which is expressed in bytes or characters stored (for example, a 120-megabyte disk drive can store 120,000,000 characters of information). Also important is how much of the storage capacity is fixed in place; the greater flexibility afforded by a unit that employs removable disks is nearly always worth the slight increase in price.

Digital.* The type of computer that uses the binary number system. Nearly all modern computers used in business are of this type.

Disks, Diskettes. (See Data Storage)

Distributed Data Processing.* A computer system made up a number of small, inexpensive computers. Each has its own information storage devices and other peripherals so that some work can be performed independently of other computers in the network. Yet all the computers can provide information to some central point. If the computers are geographically dispersed, they are linked by telecommunications. A network might also be set up to disperse data processing functions throughout a large office. Each department would have its own small system. The network approach has proven to be a much more convenient, economical approach than having one big, centralized computer.

Dot Matrix.* A method used in some printers to transfer images to paper. The characters are made up of small dots, like the lights on an electric scoreboard.

Downtime. Jargon for any time during which computer equipment is not working.

Drive. Generally refers to the mechanical device that reads and writes on magnetic media (such as disk drive).

Emulator. A program that allows a computer from one manufacturer to communicate with a computer from a different manufacturer.

Field. An item of data within a record.

*File.** A collection of information or records relating to the same subject stored in a specific place in a computer system's disk or tape storage. Just like those used by secretaries, but without the folders and usually easier to find.

*Firmware.** Instructions to the system stored in a special, nonerasable memory. Usually offers a number of choices of instructions that an operator can pick from.

*Floppy Disk.** See *Data Storage.*

*FORTRAN** (*FORmula TRANslation*). A programming language used mostly for complicated mathematical problems in science and engineering.

Hardcopy. Printed output.

Hardware. The physical components of a computer system, including all its mechanical, electronic, electrical, and magnetic parts.

Hard-Wired. A physically wired connection between two computers or other devices.

High Level Language. Programming language close to being English. The closer to English, the higher the level. Higher level languages make programming easier. Languages such as COBOL, FORTRAN, PASCAL, BASIC, and others are high level.

Host Computer. In some systems, a number of terminals or smaller computers are connected to a large computer upon which they depend to do most of the work. The large computer is the host. Some people call such a system a network, although it is really dependent on one big computer. (See *Network.*)

*Interactive.** A computer or program that is able to carry on a textual conversation with its operator. The computer prompts the operator, helping him or her through a routine, checks the information it receives for accuracy, and notifies the operator when a mistake is made. (See *Batch processing.*)

*Interface.** The place where two devices in a computer system meet and connect, or a device that permits other devices to be linked.

*Interpreter.** A program that translates high level languages into something the computer can understand. (See *Compiler, High Level Language*)

I/O (*input/output interfaces*). Used by the computer to get information; the computer's sensory and communications organs.

K (*kilo*). This is 1,000 to just about everyone *except* computer people; to them it is 1,024 or 2^{10}. Heard most often in defining storage capacity; 48K is 48,000 bytes.

*Keyboard.** The typewriter-style device frequently associated with a CRT (see Components section of Glossary) that allows entry of information into the computer.

Language. The numbers, characters, punctuation, and symbols used to write instructions for a computer.

*Line Printer.** A printer that prints a full line at a time. Gives very high speeds, but the printing quality is generally not as good as that of character printers.

LPM (lines per minute). Another way to express how fast a printer prints.

*Machine Language.** The lowest level computer language and the most precise. It is much too cumbersome for writing programs, so must have a compiler or interpreter (see above) to translate high level programs into machine language. Every manufacturer has a different one.

*Mainframe.** An extremely large capacity, complex computer system, based on one central processor.

MB (megabytes). A million bytes, or, to computer people, 1,024,000.

Memory. The memory is the place where the processor (see below) temporarily stores the computer program (see below) that is telling it what to do, along with the data that are to be processed. Memory is any material capable of assuming and remaining in one of two states of magnetization. In simple terms, memory is a large group of little switches that can be turned on and off. Each switch is a bit that the processor reads; all information in the computer is represented by groups of switches turned on and off in a certain arrangement.

There are many different types of memory, each with particular advantages and disadvantages. The important factor is the size of the memory, expressed in the number of characters that its switches can represent. The more switches, the more characters the memory can hold, and the larger the programs the processor can execute. Memory size is stated in characters (or bytes); for example, a 48K-byte machine can hold approximately 48,000 characters.

The memory of a computer is organized into two different parts: system memory and user memory. System memory is the organizational instructions the computer must have in order to do anything. This is known as overhead, since it contributes nothing to the work at hand. User memory is where the actual work takes place (where the program is held). This is part of memory that should most concern you, since it is a direct indication of how productive the system can be.

Microcomputer or Minicomputer. * Relatively small, inexpensive computer designed to perform business data processing tasks. They can do almost anything a mainframe computer can do. The dividing line between micro or minicomputers and mainframes gets hazier every day. The biggest differences are physical size and cost.

Microprocessor. * A complete CPU (see above) usually with its processing circuitry on a single chip.

MIPS (millions of instructions per second). * A measure of how fast a computer can work that takes a variety of physical factors into account.

MODEM (MOdulator-DEModulator). * A telecommunications device that makes it possible for a computer to send digital information over telephone lines.

MOS (Metal Oxide Semiconductor). * A recent technological development in manufacturing integrated circuits.

Nanosecond. One-billionth of a second; you can't blink that fast. Computers typically work at speeds measured in nanoseconds.

Network. * A group of computers interconnected by telephone or telegraph lines for communications.

Object Program. A program in machine language that is generated by an assembler or compiler.

OEM (Original Equipment Manufacturer). * Anyone who manufactures hardware used in data processing, from the small company with only a couple of products, to the full-line, full-service manufacturer, and who sells it primarily for resale.

Off-Line. * Data processing that is not done by a computer, such as the clerical work required to prepare information for processing. Can also mean the computer or some other part of the system is out of order and not working, or simply not connected to the system.

On-Line. * Any data processing work under the direct control of the computer. Can also mean a component of the system is in operation.

Operating System. * The program that is responsible for operating all other programs within the computer. It allocates computer resources, supports data transfers, and generally keeps track of all activity within the computer. Sometimes it is a DOS—Disk Operating System.

Overhead. * The amount of a computer's memory required to organize the operation of a computer system. It is important because the more overhead required, the less memory there is left in the computer to execute applications programs.

*Peripheral.** There are a great many parts of a computer system that fall under the general heading of peripherals, signifying that they are not a part of the computer itself. Included are punched card readers, interface devices that permit a computer to communicate over telephone lines, and many others.

*Plug Compatible.** Two devices that can be made to work together simply by plugging one into the other. No special interface devices are needed.

Port. The place where a peripheral device connects to the computer, for example, printer port.

*Printer.** The output from a computer system's printer is probably the closest most people will come to a computer. Printers come in a great variety, all differing in the quality of their printing and the speed with which the printing is produced. A printer's speed is expressed in characters per second (CPS) or lines per minute (LPM), usually depending on the printing method.

Character printers use the direct impact of a fully formed character to provide printed copy. Character printers deliver the best quality mainly because they use the same method of printing as does an electrical typewriter. This does have disadvantages, however; a character printer is the slowest of all printers and, due to its many mechanical components, is not the most reliable.

Matrix printers form characters made up of small dots, in much the same way as an electric scoreboard. They are generally less expensive than other types of printers and are fairly fast, although the quality of their output is usually lower. Belt printers, also known as line printers, use a rotating belt with fully formed characters on it to print a whole line at a time. They are extremely fast (into thousands of lines per minute) and provide good quality print, but they are also quite expensive.

There are so many mechanical components in any type of printer that they are normally far more susceptible to malfunction than any other part of a business computer system. Thus, when selecting a printer, reliability should be a big concern.

*Processor.** The processor is the heart of every business computer. This is the place in the system where the counting, computations, and comparisons involved in data processing actually go on. The processor or microprocessor does this work simply by being able to detect the presence or absence of an electrical charge at a specific location within its memory circuits. Each location that the computer can check represents a bit of information. These bits are tiny details. For example, finding a certain pattern of electrical charges at a certain location might represent a single digit of a number. Charges at adjacent locations might represent the other digits of the number. How many of these locations, or bits, a processor can manipulate at one time determines the speed at which the processor works. The basic number of bits is eight and is called a byte (most computers read bits in multiples of eight). A 32-bit machine (also known as a processor with a 32-bit architecture) is roughly four times as fast as an 8-bit machine, all other things being equal.

Another factor in evaluating the processor is the speed with which it can execute instructions, usually expressed in millions of instructions per second (MIPS). The reason for the large scale of this measure is that it takes thousands of instructions for the processor to perform the simplest task. The bottom line here is that when comparing processors, more MIPS mean that the system will be faster and, therefore, more productive.

Program.* Programs (or software) are instructions to the computer that are held in the computer's memory. They turn the switches on and off, and do so in a particular pattern. There are several different levels of programs. The first and most immediate level specifies the location and status of each individual switch in memory; this type of program is written in what is called machine language or assembler. Since it operates at such an immediate level, this type is the most precise and can accomplish its task in the shortest time. However, the cost of this precision is high in that it takes an extremely experienced programmer a fair amount of time to write and test such a program.

Using high level programming languages, programs are written in what closely resembles the English language, and then processed by another program called an interpreter or compiler. The compiler translates the Englishlike, high level program into a program written in machine language, which may then be executed. The final product is somewhat less precise than a program actually composed in machine language, but the effort saved in writing the program usually balances that.

There are two basic types of software: system software and applications software. System software is overhead and provides organizational information (it accomplishes no end work). It is composed of what is called the operating system along with some other programs. Applications software is made up of programs that complete specific business tasks, such as inventory control, payroll, general ledger, and word processing.

RAM (random access memory).* Items stored can be retrieved as needed regardless of their location in storage. In other words, the one-hundredth item can be retrieved without the computer having to read the first 99.

Record.* A collection of data items that are logically related. All records of a given type are referred to as a file.

Response Time.* The time that it takes for an action to be completed. Generally, the interval between executing a command or inquiry at a terminal and receiving the answer at the same terminal.

ROM (read only memory).* Nonerasable system instructions that are built into the computer. Usually used to tell the computer how to accomplish routine tasks.

RS232.* A standard plug that allows various peripheral devices such as terminals and printers to be plugged into the computer even if from different manufacturers.

Security. Methods used to prevent unauthorized access to part or all of the information in a database. An important consideration in systems where the database is shared by several users.

Semiconductor.* Any material whose electrical conductivity is somewhere between that of an insulator and that of a conductor, and whose conductivity varies with temperature. The hotter they are, the better conductors they are. Silicon is a semiconductor. They make up many of the electronic components in computers and are much more reliable than the vacuum tubes they replaced. Also referred to as "solid state" circuitry.

Sequential Access.* When information stored in a computer's memory must be retrieved in the order in which it is stored. (See RAM)

Simulator.* A program that simulates the operation of another computer. An easy way of tricking computers into being compatible. (See Emulator.)

Source Program.* The original form of a program usually in a high level language. It must be translated (for example, compiled) into machine language.

Stand Alone.* The ability of a computer to do its work independently of other computers.

Storage. Any device in a computer system capable of retaining information.

Support.* Engineering help provided by the manufacturer in fitting the system to the customer's requirements, getting it installed, and keeping it running. In jargon, it sometimes means service.

Synchronous.* In data transmission, a system where messages are sent from one device to another within a specified length of time.

Receiver and transmitter must be synchronized in order to communicate. Most efficient when large volumes of data must be transferred.

Systems House. * Usually describes an independent, third party firm that sells computer systems made up of hardware acquired from one or more manufacturers. Something like a distributor or independent manufacturer's representative in other industries.

Systems Software. * The package of programs that organizes the memory of a computer system. The most fundamental component is known as the operating system. Usually furnished by the manufacturer.

Telecommunications. Information sent and received over telephone lines.

Terminal. Any device used to put information into, or remove information from, a computer. A keyboard and screen (or printer) that provide a human interface.

Throughput. The amount of work that can be accomplished by a computer in a given amount of time.

Throughout Speed. The speed with which a computer converts input to output.

Time-Sharing. * When two or more users do work on the same computer at the same time. Most often thought of as systems where the users have only "dumb" terminals (no processing capability of their own) that communicate with a large, central computer.

Upgrade. * Substituting a larger computer for a smaller one to accommodate the growth of a business or its increasing needs for data processing. Not always an easy thing to do. (See *Compatibility.*)

Utility Program. * A system software program that helps programmers and operators perform specific types of common jobs. A program that sorts names and addresses is a common utility.

Vendor. * Anyone who sells anything to do with computers from the full-line manufacturer to the little businessperson who sells ribbons for the printer; in other words, suppliers.

Winchester. Refers to a special type of hard disk, usually not removable.

INDEX

Accounting, 29, 30, 41–42, 76–77, 174–79, 195
Accuracy, 24
Aggressive negotiations, 123–24
Airlines, 25–26
Apple II, 49
Application programs, 74–76, 194
Atari, 49
Attorneys, 90–91, 127–28, 130–31
Automobile revolution, 9

Backlogs, 31, 33, 35
Backup, 74
Bait and switch, 84
Banking, 23, 26
BASIC, 50
Bidder's conferences, 54
Billing, 39–41, 173
Bit, 50
Boiler plates, 130–31
Branch manager, 127
Buying:
    competitive, 16, 88–89
    consultants and, 44–45, 90–91
    contracts (see Contracts)
    financial leverage, 1, 16–17, 89–90
    installation, 18–19, 75, 194

negotiations (see Negotiations)
proposals, evaluation of, 3–4
Request for Proposal (see Request for Proposal RFP)
requirements study (see Requirements study)
typical mistakes, 11–15, 82–88
Byte, 50, 67

California Penal Code Section 502, 155–56
Cash Flow Application Adjustments, 43, 180
Cash processing, 42–43, 180
Chip, 50
Clerical support, 32
Client Directory, 39, 171
COBOL, 50
Commission plan, vendors, 91–92
Commodore, 49
Communications, 119–20
Competitive buying, 16, 88–89
Computer crime, 154–58
Computer Questionnaire, 38–44, 168–69
Computer Software Copyright Act of 1980, 150
Computer store owner, 128

Computer technology:
  growth of, 6–7
  human factor and, 8, 9–11
Consultants, use and selection of, 2, 44–45,
  90–91
Contracts, 5, 12, 17–18, 83, 129–45
  form, 130–31
  negotiating clauses, 130–31
  sample rental agreement, 131–39, 205–8
  status reports, 141–42, 209–10
Copyrights, 147, 149–51
Corporate attorney, 127–28
Cost, 6–8, 12–13, 85–86, 103
Cost sheets, 77–78, 198–99
Cover letter, 95, 188
CPS speed, 68, 192
Crime, computer, 154–58
CRT (cathode ray tube), 50, 66
Current workload, measurement of, 28
Customer service, 23, 25–26
Cut and paste, 35

Data storage, 50–51, 67–68, 192
Default, 137
Demonstrations, vendor, 15, 85, 107
Diamond v. Diehr (1981), 148–49
Diskettes, 67
Disks, 50–51, 67
Display features, required, 66, 192
Distributed data processing (DDP), 65–66
Documentation support, 76, 195

Edison, Thomas, 147
Efficiency, 25–26
Employee reporting structure, 32
Employee resistance, 36
Environment, 74
Equipment, availability of, 73, 194
Erasures, 35
Evaluation and selection, 3–4, 94–117,
  188–89
  cost, 103
  examples, 108–10
  form, 100–101, 105, 200–201
  optimal sections, 105–6
  scoring system, 104–6, 110–15
  team, 105, 106–7
  technical discussion, 101–2
  using model RFP, 107–8
  vendor capabilities, 102–3, 115–17
  vendor demonstrations, 107
  vendor support, 103

Failure situations, 19–23
Financial leverage, 1, 16–17, 89–90
Floppy disks, 50–51, 67
Form, evaluation, 100–101, 105, 200–201

Form contracts, 130–31
FORTRAN, 50

Games, 87–88
Gottschalk v. Benson, 148

Hardware features, 66–69, 192–93
Hardware only error, 84–85
Heilprin, Lawrence, 10
Home computers, 48–49

IBM, 27
Installation, 18–19, 75, 194
International Data Corporation, 146
Itel, 2

Kettering, Charles, 27
Keyboard, 50
Kilobytes, 50

Legal issues, 2, 146–60
  computer crime, 154–58
  copyrights, 147, 149–51
  license agreements, 152–54
  patents, 147–49
  privacy, 158–60
  trade secrets, 147, 151–52
License agreements, 152–54
Loss and damage, risk of, 137

**Maintenance, 71–72, 80–81, 103, 133–34,
  193**
Managerial training, 71
Marshall, John, 147
Meetings, 141
Memorandum, negotiating, 121–22, 128,
  202–4
Memory capacity, 50
Mencken, H.L., 10–11
Microcomputer:
  disadvantages of, 51
  growth of, 49–50
  operation of, 50–51
  (*See also* Computer technology)
Mistakes in buying computers, 11–15, 82–
  88

National Science Foundation, 7
NEC Inc., 50
Negotiations, 4–5, 16, 118–28
  aggressive, 123–24
  communications, 119–20
  contract clauses, 130–31
  memorandum, 121–22, 128, 202–4
  number one strategy, 118–19
  techniques, 122–26
  uniqueness of, 119
  vendor personnel, roles of, 126–28

New Business Memo, 39, 170

Office statistics, 28–30
Optical character recognition (OCR), 65
Oral statement of vendor, 83–84
Originator's Questionnaire, 32–34, 162–63
Overdelegation mistake, 13, 86, 125–26
Overhead reductions, 23–24
Overloads, 35
Over-the-counter mistake, 87

Panasonic Company, 50
Paperwork generation time, 32
Parker v. Flook, 148
PASCAL, 50
Patch, 22
Patents, 147–49
Payroll, 43, 181
Peak periods, 33–34, 35
Personal computers, 48–49
Personnel changes, 34
Price (see Cost)
Printer, 50
Printing features, 63–64, 68–69, 191–93
Privacy, 158–60
Privacy Act of 1974, 159
Productivity, 6–8, 29
Products currently in use, 73, 194
Project manager, 140–41
Proposals, evaluation of (see Evaluation and selection)
Proprietary rights, 146–54
Puffing, 95–96, 127

Quality of documentation, 31, 33
Quotas, vendor, 92–93

Random Access Memory (RAM), 50
RCA Corporation, 2
Read-Only Memory (ROM), 50
References, 116–17
Rental agreement, sample, 131–39, 205–8
Repetitive work, 31
Request for proposal (RFP), 3, 15, 16, 46–78, 89
  advantages of, 48, 53
  application programs, 74–76, 194
  background, 55–56, 184–86
  bidder's conferences, 54
  cost sheets, 77–78, 198–99
  disadvantages of, 53
  documentation support, 76, 195
  hardware features, 66–69, 192–93
  introduction, 55, 184
  model, 54–78, 107–8, 182–99
  Request for Quotation, 52–53, 89, 128

requirements section, 56–66, 186, 190–92
services, 69–74, 193–94
use of, 46–47
vendor capabilities, 77, 196–97
(See also Evaluation and selection)
Request for Quotation (RFQ), 52–53, 89, 128
Required word processing features, 57–64, 190–91
Requirements study, 2–3, 14, 27–45
  Computer Questionnaire, 38–44, 168–69
  consultants, use and selection of, 44–45
  employee resistance, 36
  office statistics, 28–30
  Originator's Questionnaire, 32–34, 162–63
  Typist's Questionnaire, 34–38, 164–67
Response Time, 32, 73, 144
Revision cycles, 31, 33, 34
Rifkin, Stanley, 154, 157
Risks, minimization of, 11–12
Rough drafts, 33, 34

Sales and technical support, 81
Sales representative, 126–27
Selection (see Evaluation and selection)
Services, 69–74, 79, 193–94
  maintenance, 71–72, 80–81, 103, 133–34, 193
  sales and technical support, 81
  training, 70–71, 81, 103, 193
Sharp Electronics Corporation, 50
Shopper's syndrome, 13–14, 87
Software:
  defective, 20
  optional features, 64–66, 191–92
  printing features, 63–64, 191
  selection of, 86–87
  required miscellaneous, 60–63, 190–91
Sony, 50
Speed, 24
Staff Master File report, 43, 181
Standard paragraphs, 31, 33
Status reports, 141–42, 209–10
Storage media and capacity, required, 67–68, 192
Success, examples of, 23–26
Suggestions, 34, 36
Supplies, 72, 134, 194
Supreme Court of the United States, 148–49
System compatibility, 72–73, 194

Team, evaluation, 105, 106–7
Technical discussion, 101–2
Techniques of negotiating, 122–26
Text edit and merge, 59–60, 190

Text input features, 57–59, 190
Time log, 39–40, 172
Trade secrets, 147, 151–52
Training, 70–71, 81, 103, 193
Transportation, 133
TRS-80, 49
"Trust me" mistake, 14–15, 82–83, 95
Typist's Questionnaire, 34–38, 164–67
Typographical errors, 34

Vendor capabilities, 77, 102–3, 115–17, 196–97

Vendor demonstrations, 15, 85, 107
Vendor support (see Services)
VisCalc, 50

Warranty, 135–37
Watson, Thomas, 27, 158
Written status report, 141–42, 209–10

Xerox Corporation, 2

Zuboff, S., 10

NOW ... Announcing these other fine books from Prentice-Hall—

HOW TO BREAK INTO DATA PROCESSING, by Laura Steibel Sessions. Written by a recruiter for one of the largest data processing placement firms in the world, this step-by-step guide will help those interested in data processing choose a technical school, find companies that hire entry-level programmers, successfully contact those companies, and most importantly, succeed in this highly profitable field.

$6.95 paperback, $12.95 hardcover

THE QUALITY CIRCLE GUIDE, by Donald L. Dewar. Provides a complete guide to the Japanese concept of Quality Circles as a means of improving product quality and employee motivation in American business. Includes a special leader manual instruction guide and member manual that provides step-by-step guidelines for conducting a Quality Circle meeting.

$9.95 paperback, $19.95 hardcover

HOW TO EARN MORE PROFITS THROUGH THE PEOPLE WHO WORK FOR YOU, by William H. Scott. Here's a hip-pocket guide for managers and small-business owners who want to improve their profits through enthusiastic, motivated employees. Provides lists, forms, and summary sheets to help hire, evaluate, and motivate employees.

$5.95 paperback, $11.95 hardcover

To order these books, just complete the convenient order form below and mail to **Prentice-Hall, Inc., General Publishing Division, Attn. Addison Tredd, Englewood Cliffs, N.J. 07632**

Title	Author	Price*

Subtotal _____

Sales Tax (where applicable) _____

Postage & Handling (75¢/book) _____

Total $_____

Please send me the books listed above. Enclosed is my check ☐ Money order ☐ or, charge my VISA ☐ MasterCard ☐ Account # _____

Credit card expiration date _____

Name _____

Address _____

City _____ State _____ Zip _____

*Prices subject to change without notice. Please allow 4 weeks for delivery.